CEN

D0209650

Harcourt Brace Jovanovich, c198

3 3029 00757 2597

818
W518d
1980

West
Doubl discovery

c8

AUG 1982

DOUBLE DISCOVERY

Other books by Jessamyn West

The Friendly Persuasion
A Mirror for the Sky
The Witch Diggers
Cress Delahanty
Love, Death, and the Ladies' Drill Team
To See the Dream
Love Is Not What You Think
South of the Angels
A Matter of Time
Leafy Rivers
Except for Me and Thee
Crimson Ramblers of the World, Farewell
Hide and Seek
The Secret Look
The Massacre at Fall Creek
The Woman Said Yes
The Life I Really Lived

DOUBLE DISCOVERY

A JOURNEY

 BY

Jessamyn West

HBJ

Harcourt Brace Jovanovich
New York and London

Copyright © 1980 by Jessamyn West

All rights reserved. No part of this publication may be reproduced or transmitted in any form or by any means, electronic or mechanical, including photocopy, recording, or any information storage and retrieval system, without permission in writing from the publisher.

Requests for permission to make copies of any part of the work should be mailed to: Permissions, Harcourt Brace Jovanovich, Inc., 757 Third Avenue, New York, N.Y. 10017.

Library of Congress Cataloging in Publication Data

West, Jessamyn.
Double discovery.
1. West, Jessamyn—Journeys—Europe.
2. Europe—Description and travel.
3. Authors, American—20th century—Biography.
I. Title.
PS3545.E8315Z516   818'.5403 [B]   80-7948
ISBN 0-15-126402-3

Printed in the United States of America

First edition

B C D E

For Judith Meskill and Michael Muller
who started their journey together
on June 1, 1980
in the Friends Meeting House at
Plainfield, New Jersey

Author's Note

In the journals I began to keep when I was twelve years old, I copied almost as much from others as I wrote myself. Somehow when the words of the masters were transcribed by my own hand, I felt that I had come closer to their meaning and to their authors than I could by any mere reading.

I certainly put the name of the writer after each excerpt I had set down, but the name of the book or the page number on which it had been found? No, never. I was a book reader, not a bookkeeper, and never imagined I would ever require such accounting.

Thus, though the long passage from John Burroughs was included in the very journal that accompanied me on this Journey, I do not know where I found it. I now have John Burroughs's collected works, but, while still a bookworm, I do not propose to reread all of his many books in search of the quotation for the purpose of making it, in hindsight, exact.

Rather, I would prefer to retain it and all the other excerpts, lovingly copied by me long ago, just as they appear in my journals. My vision is through the eye of memory, imperfect as it may be. If, in that view, there are minor inaccuracies, I ask the forgiveness of the writers and the indulgence of the reader.

DOUBLE DISCOVERY

"It is a great journey to the world's end."

—John Ray
English Proverbs, 1670

Outward Bound

For many years I hauled around with me on our many moves a large gray cardboard box bearing in bold blue print the words "The Emporium, Whittier, California." The box must have held originally a man's suit or a lady's coat. It was bigger than needed for corsets or Munsingwear or tablecloths.

I knew what was in the box. Beneath the name of the dry-goods store in my mother's strong, march-ahead script were the words, "Jessamyn's letters from Europe, 1929. Precious. Save."

She saved them until she died. Then they were given to me. For twenty-five years, without once being opened, the box went up and down the state of California. It was my habit to take care of what Mama considered precious, though our tastes often differed. I would have mourned, had the box been lost, for her sake, not mine.

There are those who enjoy reading what they have written. I am not one of them. When writing, my anticipation doesn't differ much from that I mean to give the reader: What's going to happen? The pleasure in such writing is greater because the writer creates. He chooses the words that make the happenings happen. Having done that, he hasn't, or I haven't, much inclination to revisit the handmade landscape.

The original Creator, I rationalize, after He created Adam and Eve, let others visit that less than perfect couple.

Letters are not stories, though they may tell a story. They are less what the writer made than an account of events that helped make the writer. Reading one's own old letters may be more egotistical than reading one's old stories: it is the difference between recalling what one did and examining what one was. What one did is often a flash in the pan; what one wrote is often, too often, the now and forever of the writer.

I finally opened the box of letters written fifty years before, more to discover who I had then been than to remember where I had gone.

Then, as now, I did not relish travel, or at least that part of it which involves the movement required to get from one place to another. The person who said "It's the journey, not the goal, that counts" was, unless he was speaking wholly metaphorically, a strange fellow. Travel is a make-do life undertaken by persons who are finding their lives at home empty. They substitute travel's necessary activities of ticket validation, plane catching, and luggage checking for the meditation, introspection, and contemplation they haven't a taste for.

Thoreau was and is my hero. He had traveled far, he said, in Concord. Of the people who were traipsing off to California in the 1850's, he said they would find when they got there that they were only "3,000 miles nearer hell."

I pitied my parents, Hoosiers newly arrived in California in 1908. By 1915, with automobile, tent, folding cots, and a Coleman stove, they were venturing the length of California. Occasionally, reluctant but dutiful, I went with them. Better, I thought, echoing my hero, to know truly the daily movement and seasonal changes of one backyard grass blade than to whiz past acres of petrified forests and sky-high stands of ancient sequoias.

I have searched my journals trying to discover why this travel hater, short on money, devoid of travel experience in anything but the family auto (which she didn't like), was so determined to get to Europe—get to England, to be more accurate. It has taken a good deal of reading to find the reason, my journals being both numerous and lengthy.

George Steiner says of diary keepers that they are "characterized by loquacity, copiousness, and temporal duration." Elizabeth Hardwick thinks that Americans "grind away at this industry [diary-keeping] as if we were trying to make perfume out of tobacco juice." I won't contradict Steiner, but "perfume out of tobacco juice" made by "grinding away" on a diary isn't a simile I find descriptive of what I've experienced in keeping a journal.

Steiner's "loquacity" and "copiousness," I certainly find accurate. If I didn't have anything to say, and this happened more often than I realized, I could still keep a pen between my fingers by copying passages from writers who did. If the libraries of the world are destroyed, a trace of what has been lost can be regained by reading excerpts copied by me in my journals.

I knew I wouldn't find in the letters any explanation of why this travel hater was traveling. The reasons for crossing the Rubicon aren't discussed in midstream.

I knew, without looking into either journals or letters, *who* was traveling: a twenty-six-year-old woman married five years; a teacher in a one-room school; the possessor of three thousand dollars; a Quaker educated in a college of under two hundred enrollment whose women students became teachers, missionaries, or wives—and sometimes all three. None, as far as I knew, ever wished to become anything else. I became a wife on graduation, and shortly after that, when the bottom fell out of the post–World War I market for dried prunes and apricots, a teacher.

Until I looked into the letters, I didn't know quite how ignorant this teacher was. The journals, laced with the wisdom of the ages, hid the fact that this copious, loquacious schoolteacher had never lived in a town of more than five thousand

population; and for the most of her life had lived on the outskirts of villages of five hundred. The journalizer was unaware
of the extent of her ignorance. Ignorance is one of the easiest
states to be ignorant of.

Not only had this letter writer never really traveled; she
knew no one who had. A hundred years before, a great-great-
grandmother, a Quaker minister, had made more than one
preaching trip to England and Ireland. And Martha Price
Griffith undoubtedly knew more about travel than her granddaughter. Like many Quakers of her time, she produced
Quakerly booklets. All of her travel tips, however, were on
how to take the straight and narrow path to heaven.

Travel agents and tour guides undoubtedly existed fifty
years ago. The consuls of foreign countries had their offices in
Los Angeles. From none of these did I seek any information.
Columbus was better informed, and certainly better financed
for travel, than I. Today's twelve-year-old could circumnavi-
gate the globe more easily than I.

Why did this travel hater travel? The journals told me. The
travel hater had no other way of reaching England.

Why England? It would not have been the choice of my
parents or my husband. My mother (who would willingly
have gone anywhere) would, given the choice, have headed
for the Irish town of Timahoe, in County Kildare. From
Ireland, in 1729, her many-times-great-grandparents Thomas
and Catherine Milhous, Quakers converted by William Penn's
followers, had headed for Penn's Woods, in the United States.

My father's people, the Wests, had been in the British Isles
longer perhaps than the Milhouses. The Wests were Celts,
those the invaders of England had been unable either to kill
or to drive across the sea to Ireland. The Celts who stubbornly
and safely clung to the West Coast of England were called,
one and all, "Wests."

I had no desire to go root-hunting, either in Ireland or along
the West Coast of England.

My husband, Harry Maxwell McPherson, Highlander though he was, had no wish to see a kilt or watch a highland fling. Samoa, Peru, Ethiopia might have tempted him. But the British Isles? As families, we had all been there long ago and had left because we didn't like it. Why go back? What would he do? If not committed to work at the university, he would go back to that part of the old American West where, in order to be a cowboy, he had sacrificed his last two years in college.

Had anyone asked me "Why England?," I don't know that I would have been able to give any answer. By training and temperament, I was loath to bare my heart to anyone, and my reason for going to England lay right at the core of my heart. I was going to England because it was the land of poets and penmen. I knew *that* without rereading my journals. But when I was asked at the monthly meeting of schoolteachers, "Do you know anyone in England?," I, playing it cool, answered, "Not yet." How could I have said, "I am going to visit the home of the poets and penmen."

In the high school and college I attended, there had been no classes in American literature. It was all English literature: Chaucer and Milton and Browning, Dickens and Eliot (George, not T. S.) and Keats. A bookworm, taught from the beginning that what he finds most nourishing is to be found in England, looks there for further food. Though they weren't taught in any of my classes, I had already formed a taste for Belloc and Brontë and Masefield, for Mansfield and Hopkins and Machen.

I was going to England, not to see the houses, or even the rooms where these writers had worked. All I wanted to do was to walk about in their world, the world they had written of: a world where heather and bracken *grew* and nightingales and cuckoos could be *heard*. *This* reason for going to England, I knew. And any reader of my journals would have known it, too. All those copied verses describing the English countryside:

The bells of heather
Have ceased ringing their Angelus.
Sleepy June weather
Has installed a drug in us.
The cry of the plover . . .

There was another reason for going to England, a reason equally discernible to any reader of the journals, though the writer required herself to be blind to it. She wanted to be a writer. To admit, even to herself, such an ambition would be a sign of madness; as preposterous as a poor loony's belief that if he jumps off a building, wings will sprout from his shoulders to support him.

A postponer is the word nowadays for the person who wants to write and does nothing about it. This state, it is thought, is comparable to one that analysts, working in other areas, discover in those longing to perform but so timid they choose indefinite postponement rather than an attempt that may fail.

This feeling about attempting to write is not uncommon. James Baldwin says, "I had been well conditioned by the world I was brought up in so that I did not yet dare to take the idea of becoming a writer seriously."

And Henry Miller, the last man one would think to have qualms of any kind about anything, writes, "To me, being a writer was like saying, 'I am going to be a saint, a martyr, a god.' It was just as big, just as far away, and just as remote as that."

I had the inhibitions of both Baldwin and Miller. In the world in which I was brought up, I had never seen a writer; nor had I seen anyone who had seen a writer. Like Miller, I thought that writers were gods. Nevertheless, though I never confessed to anyone, and certainly not to myself, that I wanted to write, one look at my journals would have convinced anyone but their scribe that those pages were the work of a would-be writer.

For what other reason could a girl have filled pages with material of this kind?

"How Short Stories Begin." Short stories began in the pages of my journal with paragraphs copied from stories published in *Scribner's* and *Harper's, The Century* and *The Atlantic Monthly.*

"How to Avoid Using 'He said' and 'She said.'" This was written before Hemingway taught writers by his example that there was no better way of imparting a character's conversation than by saying, "He said." Pre-Hemingway, I believed this unliterary. Better, I told myself, to say "He muttered" or "bellowed," "mumbled," "belched."

It was obvious that writing was accomplished by the use of words. I categorized words—Good, Bad, Appealing, Disgusting, Exotic—in page-long lists.

Plots, it then seemed to me, were the skeletons that permitted stories to move about—ahead, if possible. I had pages of ten-line plots, bare bones unclothed as yet with the flesh of anything human.

How would going to England be of any value to this young woman incapable of confessing her propensities—even to herself? For the bookworm, the pleasures were obvious. However unconsciously, she was choosing the life many a would-be writer has chosen. If you can't do it yourself, get to the place where books and writers are valued. Live in that atmosphere. See the great libraries. Hear critics analyze and poets declaim. There is a touch of voyeurism in this. The failed surgeon haunting operating rooms. The defrocked priest eavesdropping at the confessional. Perhaps more of the schoolboy peeping over the transom.

I wasn't yet failed or defrocked. I hadn't been bold enough to risk even that negative recognition. But I had been able to get myself enrolled as a student of the Summer Meeting at Oxford University. The Meeting was not a modern-day writer's conference. If it had been, I wouldn't have gone. That would have been a confession, in public, I hadn't yet been able to make even to myself: "I want to write."

How I knew that there was a Summer Meeting at Oxford,

or that I could get into it, I don't know. There is no record of it in my journal. Virginia Woolf writes in her diary of diary-keeping, "What happens is, as usual, that when I am going to write about the soul, life breaks in." I wish life had broken into my diaries more often. As it is, I have no record or memory of where or how I learned about the Summer Meeting, applied, was accepted, and had a room booked for me at St. Frideswide's, a hall occupied during term time by Catholic girls.

Not in my journal either is the reason for my having made, before I left home, a reservation in a New York hotel. That I remember. *The Atlantic Monthly,* which I read, carried an ad for a hotel that described itself as being "the ideal hostelry for a woman traveling alone." That was my state exactly, and what could be better than "ideal"? The hotel was the St. James; it was at a location that, I believe, would not now be described as ideal for women traveling alone.

The choice of means of transportation to get me to the St. James and St. Frideswide's (holy habitations both, to judge by their names) was made easy. What was cheapest? Half of the three thousand dollars would go to Max to take care of university expenses. And even as inexperienced a traveler as I was aware that $1,500 would not pay for a really grand tour.

The cheapest way to get to Chicago, where one changed trains, was by a tourist car on a Southern Pacific train. The cheapest way to get from New York to London was by a one-class four-to-the-room ship. The *Minnekahada* filled these requirements. On April 20, 1929, I devoted a single page in my journal to two lines: "I am sailing for England on June 21, 1929. Nothing more shall be added to this page. I only wish I had red ink with which to write it."

With lodging and transportation arranged for, I began to wonder about the trip.

"All this week," I wrote in my journal, "I have felt insecure, unhappy. Am I doing the right thing? Going off and leaving

Max? Though he was the one who bought my ticket in Los Angeles and brought it home to me. Maybe he *wants* me to go. These are hard times financially for everyone. Papa's oranges are not selling well. Cousin Elizabeth, so young, is dying. What right do I have to be so optimistic? Death comes in terrible forms and says, 'It is over. Hope no more. Plan no more. Torment and oblivion face you.'

"Or poverty arrives and says, 'The travel, the ease, the peace you planned cannot be. It was all a dream. Now fear and work and worry. Know the lash of humiliation that failures know.'"

Sailing date only a month away, I wrote: "I am going to England! Is it possible? I think of Mollie Milhous and the Indiana farmhouse. I think of my parents' past, so rich and varied and unexplored by me. Why do I want to enter new situations before I've made an effort to explore or understand the past?"

Sailing date three weeks away, I wrote: "This is Eden and I am a stupid Eve, leaving it of my own free will. Something is pushing me out. Have I sinned? Perhaps my expulsion is more fated than I know. Why *do* I go? Here the known cicadas sing faithfully. Here stars I can name are where I expect them to be, and bright.

"It is sad to leave a room you have made, lived in and loved. Isn't that treachery? I swear I will never forget it. I will never forget the blue dome of distant Mt. Tahquitz. Never forget the factory-made tapestry on the dining-room wall over whose picture Max and I have puzzled during many an evening dinner.

"I will never forget the far-off rustle of mountain thunderstorms, the sharp heat of summer, the smell of the dry earth after the first fall rains.

"But I will forget. Other years and happenings will push these years and happenings far back into the recesses of my mind, never to be explored again.

"God make me constant to things once loved. Transient

myself, let my memory of the past be strong and constant while I live."

From some poet I copied into my journal these lines, "All things change, we are told, in this world of change and sorrow, But love's way never changes of promising to never change."

Psychologists say that there are those who are prompted to act only by being confronted by hurdles difficult to cross. No goal, easily accessible, appeals to them. At some time, early in their lives, they learned to value struggle. If what they want is theirs for the taking, they must, to enhance it, construct imaginary barriers. Real barriers for the journey I had longed for since childhood no longer existed. The money was available, the tickets were bought, the lodgings secured, the ostensible justification for travel (school at Oxford) arranged. My husband approved; my parents rejoiced. Yet suffering was demanded to justify the trip. So I suffered.

How could I leave the seventeen pupils at Harmony, my one-room school, to which I drove each morning, with dog, five-gallon canteen of water, and clock? There would never be another Harmony for me. I knew that. We raised baby ground squirrels in the woodbox by the stove. Our Junglegym was the sloping roof of the woodshed, down which we slid on dustpans.

Who, when I was gone, would understand that Peter Mendez, slow in English, was better in arithmetic than most eighth graders?

How could I, for shallow literary reasons, be off to Ireland when my mother, who for longer years and deeper reasons than mine had yearned to make that trip, remained at home?

What assurance did I have for believing that Max, abandoned by his wife, and a "single" man among peppy coeds, would remember me?

"Will I ever have time traveling to write here again? Or will I stop wanting to? Be mesmerized by the new sights and new people? If the charm of pen and paper ever fails me, then I'll know that the road will be downhill from there on: no more glimpses of the enchanted valleys and the delectable mountains."

So, suffering and proud of myself, I suppose, because in spite of the pain and the doubts and the fears, I was going to do it.

I began to pack. I had, of course, a steamer trunk. I didn't know what to put in it, but I knew that persons who traveled by steamer had steamer trunks. So I had one.

My going-away costume was sensible if not, on a standard Southern Pacific coach, comfortable: an oatmeal-colored skirt with a Roman-striped silk blouse attached, and a hip-length oatmeal jacket that converted the dress, I thought, into a "travel suit." With this I wore a ginger-colored cloche. There is a picture of Max and me taken before I boarded the train in Pomona. Most of my face is hidden by the cloche, which hangs down about my jaws like the drooping ears of a woebegone bloodhound. What of my face can be seen *is* also woebegone; outward bound, nevermore to see my loved ones.

Transcontinental

I need not have worried that travel would separate me from my pen. True, less went into my journal, but the word output, if anything, increased. Though Virginia Woolf was right; life, as I was capable of understanding it, did keep breaking into the letters at the expense of soul. It was my belief that my parents after twenty-six years, and my husband after five, of exposure to my soul would relish a change of scenery.

I began my first letter before the train was out of Los Angeles County. I wrote constantly and I cried constantly. What my fellow passengers made of me, I don't know. What I made of them fills my letters.

"This is a motley crew of people," I wrote my mother, "a hotter, more bedraggled, harassed-by-children group of women cannot be imagined. The woman facing me looks like a lady of easy virtue: hennaed hair, ring after ring, bracelet after bracelet, lips and cheeks that would grace a Sunday-school Santa Claus. Like all such ladies, she does have a heart of gold. When I cry the hardest, she keeps her opened paper between us so that I can sob in privacy.

"When I appear to be recovering, she gives me the funnies to read. This made me cry some more: reminds me of loving care at home.

"There is a Dunkard lady with no children and a whole roasted chicken. She cuts a slice from it now and then. I contemplate making her acquaintance.

"One grandma has a two-quart enamel cup. She takes it with her every half hour to the restroom. I think she takes sponge baths in it. We all need baths. Soot flies in the opened windows; the temperature in the car is 92°.

"The lady across from me has just commented on the great basket of fruit you gave me. (It is beautiful.) She asks me if I have intestinal trouble. I tell her no.

"The porters are very kind. Ours, whose lifelong ambition has been to be a porter, tells his friends, 'Now I am a porter on the U.P. Line.'

"I'll never worry again about clothes on a train. A clean kitchen apron is the style here—and appropriate.

"There are ten thousand children in this car alone. If I would start a school to keep them occupied, the mothers would bless me.

"We are now going down the Cajon Pass. Too rough to write."

Next morning, June 24 at 9:30. "What a scene! What a scene! Ten thousand mothers and children dressing. Wise, I was up at six, washed and dressed by seven. I had breakfast this morning. Yesterday nothing but fruit, and fruit was beginning to taste too fruity! Coffee and muffins, nothing else, forty-five cents!

"I understand why Englishmen dress for dinner in the jungle. I feel the same way among these travelers. Next time I'm going to save more money and go by Standard Sleeper. The lady opposite me picks her teeth with something metallic. If you had your eyes shut, you'd think from the sound that she was knitting.

"It was 120° yesterday at Barstow. Now we are eighty-five miles from Salt Lake City. I've seen more water since six o'clock this morning than I've seen in twenty years in California: ponds, marshes, canals, rivers. Cherokee roses on riverbanks, white-faced cows, avenues of glistening poplars, mountains with snow a third of the way down. This is a beautiful land. Brigham had brains as well as sex appeal. No wonder his wives were content with their lot.

"The country outside *needs* to be beautiful to make up for the grime, dirt, and sloppiness inside. I had no idea that trains were *dirty*.

"Last night the only childless passenger in the car with the exception of me and the lady of easy virtue, a blond who lives on bananas and is reading Zane Grey's *Wild Fire* (wrong title for this weather), leaned from her upper berth, clad in rose-colored pajamas, and called to the young porter who was making up the next berth, 'Sam, if I fall, will you catch me?'

"Sam said, 'Sure. Catch you on the first bounce.'

"Wild Fire blond: 'Now, Sam, couldn't you get me sooner than that?'

" 'Sure, Queen, I get you the minute you slip.'

"I think she's slipping.

"We're twenty minutes out of Salt Lake. I'm amazed at the amount of water and the greenness. I think I'll stop off in Salt Lake, look up a Mormon, and offer to be his third or fourth."

Part of the pleasure of travel, for those who need hurdles to leap, is encountering new problems, and licking *them*. At home, with only two people using the bathroom, dressing was a simple matter. In a Tourist Pullman, travelers have to develop shrewdness to survive. In the tourist restroom, not being trampled upon by uncounted mothers and countless children was an accomplishment in itself. Time was changing as we moved eastward. I tried to avoid the restroom congestion by rising earlier than the other passengers. But 6:00 A.M. in Kansas is 4:00 A.M. in California; and for a born slugabed, congestion is preferable to getting up at that hour.

Then, as a result of some unapproved investigating, I found that the Day Coach next to our Tourist Pullman had only five passengers (none of them children) and a restroom that locked. From that minute on, I was, insofar as restrooms went, a Day Coach passenger.

In neither Day Coach nor Tourist Pullman did I learn what every other passenger on board undoubtedly knew: there was a cooler that held water for drinking. From Pomona to Chicago I drank the tepid water from the tank that held toothbrush water. Why? Was I stupid? Blind? No. I was a practicing Britisher, asking no questions, keeping myself to myself, and drinking what came to hand in the wilderness. Trivia of this kind did not go into journal or letters. But I remember.

The bathroom situation licked, though not mentioned, letter writing continued. I was still complaining of the dirt.

"It is unbelievable, the amount of soot this car collects. Next time I'm going to wear coveralls. The soap in the restroom has run out. Everyone curses the Continental Limited.

"The porter says, 'You just traveling tourist. What you expect?'

"This morning I broke down again and had a real breakfast in the dining car. Hot oatmeal and coffee. I have lost three pounds so far on fruit.

"The steward put me at a table with a hook-nosed bespectacled Australian, aged thirty-seven or eight. He wanted to know where I was going. When I told him England, he expressed pity. The English, he said, were too stiff, had too much 'side.' He says I will not enjoy myself. Instead of saying 'eighty' pronounced 'āty,' he says 'īty.' He said that 'īty-five percent of the Australians are native born. He has been traveling for five months and is on his way now to visit Niagara Falls. From the way he talks, I believe he has come all the way to the U.S. just to see the Falls.

"He told me, 'We put our watches back an hour this morning.' 'Forward,' said I. 'You are mistaken,' said he. He says that Australians and Americans are more alike than Australians and the English. I am afraid he believes, because I corrected him about the time, that I am un-American.

"After breakfast he somehow found me in the tourist section. 'I have come to apologize,' he said, 'about the time. You were right. You should not have turned your watch back.' 'I didn't,' said I. 'I left it where I had turned it—forward.'

"The Australian was an object of interest in the tourist car. He sat down beside me and busied himself brushing off soot. The grandma with the roasted chicken had found a fourteen-year-old boy to play checkers with her. The poor boy, optimistic, lost every time, but never gave up. Grandma did something I had never seen done before: she picked her nose with a hairpin. I was ashamed for my people to have the Australian see such crudeness. He watched and was impressed. 'The Americans, like the Australians, are a practical people,' he said."

"Where are you staying in New York?" he asked.

Here was a situation I had been taught to deal with early on. Strange men (this one was very strange, admiring a hairpin nose-picker) are usually up to no good. I was not bold enough to say, "None of your business." I was not willing to appear so hapless a traveler as to be on my way to New York without having reserved a room at some hotel. So I lied.

"I am staying at the Allerton," I said.

"Excellent choice," said he. "My sister has stayed there."

I wrote home about the Australian, not about my life. I tried to console myself for the falsehood by thinking: All that talk about "īty-five percent of the Australians are native born"! I bet his father was a convict. Besides, the man had been a show-off, tipping the waiter seventy-five cents for his breakfast. In his fast company I had been so weak as to tip fifteen cents myself instead of my usual dime. With him as an example, I would soon be bankrupt.

Reading, fifty years later, my account of the Australian and the "lady of easy virtue," I am struck by my ignorance. I knew nothing about "easy virtue" except what I had read in novels. The cliché phrase was used, I think, to impress the home folks with the worldly nature of my fellow passengers. The woman opposite me was middle-aged (in your twenties, a forty-year-old is middle-aged), clinking with jewelry, the gray rinsed out of her hair with henna and her lips shining with something she applied out of a little circular box. What she was doing was to call attention to herself. Virtuous middle-aged women shouldn't do that, should they? And if they did, their purpose had to be—didn't it?—to arouse the interest of men. And such an attempt indicated "easy virtue," didn't it?

The truth of the matter now seems to be that I possibly had sex on my mind more constantly than my jewelry-clinking, hair-brightened seatmate. Had she written a letter home about me, I doubt that it would have contained any speculation about my sex life. I think I obviously looked to her like a woman whose virtue wasn't easy.

Why didn't I talk to her? Virginia Woolf, trapped in conversation with a bore, writes that she was determined that she would not let that hour be wasted without learning from it something she had not known. No Virginia Woolf, I did not talk. I learned nothing. Who was she, this woman I faced for two thousand miles? A cliché! I was too ignorant to know that there are better ways of learning to write than by copying opening sentences from stories in the *Atlantic* and *Harper's*.

I can understand my action with the Australian more easily than with my seatmate. After all, the Australian was a man. I had more than novel reading to assist me in cataloguing him. No man, I had been taught, unless he was of a fatherly age, made advances to a young woman except for one purpose. The Australian was not old enough to be "fatherly"; and his question as to where I would be staying sounded suspicious.

Perhaps the fact that I was not an eye-catcher made me eager to think that the mildest kind of conversational approach masked hidden lechery. Until the Australian asked me for my address in New York, he had given me no opportunity to suspect him of anything of the sort.

Friendship, conversation, the helpfulness of an experienced traveler toward an untraveled country girl—these never occurred to me. It was sex—I hoped. I was like the old maid who, hopefully, looks under her bed each night. She would, of course, defend her virtue to the death. But it was reassuring to believe that someone wanted to rob her of it.

The journal I had with me on my journey had been begun on January 8, 1929. On page 42, I had copied this passage from John Burroughs.

"Men who write journals are usually men of certain marked traits: they are idealists, they love solitude rather than society; they are self-conscious and they love to write. Their journals largely take the place of converse. Amiel, Emerson, and Thoreau, for instance, were lonely souls lacking in social gifts and seeking relief in the society of their own thoughts. Such men go to their journals as other men go to their clubs. They love to be alone with themselves and dread to be numbed or drained of their mental forces by uncongenial persons. To such a man, his journal becomes his duplicate self and he says to it what he would not say to his dearest friend. It becomes both an altar and a confessional."

With much of this, I had agreed, at least enough to lead me to copy it. I do not now think that Emerson or Virginia Woolf or I was totally lacking in social gifts. I do not believe that Pepys went to his journal as to his club; or that Montaigne valued his tower room and pen more than his friendship with Etienne de La Boétie.

And anyone living in a family learns that while his journal may be his altar, it had better not be his confessional. Readers (and in a family, there will always be one) may not demand penance; they will not offer forgiveness, either.

Into the journal, not a letter, went some stanzas called forth, no doubt, by living in the midst of so many people, so much talk, so much clangor. I pictured a season of quiet and called the poem—that's what I considered it—"Death."

Easing, quieting, subduing the clangor of words,
Words jostling brittle shoulder to shoulder.
Pushing them apart with bland mushy silences,
Tramping them under with cold pudding feet.

Death, holding your body apart from hands that touch,
Pushing away hands forever grasping
Pushing away mouths forever seeking
Taking you from the anvil, the pressing hammer of bodies.

What is health to a dead man, or a high wind?
What are words shouted or names not whispered?
The wish for, the wish not for?
All murked over, lost in the mellowing mash of death.

Anyone who at twenty-six, traveling with a trainload of persons whose experiences would fill a library of books, preferred writing lines about death to conversation probably deserved Burroughs' description as a person "lacking in social gifts."

Even at that time, I wondered if I had chosen a mistaken way of living.

Beneath the lines of "Death," I wrote, "What do I want most? Life, of course. What will I do to secure it? In my mind, everything. In living, nothing. My best act might be to throw away this journal and talk with my fellow passengers. I need to learn more about human beings.

"This book may prove to be my gizzard, holding what I've stored here for times grinding. I may be able later to feed on what I stole from less thrifty hens and cocks."

Cock was still a barnyard word in 1929.

"Dearest,

"We stopped at Green River, Wyoming, for thirty minutes last night. At eight o'clock, it was still very light. All the townspeople were out to see the train pull in. All the passengers walked about eating ice cream cones (except me) and making eyes at the town bums (except me). The Green River really is green and wide, and looks deep and cool. The buttes outside town are bottle green. If California had anything as green as the mesas here, we would call it a park and put in picnic tables. The clouds rise high here, heavy and rounded as carved marble. I love this open land, no orchards hiding its swell and curve."

"Dear Mama,

"Papa's telegram arrived yesterday telling me that the coat I had forgotten had been sent air mail to the St. James. When the telegram was delivered, every woman in the car came down to ask the news. They had already decided that because of my prolonged crying, my incessant writing, my diet of fruit, and last of all because of my Australian visitor from Standard to Tourist, that something ailed me. A visitor from Standard to Tourist was like a man from Fifth Avenue coming down to the ghetto.

"One woman has a child who must be almost two. It runs up and down the aisle like an antelope. She is still nursing it, as unself-conscious as a nanny goat. With one hand she keeps her breast and its mouth in contact; with the other she picked up Papa's telegram and read it.

" 'So your father is still alive?'

" 'Yes, of course. He's only forty-seven.'

" 'From all your crying, we thought your whole family had been wiped out in some accident.'

" 'Oh, no. I was crying because I was leaving home.'

" 'Were you kicked out?'

" 'No, no. I'm going to England, where I've always longed to go.'

" 'Why were you crying, then?'

" 'Homesick,' said I.

" 'You can turn around at Chicago and go back.'

"I didn't think I could explain to her that I was crying because I was leaving, but wouldn't go back if I could. Lola—that was her name—wears a kimona all day long and talks with a speed rivaled only by the click of the wheels. Somebody in California loves her, though. She is on her way to Minnesota to show her mother her little nursling.

"Everyone in the car has been down to ask me about papa's telegram, my destination, age, etc. I really am nice to them, give them some of my fruit, take care of their kids, try not to wince when they whang them over the ears, pretend an interest I don't have in the power of their home radios. But oh, I never dreamed travel would be like this."

Into the letters went the travelers and the landscape. Into my journal went my feelings. The letters were written to inform the stay-at-homes of the world east of California. The journal was written to declare to someone—me?—what I thought. Or perhaps by writing to discover what I thought.

Virginia Woolf, in one of her letters, which were populated with the hundreds of people she met, declares that Ottoline Morrell's journal, which is "inner," is a failure. I prefer Virginia's journal, less inner, to Ottoline's because Virginia is a better writer. But I prefer all journals to letters because they *are* more "inner." Letters tell you what the writer thinks of the recipient; journals tell you who the writer is.

My feelings were an old story to my husband, mother, and father. What was new to them was the country I was traveling across and my fellow travelers. I felt I had been commissioned by them to spy out the land, and that I owed them a daily report, though there was never any sense of compulsion in writing to them; there was a sense, instead, of gratitude. I wanted to tell and I had somebody who wanted to hear.

Mother wrote, "Your letters are most satisfying. You touch things great and small and fill the void of wondering. Grandpa [mine, not hers] and I both get so excited, the tears roll down our cheeks as we listen to and read your letters aloud. Grandpa said he was pleased to get your card and to have the post-master and mail carrier know that he had a granddaughter bound for foreign countries. God bless and keep you safe is my desire. Desire is prayer."

Father, quiet and self-contained, wrote, "We've read and re-read all your enclosures. This morning as I read your letters, I couldn't keep the tears from flowing, and even now I can hardly keep them back. Love, Dad."

With such an audience, untraveled and travel-hungry, who would waste time and paper writing them of the sound of wind? Of the difference between the sound of a train whistle heard inside a train and that sound carried on the Santa Ana wind from far away across the barley fields to a listener in a sleepless bed?

"Will the whistle of a train ever be the same to me again?" I wrote in my journal, "now that I've heard it from inside a train? What did it say to me as it moved north from Richfield with its load of tankers? Passing through Hemet with its car-loads of apricots and peaches? Well, it didn't say apricots and it didn't say peaches. Or oil. It said far, distant, farewell. It said mysterious, dangerous, adventurous. It was a cry in the dark from something I didn't understand going some place I didn't know.

"It was nearest, in the feeling it gave me, to the feeling I had when I went out to the barn to hear the Santa Ana wind whistle through the cracks. Wind, I knew, was nothing but air moving; but sitting alone in the dark, on a bale of barley, it sounded to me like the lonesome cry of the universe, of the whole world moving, without ever having willed to do so, endlessly round and round.

"The wind will still sound the same, I hope. But now that I know what a train really is, a string of boxes with seats carrying bedraggled mothers and crying young, will trains have lost their mystery? Will the whistle of a train be just a machine's release of steam, not an invitation to the unknown?"

What I thought of train whistles and the sound of wind blowing through the cracks of a barn didn't go into the letters. There would be time for that, if I could find any listeners, when I got home. Meanwhile, I had reached Chicago, where I changed trains after a four-hour stopover.

"Dearest Mama: 9:00 A.M., out of the Continental Limited and into the station where I'm to catch the New York Central. All my bags are checked. I bought this paper and envelope for 5¢. I spent my first hour here walking about the station saying, 'This is Chicago, this is Chicago.' If I hadn't done that, I would have forgotten it. Chicago people look just like Los Angeles people, except that L.A. women are more brightly dressed.

"Last night in Boone, Iowa, I had a ham sandwich for fifteen cents. I had a bowl of hot oatmeal in the station this morning for the same. It is cheaper to eat off the train than on it. Thanks for all the fruit. It saved me piles of money and made me a living curiosity to my fellow passengers. An hour before train time now. Just time to write Max."

"Max, I'm in the Chicago RR station, writing at a table with a young novice nun. She is turning out dozens of postcards. Wonder what she says to her friends out in the world?

"Iowa, yesterday, was jungly green with rivers hopping along unhampered by California dams.

"At dusk last night it rained. We went through Iowa villages where the house lights gleamed like fireflies caught in a dark green net. The rain, the lighted houses, families I could see eating their suppers made me so homesick that if my ticket had said L.A., not N.Y., I'd be on my way home now.

New York

I continued next day to Max.

"State of New York. The lady across the aisle just told me that we were in the Mohawk Valley and that the river we are following is the Mohawk. It looks like the Busch Gardens of Los Angeles would look if spread out all over the Santa Ana Canyon. Never have I seen its equal. How do people work? I should think they would do nothing but roll in the grass and swim in the river and stare.

"This train, compared with the one I left in Chicago, is luxurious. No dirt. Large dressing rooms with *chairs* and full-length mirrors. There are even mirrors in the berths; and lights! People complain, but they should see what I just left: two-by-four bathrooms always one-half inch deep in water and worse.

"I had dinner on the train last night. The charge was so monstrous I have sworn not to eat a bite until we reach New York City at three-thirty this afternoon.

"The menu was: 1 Baked Potato (small)
                  1 Dish Creamed Cabbage (ditto)
                  1 Slice of Bread
                  1 Piece of Pie—Green Apple

"For that, $1.40. Isn't that terrible? If I were to eat as I am capable and inclined, my dinner would have cost me $2.50 at least.

"I am starving at this very minute. Oh, to be back in steerage with my basket of fruit.

"There goes a boat, a noble yacht, I think; and I waste time telling you about my empty stomach. I'll eat the minute we get into the station, then write you something more edifying from the St. James."

I ate the minute I got to Grand Central Station, but the letter I wrote from the St. James was no more edifying than the last. It also had to do with money. I think this harping on the cost of things had less to do with any mean-spiritedness of mine, or even with my quite sensible understanding that unless I was economical I would find myself stranded and penniless in Europe, than with my latent writer's desire to put a little conflict into my story. Long stretches of scenery and even characters as entertaining (to me, at least) as Lola and the Australian were no substitute for action. "How is our girl making out in her battle against the hostiles?" And to me, there was no pretense in depicting the waiters, porters, and taxi drivers as modern-day muggers. I was truly astounded and enraged by them and determined not to be bilked.

"Your daughter is safely housed in the St. James. I found that it was just a few blocks from the station. My taxi fare was forty cents. I knew by now that I was supposed to tip the taxi driver, but I was determined not to. I have already spent more money on tips than on food. So I gave the taxi driver his forty cents and started to follow the St. James man, who had my bags, into the hotel. Before I could take two steps, the taxi man jumped in front of me and said, 'Where's my tip, sister?'

"Rather than create a scene I gave him a quarter, the smallest change I had. Never again will I be caught with no change smaller than a quarter. The minute I go downstairs I intend to get a supply of dimes and follow Rockefeller's example. People who demand tips will have a dime put into their hands before I vanish in the crowd. I don't mind paying bag-carriers, shoe-shiners, who get no other pay; but I refuse to support taxi drivers and waiters in luxury while I starve.

"This morning I was awakened by the phone. 'A telegram for you,' said a voice. Fearing some accident, I said, 'Read it, please.'

"It was from Max and when she got to the love and kisses, the poor lady said, 'I think I'd better send this up to you.' By that time, I thought so, too.

"It's 9:00 A.M. now. Six in California. I've marked in a little book the walk I want to take, besides the places I have to go. One thing I'm going to do even if I have to tip for it: I am going to walk up the steps of the public library and touch each lion on his head. I'll write you again tonight."

"Max, I will never travel again without you. The train pulled into Central Station at 4:00 P.M. Central Station is a madhouse, a beehive, an ant hole, a Tower of Babel. It made me dizzy just to see such swarms of milling people.

"My room here isn't bad—on the inside looking out onto what is called a 'court' but is really just a hole between buildings. All last night I kept waking thinking, gee, the train's making an awfully long stop.

"At dinnertime the desk called me asking, 1) Are you comfortable?, 2) Do you want a drink sent up to your room?

"Since this place is plastered with signs saying, 'Help us keep the Prohibition Amendment,' I don't know what they would send up. Root beer? Ovaltine? Anyway, I didn't take a chance. Probably cost fifty cents just to tip the waiter who brought it up.

"This really isn't such a bad room for $3.50: desk with reading lamp, cretonne curtains, full-length mirror, and spittoon if I need to spit.

"Of the $25 cash I started out with, I have $15 left. This will pay for room and food and get me to the boat shipshape. Now that I am so far away from home and everyone is so crazy for money, I sleep with my purse in bed with me."

"Mama, I've already told you about the beginning of the day, the telegram from Max, etc. Now it's 8:00 P.M. I'm surprised to be back here alive after the day I've had.

"This morning at the desk downstairs I asked for directions to get to the Irish Free State Consulate and the Mercantile Marine Offices. I said I intended to walk there.

"The lady at the desk screeched, 'Name of the Deity.' [Actually she said, "My God," but I tried to protect my mother and father from the roughness I was encountering.] 'You ain't a marathon runner, are you? It's ten miles if it's a foot there.'

"Another lady joined her and said, 'Your best bet's to take the subway.'

"A third lady said, 'Name of the Deity, she'd get killed if she's never been on the subway before.'

"A fourth lady said, 'Come with me and I'll show you where to take the elevated.' She took me down Sixth Avenue a block or two, showed me a platform, told me to climb up to it, board the first train that came along, and ride on it to the next to the last stop.

"So I climbed up to a dirty crow's-nest, bought a nickel ticket, and jumped, as I had been told, onto the first train that came racketing along. After we had made one hundred turns and traveled ten or fifteen miles above the dreariest streets I have ever seen in my life, I began to get worried. I asked the conductor to tell me when we came to the next to the last stop. He said he would tell me exactly which way to go to get to Broadway.

"When I got off, a man who had heard what the conductor told me, got off with me. 'If you go the way the conductor advised,' he said, 'you'll have to pay extra fare.' I pretended I didn't hear him, but when he actually took hold of my arm, and not gently either, I wrenched it away from him so hard he almost lost his balance. I was ready to kick him someplace where it would hurt, but when he saw how strong and determined I was, he moved off quickly in the opposite direction. He must really have thought I was a greenhorn. There could not possibly have been a fare of any kind. All I had to do was to go down the stairs, cross the street, turn to the left, just as the conductor had said, and there was Number One Broadway, the address I wanted.

"First, I went to the International Mercantile Marine, which was a good thing, for I found that I should be on board when my trunk was delivered in order to identify and accept it.

"Next, I went to the Irish Consulate on the twelfth floor of the same building to get my Irish visa. The man in charge (Consul?) was the shortest-tempered human being I ever saw: a black-haired Irishman with a cigarette behind one ear. He seemed to hate us all, and there *was* a mob for him to take care of. I was far back in line and, having observed the others, had my stuff ready for him. He proceeded to stamp and write in silence; then suddenly, in a brogue I didn't at first understand, he growled, 'Married or single?' What I said was 'I don't understand you.' What he thought I said was 'I don't know.' 'Name of the Deity,' he screamed to the whole roomful, 'she doesn't know whether she's married or single.' 'I do, I do,' I told him. 'I'm married.' He acted like he would either jump out of the window himself or throw me out; but he gave me my visa.

"Leaving there and going by subway this time—I'm getting bolder and bolder—I went from One Broadway to 218 Madison, to the offices of the International Student Federation. Because I'm not yet registered at Oxford, I wasn't eligible for any of their services.

"Then to the library, the place I'd been heading for all day. First I went to the General Literature Room on the third floor. Then to the Art Gallery, where I saw Stuart's 'George Washington,' Turner's 'Evening on the French Coast,' and Andrea del Sarto's 'St. Thomas and the Angel.' I didn't forget the lions coming or going.

"Next, to Brentano's, the famous booksellers, where I bought a copy of the English magazine *John O'London's*.

"Next, food. My first meal of the day. A magnificent meal for forty cents. A ham omelet, mounds of French fried potatoes, two rolls, three pats of butter, a glass of milk. Up to this time, I have lost five pounds; now I fear the tide is turning. New York is a dirty, grimy city, full of lechers, but it is a great place to eat.

"I hate to admit it, after all that eating in midafternoon, at seven o'clock I was hungry again. I ate with more restraint this time, just a sandwich and a glass of pineapple juice.

"Now I have washed my hair (in New York you have to wash your hair every time you step outside), shined my shoes, packed my suitcases. We must be on board the S.S. *Minnekahada* at 1:00 P.M., and I intend to sightsee from 8:00 A.M. until 1:00 P.M. The only trouble is, it will cost me a fortune if I take a taxi, and break my back if I walk and carry my bags. Maybe I can do a little of both."

"Dear Husband: Leave-taking day. 11:00 A.M. I've been out sightseeing. The lady who showed me how to get on the elevated yesterday advised me about the best way to get to the ship. A taxi from here would cost $3.00 at the very least, she said. So I am going to carry my bags a block and a half to catch a streetcar. Then I go to 16th Street, where I get a taxi to the ship. I will save one dollar that way, at least.

"*The Atlantic* said this was a hotel for women traveling alone. There are certainly plenty of women here. They are not travelers, though; otherwise they wouldn't know so much about how to get around New York.

"I'm so excited, my hand shakes. I'm scared as a rat leaving a ship, not getting on one.

"The toilet here keeps running just like ours at home. I wake up in the night and dream I'm back in Hemet. Oh, honey, don't we have a home any more?"

Camus wrote in "Love of Life," "What gives value to travel is fear. It breaks down a kind of inner decor in us. We can't cheat anymore—hide ourselves behind the hours in the office or at the plant (those hours which protect us so surely against the hours of being alone.) . . . Travel takes this refuge from us. Far from our own people, our own language, wrenched away from all support, deprived of our masks (we don't know the fare on the tram), we are completely on the surface."

I only half understand this; and perhaps would understand it better if Camus had said, "What gives value to life is fear." What we undertake without anxiety gives little satisfaction if accomplished. I could understand it better if travel were not depicted by Camus as an enterprise that robs us of the protection office and plant give us "against the hours of being alone."

Elsewhere, Camus wrote, "Enjoying oneself alone is impossible." This is very strange, but understandable. Less understandable is the great difference between Camus' feeling about travel and mine. We were both traveling alone, he at twenty-two, I at twenty-six. Had he been traveling in a Southern Pacific Standard Pullman, as I had been, or about to set sail on a single-class tourist ship, "a schoolteacher's ferryboat," as I was, he would have had no hours alone.

In New York, however, I did experience fear, lose my decor, and anger conductors with my lack of knowledge of tram fares. My fear had nothing to do with the loss of protection of plant or office. No such loss existed, even when sleeping. On the train, the lady of easy virtue slept in the berth above me. On the ship, I shared a pantry-sized stateroom with three other women; the four of us were wedged as compactly into bunks as sardines into a can.

What frightened me in New York were the people—not as individuals, but as a swarm, a horde, a tide. I had never seen so many people, most of whom appeared to be angry, bitter, and discouraged; they all appeared to be late for an appointment they did not want to keep but were fearful of being late for.

People in a city weren't a new experience to me, of course; but never had I seen so many, so hurried and seemingly so sorry to be where they were. In Los Angeles, the streets were wider, the buildings less tall. There were even some trees. It had never struck me when in Los Angeles that it was a cage filled with maddened animals trying to get out.

As one country-born, I would have been more at home in a jungle or a desert than in a city. There I would have found more of what I knew: sky, earth, water, animals, vegetation.

The *Minnekahada,* carrying more passengers per square foot than any city, did not depress me as New York had done. It seemed somehow, crowded though it was, a home. It was surrounded by the sea, the universal symbol of solitude. The minute I left the streets and boarded it, I felt more serene. Boarding the *Minnekahada* made it easier for me to understand the Ark. Its passengers had no doubt been crowded also. They endured (or, if they were Camus, enjoyed) each other, tranquilized by the rhythmic wash of the water they now lived on.

The Atlantic

"Dearest Maxwell,

"1:30 P.M. Safely on board the S.S. *Minnekahada*. The boat doesn't sail until 4:00 P.M., so letters written now will be mailed. Now that I've arrived, I feel tiptop, cool as a cabbage. I haven't found my room or roommates yet. I'm writing this in the library, where they are unpacking lots of new books.

"I rode a streetcar for five cents to 16th Street. The taxi from there cost thirty-five cents. I tipped the driver ten cents out of relief.

"This is a nice big clean boat after that hot dirty train. The average age here is forty-nine and a half years, matrons weighing 162 pounds; though there are some sixty-two-year-old professors weighing 113 pounds.

"Honey, I look all right. I see ten people right now who are less well dressed for travel than I.

"I must turn this letter in if I want it to be mailed. People are standing at the railing already waving and throwing kisses to their dear ones on the dock. I am going to wave and throw kisses, too, to my husband back in California, studying hard to be a legal school administrator."

· · ·

"Dear Ones and All,

"On the boat—ship, I should say—with nothing but water beneath me—which I try not to think about. I am writing this in the library, which is only a few steps from my room.

"My room is a cubbyhole with four shelves for berths and two hooks for the clothes of each person. During the first years of the war this ship was a mule and horse transport boat. When America entered the war, it was hastily converted to a transport for humans, which accounts for these cubbyhole rooms. It is called 'the schoolmarm's ferryboat.' After the train, it looks good to me; but most people complain.

"Two of my three roommates are elderly ladies, and I don't mean forty-five, but sixty at least. Both are teachers and have been abroad many times. Mrs. Ferguson, who sleeps in the berth beneath mine, asked me not to tell anyone that she is a teacher. She should have been a secretary for a year, like me, and she would be proud of being a teacher.

"Miss Rabot, another teacher, who is slightly lame, has the upper berth opposite mine. She can't get in or out of her berth without the help of a ladder. The room steward who brings it to her is furious because of the bother. 'If madam wants her stockings washed at 3:00 A.M., just let me know. I've been on this old tub five years. On this crossing, eight hundred old ladies who can't get in and out of their berths! Speed the day I leave.'

"Miss Rabot doesn't give a fig for saucy stewards. 'There are eight hundred passengers on board,' she corrected him. 'Not more than four hundred of that number are old ladies.'

"The youngest of us, aged twenty-three, another teacher, should have had the upper berth. Her name is Rose Bruno. This is her first trip abroad, and she says her father told her she would be disappointed. 'The grass looks the same in every country,' he said. I'm afraid it will be true.

"The man who has the deck chair next to mine, a Mr. Trask, is some kind of employee—that may not be the right word—

but he gives inspirational lectures over KHJ in Los Angeles. I am his audience now. First of all, because I was eating a chocolate candy bar, he tells me that I should not eat chocolate because it is constipating. No man has ever used that word to me before, not even Papa. I chomped away and pretended I hadn't heard what he said. I don't intend to discuss my bowels with strangers.

"When he asked me where I was going and I told him, he said, 'What discretion, what foresight! How did one so young have so much knowledge of what is best in England?' He is very heavily flattering. When I said that some of my forebears had come from Ireland, he said, 'Oh, you warm-hearted Irish, with your charming fancies.'

"Well, he isn't mine. He misses his radio audience, I think. And he is so short, round, and bald, I suspect he knows that only by flattery will he be able to win attention.

"He said, 'If you have an hour or so to spare, I would like to show you my slides of sights not to be missed in London. Foreknowledge increases interest.' This wasn't an invitation to 'come up and see my etchings,' I'm sure, but a real desire to instruct. This ship is loaded with people who are full of advice. I have just been talking with three ladies fifty-five to sixty-five, professors at Wellesley on sabbatical leave. They asked me if I had a woolen bellyband to wear in England. Said one should never travel in England without one. We have ours on now, they said, and we feel most comfortable. Think of acquiring a habit like that! They also wanted to know if I had plenty of woolen underwear with me. I certainly have plenty of everything else. Miss Rabot and Mrs. Ferguson think the Wellesley ladies are nuts. Each has been to England many times, always without woolen bellybands, and they have never had a bad cold even, let alone pneumonia of the stomach, whatever that is. They think the Wellesley ladies are showing off as world travelers and college professors. 'If you aren't cold now, you won't be in England,' they say."

.　　　.　　　.

"Dear Max: I told you when I first got on the boat that everyone was elderly. That wasn't true. The elderly, being cautious, like me, got on early so they wouldn't miss the boat. Young people, more willing to take a chance, came on board as late as possible.

"In the room just across from me are four beautiful young men, three of them seminarians heading for the priesthood. They are to be ordained next June. O the pity of it! Carmen should be with me to convince one or two of them of the error of their ways. The fourth, the largest and handsomest, is conducting a tour and has done so for four or five years, though he doesn't look over twenty-four or five now. His roommates are part of the tour. They look to be Irish, big aggressive faces, commanding noses, snapping blue eyes.

"At night, after the dancing is over, the four come down to their room, with their girlfriends, or at least friends who are girls, have food and drink sent down, and sing and dance some more. Their door is always wide open, and I lie on my bunk and watch them as if they were a living movie. The youngest priest-to-be, perhaps eighteen, was brought to his room dead to the world last night. Later he was retching and sick, later still talkative. His friends put cold towels on his head as if he had a sick headache—which I suspect he did. They were kind to him, not blaming him. Is this better than the Quaker way?

"Everybody on this ship smokes, women just as much as men. I bet I've been offered a cigarette twenty times.

"Last night was the Fourth of July and someone at our table in honor of the occasion ordered champagne for all. I took a quick swig to celebrate Independence, and it just about killed me, it was so terribly sour and bitter. It did make me feel pleasantly warm inside, as if I had already put on one of the Wellesley ladies' bellybands.

"There is a lot of lewdness going on on this boat. They have put the lights on on the upper deck to 'prevent promiscuity,' so the purser told me. I'm glad you aren't here. There are 700 women and 150 men, and of the 150, only about 50 look capable of promiscuity. You would be pounced upon."

Some matters did not go into my letters. One was my real wish that I could somehow be invited to partake in the fun going on in the room across the hall. Our room, the room of the four schoolmarms, has a sepulcher beside it. Mrs. Ferguson, who did not want it known that she was a schoolteacher, felt that this fact was somehow obvious; otherwise, why would she have been housed with three other teachers? She tried to indicate that she wasn't an ordinary schoolteacher by avoiding Miss Rabot, Miss Bruno, and me.

Miss Bruno had two occupations that kept her busy: she was seasick a lot, and she had been accepted as a volunteer to perform in the final night's concert. I don't know why. Hearing her sing "Danny Boy" was almost as disturbing as hearing her be seasick. I admired her grit. She never complained about her seasickness; or the fact that she couldn't remember the words of "Danny Boy." I held the music and prompted her when she forgot. Together we would have made a good team. I couldn't sing, but could memorize.

Miss Rabot cried a lot. I was able to see how unpleasant a spectacle I had been on the train from Chicago. Crying indicates anguish: if you don't know why, only that somebody hurts, there is nothing you can do about it. This is painful.

Since I wasn't invited to join the seminarians, and since I couldn't dance, sing, or drink, I don't know what I would have done had I been invited. All I could do was to gaze from our cubicle of seasickness, sorrow, and scorn and envy those who knew how to be merry.

I could, of course, walk the deck, sit in my chair beside Mr. Trask, or admire the sea. Mr. Trask was also going to be one of the performers in the final evening's entertainment. There was nothing wrong with *his* memory. He would, he told me, remind the passengers who would be leaving the

Minnekahada for France on a tender named *Sir Francis Drake,* while we proceeded to London, what Sir Francis had said when the Spanish Armada came into view. Sir Francis was then bowling. He kept right on, saying, "There is time to defeat the Armada and finish our game of bowls." Which is what he did. Mr. Trask—his first name was Waldemar— was no seminarian, and when I talked to him I felt that I should be taking notes preparing for an examination that he would give at the end of the voyage. But he wasn't seasick or sorrowful and he didn't scorn me because I was a teacher. He had also stopped worrying about my being constipated. I spent more time looking at the sea, or writing about it in my journal, than I did listening to Mr. Trask. I wrote sitting in my deck chair, and Mr. Trask, who took, I think, my writing in my big hardback book to be some kind of study, didn't interrupt me. I never sent reports of the sea home in my letters. I believed that my parents felt about water as Miss Bruno's father did about grass; they thought that sea water, call it Atlantic or Pacific, was pretty much the same everywhere.

I tried not to let myself forget that I was at sea. It would have been easy to do so. The sea was calm. I was never seasick. There was little sense of any progress being made. Except that there were more men present than at the St. James, and no signs saying, "Help us keep the Prohibition Amendment," I could easily have believed that I was in a hotel, not on a ship. I labored to prevent this. The chief point of my journey was to get to England. It would be wasteful, and God knows I was thrifty, to forget that getting there involved a sea voyage.

"Remember," I urged myself in the journal, "that beneath you as you travel lie the bones of brave sailors who crossed the Atlantic before it was known that the earth was round. Remember that beneath you there are as many strange animals as prowl the jungles. Try to see the changes in color of the sea from morning to night and think of the right names for each shade."

Though I hadn't discovered it at that time, my favorite views are of desert or high mesa and the sea. Both have elements in common. Most obvious, of course, is the openness: a great expanse uncluttered by buildings or vegetation. They have stayed free of the imprint of man. A ship now and then, a camel or sand grouse. But desert and sea are the planet before stop and go signs and billboards were put up; or drive-ins built. They also attract me because of their menace. They can kill you. Here I understand Camus. They have destroyed many. When you go onto the desert or put out to sea, you gamble a little. You take a chance. Travel on desert or sea challenges. It is not like driving through the equally flat, but tame and cultivated fields of Kansas, Illinois, and northern Indiana. Desert and sea are solitude made visible. (This is what Camus didn't like.)

A mountain on the horizon is desirable. In the mountains at levels I am able to attain, one encounters trees. Unlike the poet, I thank God that only He can make a tree. If man could, the savannahs would never have replaced the forests; and it was only when this happened and apes climbed down from the trees that they became men. A forest frightens me— not with the delightful tingling menace of desert or sea, but with the numbing oppression of a crowd. There are individual trees I could caress. Emerson said he would as lief grasp the limb of a tree as Thoreau's arm. I would rather. Thoreau, I feel, would object. The tree never winces. There is a eucalyptus halfway between home and St. Helena, with a great bone-white trunk and slippery green fish-shaped leaves, that I would gladly embrace. There are trees, monumental as temples, that should never be felled. I have stood beside the room-sized stump of a fallen sequoia as sorrowful as if it marked the spot where a hero had been cut down. But the forests from which we have escaped? I have no desire to return to them. The tract houses they were felled to build, aesthetically less pleasing, frighten me less. Men live there.

None of this went into my letters, or even into my journal. It is part of the discovery one makes in remembering and writing.

Mr. Trask did go into my letters. My parents had listened to him on KHJ and would rejoice, I believed, to think that travel had brought me to the side of so much rectitude and inspiration.

I attributed rectitude to Mr. Trask, judging this attribute wholly by Yorba Linda standards: that is, was he or was he not "up to no good" in relationship to young women? Anyone, I thought, who upon looking into a mirror and seeing the face Mr. Trask saw, florid, hairless above and jowly below, would instantly decide that he would never succeed as a sexual predator. I had looked into a mirror and had been instantly convinced that a career as a *femme fatale* was not for me. Mr. Trask, a KHJ commentator, was certainly my equal in common sense, I believed, and would hence devote himself wholly to commentating and make no passes at young matrons traveling alone. I had not felt this about the Australian; he was bold and not uncomely and I had lied to him about my hotel. I trusted Mr. Trask and, far from hiding my London residence from him, I told him that I had no hotel reservation there. Mr. Trask, who had been in London many times before, said, "I know just the place for you, the White Hall Hotel. When we arrive, I will take you there myself."

Meanwhile, there were, in addition to my roommates, Mr. Trask, and the seminarians, others I could write home about.

"There is an E. D. Burdon on board," I wrote home. "She is, she says, a former washerwoman. How she got to be a world traveler and poet from that beginning, I don't know. She has the build and muscles (she is forty-five or fifty, I think) to have been a washerwoman. And anyone can, I suppose, be a poet—if inside he is a poet—no matter what his job is. It takes money to be a world traveler, and where that came from, I don't know. She wrote—she asked me if she

could—some of her poems in my journal. I'll copy a couple
for you. She's no Milton, or even Longfellow, but I've read
worse verse in magazines.

Prohibition

Now that prohibition's here
You can get no wine or beer
Not a single drop
Nothing with a kick in it.
All that has a stick in it
Is a lollipop.

A Kiss

A kiss: Who'll define it,
A kiss: Who'd decline it,
If offered by someone we love?
Of lips it is but a contraction,
But oh! what intense satisfaction,
Just try it if the truth you would prove.

And so if a kiss you are offered,
Accept it as quickly as proffered.
And I think that with one
You will fully agree
'Tis as hard to decline
As it is to define:
A kiss.

Mrs. Burdon is always careful to put her name in big bold
letters after the poems she writes in my journal. I am not sure
whether this is sensitivity on her part, she thinking this Quaker
lady would not care to be thought the author of verses on
liquor and kisses; or whether she considers printing them (she
prints) in my big legal-looking journal the next thing to
publication. Well now, you have read (I hope) two, so she
has added to her readership."

"The drama has gone out of eating as a subject to report.
There is no longer a struggle to get as much as possible for

as little as possible. There is a different dessert every night. It is always bread pudding, but with a different name each night and with a different sauce.

"I got up at 5:30 this morning. Land had been sighted at 4:30 but no one had warned me. I was out on deck in five minutes decently, but not neatly, clothed. The sky was red, and against it the mast of a ship could be seen—a beautiful sight. The cliffs of England were now visible. At 6:30 we anchored, waiting for the tender that would take 250 passengers to Plymouth. The land rose in a gentle but continuous undulation from the water. The fields, outlined by hedgerows, could be plainly seen. If Ireland is the Emerald Isle, I don't know the name for this. Is there anything greener than an emerald?"

The passengers, once aboard the tender, gave three ringing cheers for the *Minnekahada*'s Captain Jenner. We then continued on our way along the green Devon coast.

"The people for Boulogne have breakfast at 4:00 A.M. tomorrow morning, then board their tender at 6:00. We land in London tomorrow at 3:00 P.M.

"I feel sorry for Europe, all these people descending upon her shores. But our hard-earned money will go into her coffers.

"I had one of my pound notes changed into silver and bills of small denominations. One pound equals a

ten-shilling bill =	2.50
2 half crowns =	1.24
4 shillings =	1.00
2 sixpence =	.12
Total	4.86

Something wrong here, in my addition.

"Bath call. I get a bath every other night at 10:00 P.M. The bath steward bangs on my door and says, "Bath for Number 58." I am Number 58. The tub is filled, steaming hot, but with salt water that won't make suds. After thirty minutes, you are kind of fishy-smelling, but clean."

London

"Next morning. We are two hours from London, sailing, moving anyway, up the Thames River. Those of us who are left are writing farewell notes, playing solitaire, or watching the scenery: which is flat green meadows, occasional groves of trees, some sheep, many boats, a few factories. Two hours more! The destination toward which I have been traveling all of my life is almost at hand."

"London, England
"Friday Eve, July 12, 1929
"Something will have to give: letter writing or London. There isn't time for both. Because it's daylight until 10:30, I put off writing until dark—and by that time, I'm too sleepy to be coherent.

"When last I wrote you I was traveling up the Thames, past factories and foundries. After three hours of that, we finally reached the piers where we docked. There stood Englishmen in bowler hats, just as I had expected them. Only one of my suitcases was opened by the customs officer, after a look at my innocent freckled face. Then a cockney porter I couldn't understand at all, but who could evidently understand *me*, crammed me and all my luggage onto a train and into a compartment, where, by chance or plan, was Mr. Trask. He was not going to the White Hall Hotel, which he had recommended to me, but was going on to some fancier place; he said his taxi would go past the White Hall and I could ride with him.

"I did, and at the hotel he said he would run in and see if there was a room he could book for me. I was glad to have him do this. The St. James was the only hotel I had ever been in, and this, unlike it, was not for ladies traveling alone.

"Mr. Trask booked a room for me, tipped the porter who took my luggage out of the taxi, and was off to his own hotel. Be sure to watch KHJ in the future, and you will hear the voice of the man who was so kind to your daughter. The White Hall is exactly what I needed. Cheerful, clean, and cheap. It costs only 6/6 (six shillings sixpence), which equals $1.62 for bed and breakfast.

"Now I am going to abandon chronology for a while and just list some things I have noticed so far.

"1. You should see English people eat! They work very hard at it. Every bite they take is first pushed with one implement onto another and then into their mouths.

"2. Our ice cream is called 'cream ice' here. It is very creamy, but not sweet. People sugar it.

"3. A menu at a confectioner's is called a 'tariff.'

"4. Water is never served with a meal.

"5. Pop is called 'aerated water.'

"6. When I ask for a glass of milk, it comes heated.

"7. Coffee is always served with hot milk, not cream.

"8. Marmalade is always on the breakfast table. And we are the ones with the oranges. Why is this?

"9. I asked for grapefruit and it came in a dish chopped up and looking like apple sauce.

"10. Liberty's is the only store that can compare with any shop in Los Angeles. Most could take lessons from J. C. Penney. Windows are crowded, nothing properly displayed.

"11. Women wear afternoon dresses on the streets.

"12. Derby hats and canes make men look sophisticated.

"13. London is a man's town. Never do you see the crowds of women on the streets you see in any American city.

"14. Nothing but American movies: *Showboat, Broadway Melody, Fox Movietone Follies.*

"15. There are ten thousand buses.

"16. I saw a Buick and it looked like a tank.

"17. *But* in the Mayfair-Berkeley district I saw more Rolls-Royces, Hispanos than I expect to see again in a lifetime.

"18. Houses here are all connected with each other.

"19. London is having a hot spell. Not to a Southern Californian, though. Drought, too.

"20. I bought lavender of a buxom lady on the street who was singing a song about it.

"21. Sidewalk artists are thicker than dry cleaners in Anaheim.

"22. Also hurdy-gurdy players.

"23. English money is simple. I could be a clerk in any London store this very minute.

"24. London abounds in "greens," "parks," "squares."

"25. London is easy to get about in. London bobbies don't think you are stupid because you don't know the town. In New York they thought I was stupid. All except the ladies at the St. James. They knew I was just ignorant.

"Tomorrow I am going on a bus tour of London. I am soft after two weeks of sitting on trains and boats and in hotels. I actually have blisters on both heels, just from walking. I did see a lot, blisters and all: Tate Gallery, Westminster Abbey, Houses of Parliament. Tomorrow we'll see the Tower of London, the beheading block, Dr. Samuel Johnson's home, London Bridge. The tour costs only two shillings (50 cents), and is cheaper than seeing a doctor about my feet."

"I forgot that tomorrow was Sunday. I went this morning to the Friends Meeting House: the Meeting House proper occupies only a very small proportion of a really large and

imposing building. What the rest of the building is used for,
I don't know.

"The interior is arranged in a strange way as compared with
any Friends Church in Southern California. I will draw you
a picture: The  people in the
center section face each other
as do the people on the side sec-
tions. There are no chairs, only
benches. These may be made for worship, surely not for comfort. The room, walls, and benches are a subdued brown, and
the only light is what filters through heavy red curtains that
cover the long windows. I entered, sat down (x marks my
place). Since all heads were bowed, I bowed mine. After about
fifteen minutes, I ventured to open one eye. I then saw that
heads weren't really bowed, only inclined in meditation. Becoming bolder, I glanced about and in so doing saw that there
was no pulpit, no organ, no choir, no minister. Again I
meditated, but with a stealthy eye on my watch. When I had
exhausted my store of thoughts, I glanced around again. I was
the youngest person there.

"At 11:30, a mite of a man in gold spectacles which permitted him to look out, but with whiskers so enveloping we
could see nothing of him but his specs, got to his feet and said,
'A dumb world is a dead world.' So saying, he sat; nor did
all of my ardent internal encores persuade him to further
develop this truly rational thought.

"However, his example brought a lady from Philadelphia
(she told us) to her feet. She said, 'Strive always for the vision
as yet unfilled.'

"Suddenly everyone rose and I could hear someone speaking
but could not understand what was being said. The amens,
when the speaking ceased, told me that what we had been
hearing was a prayer. I didn't care for the standing. Prayer
shouldn't be treated like the national anthem. At one minute
of twelve a lady said, 'Spend not your money for husks,' which

is also my motto. At twelve exactly, another lady said, 'There will be no meeting tonight.' People then shook hands with each other and began to leave.

"I didn't realize that I was in a Silent Meeting until the man with the whiskers said, A dumb world is a dead world. Here I was, a birthright Quaker (and the Silent Meeting is considered by most to be a Quaker birthright), and I didn't know one when I was in it. Did you ever go to a Silent Meeting?

"After the service was over, it was like any Friends Meeting. Because I was a stranger, I was made welcome. They told me there was a Friends Service Council, whose purpose was, among other things, to help traveling Friends. The Council had its office in the Meeting House building and if I needed advice or help, I shouldn't hesitate to call on them. So far, I haven't needed help, but I now know where to go if I do."

I didn't find out a minute too soon. Next morning the head housekeeper or manager, whatever she was, of the White Hall, said, "Well, Mrs. McPherson, I expect you've been looking forward to today."

I hadn't, so I said, "Not particularly. Why?"

"This is the day your husband rejoins you. You surely haven't forgotten?"

"My husband is at home in California. What do you mean, 'rejoin'?"

"He was with you when you came. He registered for you and for himself."

"That was Mr. Waldemar Trask. He is a KHJ commentator. I never saw him before I met him on shipboard."

"Mr. Trask registered as your husband."

"He is old enough to be my father."

"Some husbands are. This Mr. Trask is also old enough to have some coin. He paid for your room in advance."

"I didn't know it. I'm leaving, at once."

"Where will you go?"

"I don't know. And if I did, I wouldn't tell you. You knew all along that man wasn't my husband."

"I thought you did, too."

"What are you?" What I had in mind were literary terms like "madam" or "keeper of a house of ill fame," but I didn't have the temerity to be so outspoken.

"I'm what you Yanks made me, that's what."

"I never set foot in London before."

"The war, the war. We got used to it. It was partly good-heartedness. Some were just boys. They might never be back. So, if a doughboy said, 'Mr. and Mrs.,' why not? Might be their only chance to say it."

"Mr. Trask's no boy."

"No, he ain't. But he has plenty of money."

"You mean he's been here before?"

"Many's the time. And is somewhere right now, or I miss my guess."

"As a husband?"

"Maybe. Maybe not. Some don't care."

I didn't shed tears, but my chin shook so I couldn't speak.

"There's nothing to cry about. You're not hurt except in your pride. And you got a good clean room free."

"Not free. I'll pay for every cent of it. And I'm leaving this minute."

"Where are you going?"

"You'd tell Mr. Trask."

"Trask don't have to go chasing around strange hotels looking for girls. The truth of the matter is, you don't know where you're going."

That wasn't the truth of the matter. I knew exactly where I was going: to the Friends Service Council.

"This is the tourist season. The hotels are full. You'll go chasing around hunting a room and fall into the hands of someone a lot worse than Trask and the White Hall."

"I couldn't."

·   ·   ·

My bags were packed (my trunk was still at American Express), my room paid for, and I out of the White Hall in thirty minutes. In thirty more, I was at the offices of the Council for traveling Friends. I was ashamed to tell them my story; and I have never told it to anyone until now. The Council, evidently of the same opinion as the New York police, though as kind as the London bobbies, gave me a card of introduction to The Penn Club at 8, 9, and 10 Tavistock Square, London W.C.1. The Club was for traveling Friends, and I surely qualified. The Club at the minute was filled, but a Mr. George A. Walton was going to be away for a week and he might be willing to sublet his room. The Council could not make this decision. I would have to go out to the Club and apply to the manager in person.

I was more than willing. Money for taxis meant nothing to me now. I was shamefaced and running away from a disgrace. I knew about Mr. Walton, whose room, if I was lucky, I would be occupying. I had been given a folder at the Friends Meeting on Sunday announcing a July series of lectures on "International Understanding"; George A. Walton (of Pennsylvania, U.S.A.), head of George School, in Pennsylvania, would lecture on "American Education."

Tavistock Square did not mean anything to me then, let alone Bloomsbury. Virginia Woolf in 1929 was living at 52 Tavistock Square, and I may have passed her and Leonard pacing the street together. She, who deplored "the predominance of sexual love in 19th century fiction and its growing unreality to us who have no real condemnation in our heads any longer for adultery as such," would not have taken my running away from Mr. Trask as anything but comic. I may have been mistaken in thinking that Mr. Trask had adultery in mind. But the idea, and it was repulsive, had entered *my* mind when I found that he intended to return to the White Hall.

Copulation outside marriage, Virginia wrote in a letter to

Vita Sackville-West, did not offend her; but Trask surely would have. "I felt like vomiting," she writes, "after encountering in the street people with faces base, vulgar, empty." And I certainly did not look like the woman she most admired (though I share her name), Sackville-West, a woman like "a ripe fig, with legs like white columns."

Nevertheless, I would that we had met. We had one subject in common: headaches. No word occurs more often in my journal than "headache"; no word more often in Virginia Woolf's letters. I would no more write in my letters of headaches than of hemorrhoids. Pain at the top may be more seemly than pain at the bottom; but pain is pain and unless you have Virginia Woolf's great narrative power, all aches, pains, twinges, and seizures are best left out of letters.

Not a word of my reason for leaving the White Hall for the Penn Club went into either my journal or letters home. Once I saw the Penn Club, I was glad that Mr. Trask had deposited me at the White Hall, not in Mr. Walton's room at the Penn Club. I was so enamored of that room, the Club, and its location that Mr. Trask might have been a price I was willing to pay.

"Mama, I have now moved to the Penn Club, a place ten thousand times more agreeable and appealing than the White Hall. I found it through the Friends Service Council. My room is one sublet to me by a Mr. Walton, head of George School in Pennsylvania. It is a beautiful room, twenty by twenty at least, with a fireplace, two huge mirrors, an ornate but usable desk. French doors open onto a balcony which overlooks a park across the street. The park is private and may be used only by persons living in the houses that surround it. The gate is kept locked and can only be opened by those who have keys. I have a key.

"Behind the Club is a typical English garden—high brick walls covered with ivy, graveled walks, a sundial, and borders with masses of old-fashioned flowers. Here the Club members sit after dinner smoking—English Quakers are much less strict than Quakers in Yorba Linda—drinking coffee, ginger beer, and lemon squash. Living in London is about like being at the North Pole. Daylight half the night. Men in white flannels go across to the park at 9:00 P.M. for a game of tennis. Think of that!

"Last night I went to a musical called *Awake and Dream* with a San Luis Obispo schoolteacher who is staying here. The tickets were $3.50 and worth it, I guess; though at this rate I'll soon be broke and English Friends will have to take up a collection to send me home.

"The show was beautiful but the audience interested me more than the play. People smoked and talked during the whole performance. The theater was blue with smoke. In the middle of the performance, there was a fifteen-minute intermission during which food was served. Not free, of course.

"Never have I seen so many evening dresses or such sophisticated ones. Not even straps! Held up by magic. Every man in full dress. Not tuxedos, but long tails, silk hats. In Los Angeles, if any people do dress like that, they are in their cars until they reach their destination, not walking the streets as if they were in an outdoor ballroom.

"My room here is eight shillings and sixpence for bed and breakfast, or about $2.10. More than I had hoped to pay, but, oh boy, is it worth it! My eyes are closing. I'll write more tomorrow."

"Here it is 10:30 before I get started writing. I wish you could see how pleasantly I am situated. My (Mr. Walton's) long table is drawn up to the window that faces the park and my books (from the library downstairs) are ranged on it in neat rows. Also, I bought two books. I shouldn't do it. They cost too much, and carrying my suitcases already breaks my back without making them any heavier. The two I bought are De la Mare's *Come Hither*, and Logan Pearsall Smith's *Selections from Santayana*.

. . .

With Logan Pearsall Smith I was once again close to Bloomsbury without knowing it. I admired Santayana, and by buying Pearsall Smith's *Selections from Santayana,* I thought I'd have the best of both men. Virginia Woolf knew and did not care for Smith for a variety of reasons: he was "little, censorious, mildly buggeristical." Also, he was born in America and hence had in his veins "the American salt I don't relish, something coarse and briny," which Virginia found more forbidding than the "buggeristical" strain, which if purged from Bloomsbury would have emptied it of half its men. Pearsall Smith was also of a Quaker family, God worshipers, which fact Virginia found ridiculous. So perhaps it was just as well I never had the opportunity to compare my "coarse and briny" headaches with Virginia's more civilized pains.

I wish I had had that opportunity, though; in addition to my coarse brinyness, the result of the "American salt" in my veins, I had other qualities Virginia Woolf found disagreeable.

Even the English, when they were "lower class and poor," had in her opinion "hideous voices and clothes and bad teeth." (Virginia's own teeth weren't perfect. She speaks of clapping her front teeth into her mouth on the arrival of visitors.) In addition, the poor "didn't have much notion how to express their feelings."

My teeth were all right, but I was poor; and in Virginia's opinion undoubtedly lower class. Add to these disabilities my Quakerism and I might, had we met in the few blocks that separated us, have reached immortality via a report in a Virginia Woolf letter.

Of Quakers, she wrote to a friend, "Quakers are notoriously long-lived and unsusceptible to shock. They stand any amount of strain and have practically no feelings."

I still wish that by some miracle we might have met. Virginia Woolf enjoyed talking, and learning from her talk. She would have learned at once that, Quaker though I was, I was capable of shock and brimming with feelings.

I would also like to have told her about my adventure, if that is the name for it, with Mr. Trask. She was fifteen years older than I and a thousand years wiser. She wrote that copulation outside of marriage did not offend her. Mr. Trask, I think, *would* have offended her, copulating or noncopulating. I found him offensive for reasons she might not have shared. She was no romantic, and advice about avoiding constipation might have struck her as no more than sensible and down to earth. When Lytton Strachey, seeing a spot on her sister Vanessa's dress, asked, "Semen?," Virginia is not reported as being offended. The two words do, however, suggest a different range of activities, one more typical of Bloomsbury than the other.

Headaches were the subject we might have talked about most easily. I am amazed at the number of times Virginia speaks of them in her letters. She calls them a "sickness," as I would speak of a case of strep throat or a bout of the flu. I called mine "a pain in the head"; and since they were often daily, I could not treat them like a sickness and take to my bed. But then, my headaches have never, so far, at least, been the forerunners of madness. I wrote of them in my journal only. Is this an indication that old John Burroughs was right, that I *was* a "lonely soul," able to communicate only with myself? I did write from England, in one of my letters to my mother, "I have had only two headaches since I left home." Travel evidently provided my head with so many concerns that there was no opportunity left for it to relax and ache.

Years ago in a piece of writing I mentioned my headaches. From far-off places came letters, one from a man in Australia who had to take a boat to reach the pharmacy that would give him the exact name of the concoction that earlier had cured his migraines. The headachers of the world are evidently legion. Their many responses made me think that since other persons sharing handicaps, grievances, and goals are organized, headachers of the world should form a league. Their initials would be HOW. *How* to get rid of the damned things. Left-handers are organized, gays share their troubles, parents without partners get together. High-IQers meet in Mensa to avoid the tedium of mingling with those in lower brackets. There are undoubtedly more headachers in the world than there are people in all of these other groups put together. We get less sympathy than the others. Our affliction, while painful, is neither very interesting nor very frightening. We probably imagine most of it. Was anyone ever known to die of a headache? It is the universally accepted excuse of the sexually non-co-operative wife.

One reason for the lack of sympathy a headacher gets, however, is that he doesn't like to be organized. The very thought of it makes his head ache. So we'll probably have to struggle on alone. No one will ever stage a telethon for us, or tell us we'll be fine if we eat less cholesterol and more bran.

Yet the person who has never had a headache, except as the result of too much drink or congested sinuses, strikes me as scarcely human. Just as the emergence of Homo sapiens was marked by increase in brain size, so it seems natural that this expansion in so exposed an area atop all the rest would, naturally, be more vulnerable to pain. Hens, I suspect, do not have headaches, having so little in that area to ache with.

I have long tried to find in Thoreau any mention of headaches—without success. He has cheered me (apart from his writing itself) in other ways. He was born, like me, near the center of July. And the July-born are not well thought of astrologically. We are called the "doormats of the zodiac"; and in a book entitled *Astrology for Cats,* I read that "the Cancerian cat is a fraidy cat."

No one I know, with one exception, has ever called Thoreau a "doormat" or a "fraidy cat." The one man who did so is almost the only man who could do so and be forgiven; and until I read Robert Louis Stevenson's life, after I had read his stories, I did not forgive him. But for a man with Stevenson's ailments, who in spite of them pursued and won a hesitant bride, defied disapproving parents, circled the globe, paid his way with his pen, Thoreau at Walden, two miles away from home and supper, writing in his journal instead of composing something salesworthy, seemed justifiably, as Stevenson wrote in his essay, "to possess none of the large unconscious geniality of the world's heroes. His thin, penetrating big-nosed face . . . conveys some hint of the limitations of his mind and character."

Had Stevenson kept a journal as did Virginia Woolf and Thoreau, I would have discovered his worth sooner. Are journal keepers journal readers? Or are most too self-centered for that? Are they, as my mother's question to me indicated years ago when she brought me from the library someone's journal, affected with limitations of mind and character?

"What," my mother would ask, handing me the journal I had asked for, "was the matter with this man?"

Whatever it was, Virginia Woolf and I were both afflicted with it. I missed my chance fifty years ago on Tavistock Square to speak to her. She speaks to me often now in her journals and letters. And it is probably just as well that I don't have to encounter in them her scathing report of the briny coarseness of Trask and the downright stupidity of West.

"Dear Mama: I went to the library at the Friends Meeting House this morning. They have enough letters and records of early Friends to stock a small library without any other books at all. I did so much copying I have writer's cramp. I'll bring everything home, not try to copy what I copied in my notebook once again here. Since the Quaker marriages were not officiated over by any minister, not even their own, they were in the eyes of the law a bunch of bastards. But you know all this. In any case, the Quakers themselves made records of everything and kept them all. So the library here is bulging with letters, notebooks, booklets, affadavits. Mr. Milligan, the librarian, said I'd find more complete accounts of the Milhouses who were Irish in the Quaker Meeting House in Dublin. But he had plenty for me.

"I was struck by the fact that I was in London copying the facts of Thomas and Sarah Milhous's leaving for America exactly two hundred years after their departure in the summer of 1729. Mr. Milligan said that the Milhouses were originally north of England people who had fought with Cromwell and had been given land in Ireland by him at the end of the war.

"In Ireland they were converted to Quakerism by missionary friends of William Penn, perhaps by William Penn himself. The Welsh Griffiths, one of whom later married a Milhous, sailed in 1682 to America on the same ship that brought William Penn to America. I'm glad the Penns caught up with us. I'd rather be a Quaker with Penn than a soldier with Cromwell.

"Edith Price Griffith (whose daughter Elizabeth married our [mine anyway] great-grandfather Joshua Milhous) was a Friends minister who made more than one preaching trip to England and Ireland. I laughed to read one letter about her that Mr. Milligan showed me. Someone at whose home Amos and Edith had stayed wrote that when Edith came in weary from preaching, her husband would fetch her house slippers for her, and draw up her chair to the fire, just as good wives are supposed to do for their husbands.

"No wonder Quaker women are so independent. I must copy this letter for Max, so that he will understand that I have the blood of women who were accustomed to being waited on by their husbands in my veins.

"It is a strange thing to be reading these hundred-year-old letters and at the same time mourning the fact that no one will now write a letter to me. Where are the letters from home? I don't worry much about Max. His mother long ago, when Max was in Inyo County being a cowboy and failed to write, said, 'McPhersons don't write letters.' She knew what she was talking about. But Milhous-McManamans write. At home you send me three letters a week. What has happened?

Are you well? Nonsense, asking a nonwriter to tell why she doesn't write.

"The trouble is that even if you do write, I'll be out of touch with American Express in London, who take care of my mail. I've already bought my tickets from here to Edinburgh, Glasgow, and thence by boat to Belfast, Ireland. In Ireland I travel from Belfast to Kildare to Timahoe to Dublin. Then across to Hollyhead, England, and on to Oxford in time for the beginning of the Summer Session. My ticket pays for a two-day conducted tour of the Trossachs, which includes steamer trips the length of Loch Lomond and Loch Katrine, and a ride in a horse-driven something through the Trossachs. Meals are included. The cost for all this is $40. Hair raising! But maybe, considering the territory covered and the food provided, not unreasonable.

"I love my room here so much so that if Mr. Walton weren't returning, I'd be inclined just to stay here, drink ginger beer, read, and explore London until time to go to Oxford.

"Oh, why doesn't somebody write? At least I'll have the solace when I reach Dublin of reading some more two-hundred-year-old letters, if not addressed to me, at least written by my forebears."

One line written in my journal at that time was the result of more thought than its brevity suggests.

"Why do I feel so much more comfortable and at ease in London than I did in New York?"

Myths about people exist everywhere. Easterners believe Californians to be a semitropical people, slow and languorous in their walk and amorous by nature. I have had a New Yorker in San Francisco ask me if his walk was too brisk for me, believing evidently that a loll or a stroll was all that my tropical blood could endure. Even native Californians, accustomed only to the north, have a myth about Southern California. Joan Didion, born in Sacramento, now living in

Southern California, writes of the Santa Ana wind like a native son of New England, not the Golden West. She is as romantic about the Santa Ana as I am about snow.

"It is hard for people who have not lived in Los Angeles to realize how radically the Santa Ana figures in the local imagination," writes Didion.

Nonsense!

For twenty-five years I lived far nearer the epicenter of the Santa Ana wind than the people of Los Angeles. First in Yorba Linda, at the mouth of the Santa Ana Canyon, down which the Santa Ana wind funnels; then in Hemet, near Mt. San Gorgonio, at the base of which, in the Mohave Desert, the wind Didion calls "malevolent" has its cradle.

While the child Didion was living in Northern California, I, in Yorba Linda, was living in a two-story wooden house built on the one hilltop of a barley-field ranch. No orange trees had yet been planted; there were no eucalyptus wind-breaks to protect us. Before a Santa Ana began to blow—and we could tell when one was coming by the pillars of dust that were piling up far to the east, out San Gorgonio way—my father braced the house on the west side with half a dozen heavy planks. In a bad blow, he bedded his four children down in the cement weir box, empty then, but which would hold water when the pumps went in and the irrigation systems began working.

But, children in the weir box, parents in the stable, the house stood steady, never lost even a shingle. Upstairs, where the beds stood on uncarpeted floors, the house did rock enough to cause beds moving east to west to leave, like the glaciers before them, tracks of their movements. It was a sturdy house, though built by a noncarpenter on top of a hill; and it needed to be, since it was about the first object of its height the Santa Ana, in its malevolence, met after leaving San Gorgonio.

Didion writes of the Santa Ana in a California way: as a wind stronger, more furious and destructive than the winds of other states. In Yorba Linda we did not thus experience it. Rapine, wrecks, and migraines were no more numerous than usual when the Santa Ana blew. We propped up our houses, slept in our weir boxes, and delighted in the dance of the outsize tumbleweeds.

Lovers of solitude are perhaps wind lovers. Hillaire Belloc says, "A man is never alone who loves the wind."

Bryher writes of a friend, "She loved the wind. I suspect she must have had a Celt among her ancestors."

What the connection between Celts and the wind is, I don't know. But Bryher's opinion illustrates the myths one group of people has about another.

New Yorkers, as I have said, believe that Californians are slow of pace and given to siestas. The English believe that Americans are loud-mouthed hustlers, with little regard for civilized dignity.

Perhaps so. In any case, I was more at home in London than in New York. New York Americans were on their way, and I, ignorant and stumbling, got in their way. Englishmen in London had arrived. They had had centuries to accustom themselves to visiting colonials and knew how to do so cheerfully. In New York I had been yelled at as stupid. In London, recognized as merely ignorant, I was quietly helped.

In my first week in London I did not visit the homes of my heroes. I walked about their city, content to experience their sky over my head, their river at my feet, their towers and bridges on my horizon.

"Was I afraid reality would shatter my dreams?" Ben Hecht had written in *Gargoyles*. And I had copied into my journal these lines: "If you hold something in your arms, you haven't got it. It's what you can't get your fingers on that you own. What you dream about, you own most."

So, living at the Penn Club, where I was absorbed in a modern England I knew nothing about, I continued to dream about (and thus own?) the London whose writers had brought me to England.

•   •   •

"Dearest Ones and All, as Aunt Lib always said: I have now paid for my ticket for Ireland. Otherwise I might never leave here. Breakfast comes with the price of the room and it is so large I'm not hungry at lunchtime. Besides, I am never here at lunchtime. Dinner is strange but delicious; the dessert is called 'a sweet' and after it something like macaroni and cheese, which is called 'a savoury,' is served. Coffee and soft drinks are brought to us in the garden. I drink ginger beer. Don't tell Papa, who doesn't like anything with the word 'beer' in it.

"A man here who is in Parliament told me that if I wanted to I could stop over at all the sizable cities between here and Edinburgh; he said that it would be a pity to miss Cambridge, Ely, Lincoln, and York. I think he is right—though I'm learning to take a lot of advice with a grain of salt. These are all great cathedral cities, and York and Lincoln are also old Roman fortresses. It will cost me only about two dollars a night more for bed and breakfast in each of these cities. I'll carry my own bags, tip no one unless it is shaken out of me, and dine in the evening in my room on meat pies bought in pastry shops.

"My blisters are now completely well. I've stopped walking and have been taking tours. The tours save my feet but they lacerate my heart. The tour leader has said his piece so many times about the Old Curiosity Shop, St. Paul's Cathedral, and the spot where Mary, Queen of Scots lost her head that he had as well be reciting the multiplication table. I stand at the back of the tour group and try not to hear a word the leader says. I want to know where I am, of course. And I want to stand on unblistered feet; then I want to think my own thoughts."

"Dear Max: You have heard it said that it's the journey, not the goal, that counts. Maybe for some, but not for me. A journey is the price, and a very dear one, you pay to get to a place like the Penn Club. If Mr. Walton weren't coming back, I might just stay here indefinitely and travel no more. I might stay here even if he did come back, but I doubt that the head of George School wants a roommate.

"There are many Englishwomen here. They understand me perfectly. I am never sure what they are saying to me. The English speak very fast; they have a rising inflection; no single word is stressed and no emotion is shown. Of course I think our way of speaking infinitely more attractive, both as to sound and as a means of conveying ideas.

"There are people of all nationalities here. At the table tonight I talked with an Austrian professor who was for three years a prisoner of war in Russia. I asked him if he had read *All Quiet on the Western Front.* He had. I asked him if war prisons in Russia were as bad as the German ones portrayed in that book.

" 'Oh, yes,' he said. He has an accent but I can understand him much more easily than I can the English ladies. 'A book can never dare tell of the awfulness of the prisons. It was hellish. And I was an officer. Of what the common soldiers endured, I will not speak.'

"It is 1:30 A.M. and I am writing with my eyes closed. The San Luis Obispo lady and I went to see *Journey's End* tonight. It is the most talked-of play in London and New York; and it was the greatest modern play I've ever seen. There are no women in the cast. The entire action takes place in a dugout about forty yards behind the front-line trenches. There is a constant boom of guns, whine of shells, smell of smoke. I came out feeling I had served for two or three years in some war myself. At the end of the play when the orchestra played 'God Save the King,' as it does at the close of all functions, I was ready to do all in my power to save him.

"I am asleep. 1) There are no streetcars in London. 2) There are millions of buses. 3) There are hundreds of horses. 4) A bus stops when signaled. You ride high above crowds. For tuppence you can ride miles. 5) At some streets there are

officers directing traffic; at others, none. It is a wonder so
many Britishers are still alive. 6) There are raised places of
safety for pedestrians in the middle of each street. You run,
climb on one of these, watch for a chance, then run again.
7) I have never encountered such courtesy. The answer to
every question is closed with 'It's been a pleasure to help you'
or 'I wish you a pleasant afternoon.'

"I've been undressing as I write. I can undress faster than
I can write. Now I'm ready to sleep—in bed—not writing.
See you in the morning."

In the morning I continued.

"I have seen the damage—the rubble isn't cleared away—the
weeds growing about the vines climbing over the ruins of
buildings and homes left after the German air raids. I see
them and say to myself, silently, 'Here people died, were
burned to death, lost all their belongings; while we in America
prided ourselves on staying out of the war. I am ashamed of
our tardiness and of our pride in our peacefulness.

"I spent three hours in Westminster Abbey. It is impossible
to believe that such a building exists. Every block of pavement
covers the bones of a dead man. At first I was loath to tread
on what once lived. It is impossible not to. At first I tried to
read all the inscriptions. I had to give that up, too. Not only
the pavement, but the walls are covered with plaques, lined
with statues and bas-reliefs and inscriptions.

" 'Contiguous with this plaque lies all that is mortal of
Gerald Geoffree Neville who died at the age of nineteen
defending his Majesty's frontiers against the French in the
New World.' That isn't exact. Tomorrow I'm going back with
a notebook and copy dozens of inscriptions. Oh, the pity of
those thousands of young men dead in wars long forgotten—
dead fighting against her Majesty's enemies in the Punjab,
drowned off the Carolines, fallen in an engagement with the
revolutionists, fallen in battle in South Africa, gloriously dead

in an engagement of her Majesty's forces in Crimea. Name of the Deity! Name of the Deity!

"England is built upon a foundation of the bones of her young men. Not hundreds, but thousands, of inscriptions; monuments 'erected by his yet living widow,' by 'a sorrowing mother,' or by 'the officers of his command.' The graves of these men affected me far more profoundly than the graves of the illustrious dead: Chaucer, Ben Jonson, Butler, Hardy. They had their lives and had their time; they said their say and were heard. They rest now, universally honored. I shed no tears on their graves. But I will say ten thousand prayers and shed ten thousand tears for those whose lives were sacrificed before they ever lived. 'Dead at nineteen in the New World fighting the French'! Name of the Deity! Name of the Deity! Empires are not worth this price.

"The dead in the cloister have been dead so long, I decided they must be used to it. Norman abbots of the cathedral dating from 1066 are there. Crusaders of the eleventh and twelfth centuries. I sat in the cloister with the birds, the fountain, the green grass on one side of me and these thousand-year-old dead men on the other. I wanted to be home in Yorba Linda, where everything is either alive or out of sight and uninscribed.

"I hadn't exhausted the cathedral, but I had exhausted myself. I headed for Trafalgar Square. As I stood on the bridge over the Thames first, Big Ben struck six. At Trafalgar Square there was a public meeting of miners. Impassioned speeches of which I couldn't understand a word were being made. Why can't I? English is my mother tongue. Is it my Indian blood refusing to understand a word of my former persecutors? But I can read. There were posters everywhere. 'In memory of Maggie's victims.' 'We will not starve in the midst of luxury.' 'Maggie must not grind us down.'

"I asked a policeman who Maggie was. He didn't know. I asked two other men; they didn't know either. Finally I was told, 'Maggie is the Home Secretary.' I never did find his real name, but I can tell you one thing: the miners hate him, and whatever the speechmakers were screaming, the crowd approved. There were at least twenty Bobbies present. They may not have known who Maggie was, but they were going to see that his opponents did nothing worse than bellow.

"By the time I got home, I had walked so much and read so much and cried so much, I was starved. When I was asked if I wanted a salad, I said yes. I wanted everything on the menu. The salad was a boiled custard with fresh fruit, strawberries, peaches, etc. in it. When I had finished that, I asked for my dessert. I keep forgetting that here, a dessert is called 'a sweet.' 'You have had your sweet,' the waitress said. I wondered if I had been in such a stupor of weariness that I had eaten my sweet without knowing it. 'What was it?' I asked. 'Your salad. You ordered it and ate it.' So a salad is a sweet here! And that was the end of my meal."

Cathedral Country

It was fortunate for me that Mr. Walton was returning. Otherwise I might never have had the backbone to leave. The Penn Club was too comfortable and London too large and history-soaked for me to give either up voluntarily. But my ticket was bought and my decision wise to use the two weeks before Summer Session began visiting Ireland. In Oxford, I'd be once again near London.

From the Penn Club I wrote Max, "This is my last night here. I write you from my bed surrounded by books from the Penn Club's wonderful library—which is something I know you don't like. I don't blame you. Men have gone to bed with readers, but I have never heard of any who enjoyed bedding down with a woman *and* a bedful of books.

"My first stop is Cambridge and I'll write you from there tomorrow night; though you know more about where I am than I know about where you are. Have you gone up to Berkeley yet? If I had a drop of mean blood in me, I'd stop writing to you and Mama and let you worry about me for a change. If you did worry, I'd never hear—and I like to write—so I guess I'll just keep on."

.   .   .

My first stop, as I'd told Max it would be, was at Cambridge. I refrained from writing to anyone of the embarrassing mistake I made when I arrived there. "Where," I asked a resident, "is the college?"

My idea of a college was based on the one I knew, Whittier, with its single building (not counting the gym), called "Founder's Hall."

"The 'college,' as you call it," I was told, "is everywhere. Cambridge University is a collection of colleges. Which college in particular did you want to see?"

"All," said I, not knowing what I was talking about.

"In that case, I hope you'll be here a fortnight. But since you're very near King's College Chapel, I suggest that you start there."

And that's where I started; and beyond any other building I've ever entered, it has stayed in my memory. The reason for this is, I think, that it was a place to smell as well as to see. The chapel was filled with masses of lilies, remaining, I suppose, after some Church of England celebration.

"Dearest, dearest Mama: I write you from King's College Chapel, Cambridge. I feel that it is almost sacrilegious to be holding anything so materialistic as a pen and notebook in my hand. Never, *never* have I set eyes on anything so beautiful, so inspiring. Westminster Abbey was noble, rich beyond all compare; St. Paul, magnificent, awesome; but this is somehow more significantly beautiful. Is it because of the scent of lilies? Or because, as I write, music is being played that almost shakes my fingernails loose from my fingers.

"Is it impossible for us, on the last frontier, to understand how mere building materials, glass, stone, wood, can be so combined as to appear to be man's most impassioned prayer? If all buildings were like this, a Martian could easily believe that our world was peopled by angels.

"King's College is one of the oldest and most distinguished

of the many colleges at Cambridge. Formerly only Eton students were permitted to come here. To think that this was the 'church' of college boys! Probably they thought chapel was as much of a bore as we did at Whittier. Whatever they felt, it is a perfect thing. I wish you were here seeing it for yourself, not getting it secondhand in pen and ink.

"I am now in one of the smaller rooms. It contains a memorial to those fellows of the college, two or three hundred of them, who died 1914 to 1918. Rupert Brooke was one of them. He wrote, 'If I should die, think only this of me: / That there's some corner of a foreign field / That is for ever England.' If I keep going to chapels and cathedrals, I'll cry all the way to the Scottish border. Cry up there, too, maybe.

"Another stopping place to rest and write—in the garden of Christ College now. Before I write 'lovely,' 'exquisite,' etc. again, so that you will think that the mere sight of anything English starts the soft soap to flowing, I will tell you that I rode here this morning from London with two lunatics in my compartment. Talk about American flappers! Those two girls giggled one and one-half hours and sixty miles without stopping.

"I am eating my lunch as I write: three oranges for 6d (12¢). That's cheaper than California. Since I wrote you in King's College Chapel, I have watched part of a cricket game (resembles one-o'-cat in method of running), lawn tennis, and walked along the river Cam at the back of the colleges. St. John's College alone has more lawn and more lawn-tennis courts than the entire city of Los Angeles. This is the 'long' (long vacation) and the colleges are not in session. The cricket fields and tennis courts are filled just the same.

"At every quarter-hour the chimes of the clocks in the different colleges ring out. The trees rustle, rustle. The wind is sweet with the smell of damp earth and blossoming flowers. I have spared you a listing of the names of all the flowers that grow here. But I am going to ask the gardener for one pansy to send you, a pansy that bloomed in Christ Church garden, in English soil and beneath the English sun, which was very hot today.

"I have no idea where I am in relation to the rest of the town, but I seem to have been hitting all the right places: King's Chapel is thought to be the most beautiful building here; this garden is its most famous. The garden closes at four, so I must pick up my orange peels, my pansies (the gardener gave me two), and be off to Queen's College Chapel, about which I will try not to rave."

I raved.

"Max, I asked Mama to send you my letter from Cambridge. The letter was so long and I stayed so late sightseeing that, now that I'm at the Bell Hotel in Ely, I'll write you about Ely, not Cambridge. I got a train at six o'clock in Cambridge and was in Ely at 6:30. I had no idea where to go. There was a bus from the Bell Hotel at the station. I asked the driver the price. When he said 'five and six,' I hopped in. This hotel and this town are the quaintest, oldest, most lovely yet. (I'm really trying not to use those words so often.)

"The sixteen miles between Cambridge and Ely were flat and green—no orchards, hay, natural grass. Some wheat with red poppies blooming in it that reminded me of Flanders' fields and the war. There were also fields of *cultivated* mustard, a peculiar sight to a Californian.

"I have walked ten thousand miles today. I'm going to bed. I'll write in the morning."

"Morning. At least I don't even *want* to use 'quaint' or 'lovely' about Ely Cathedral. It is grave, lofty, awesome. Enormous in size, cold as a dungeon. It is a serious, even a forbidding, dream materialized. I spent the morning there, attended a service one hour in length. The old Quaker who said 'a dumb world is a dead world' would have enjoyed it. There was never a minute's silence, though for all I could understand, there had as well have been silence. Whether English or Latin was being used, I couldn't tell; all was chanted in very high voices with a curious falling note at the end as if the news of the death of the One we loved on the cross had just come to us. The choirboys, deans, bishops, whatever they were, wore robes, like angels—or doctors of philosophy. And all this sound, and all these costumes (that's not the right word) in the heart of what appears to have been built by monstrous trolls thousands of years ago—and abandoned."

"Sudden change. I found that to go to Peterborough I would have to pay $2.50 to get back to Lincoln, so I am now en route to Lincoln, where I am scheduled to arrive at five-something.

"From Ely to March (where I am now), I had the compartment to myself, so I changed my shoes, repacked my suitcase, combed my hair. Now I have two walrus-mustached Englishmen of sixty-five with me—one talks like a titmouse newly hatched, the other bellows like a bullfrog. But they know this country and I like hearing about it. We are passing through fenlands now, England's main agricultural district. Green stuff goes from here to London and Scotland. In the winter, the English gentlemen tell me, this land is partially flooded. Great herds of horses are grazing here now. Here in wintertime they used to have their skating contests. The small man lives in Cambridge and he says that last winter the Cam in Cambridge froze over and he skated on it and felt like a boy again in the fens."

"Max, this is Spaulding and never have I been more surprised in my life. I've been talking to these two men, mostly the smaller, older man, who lives in Cambridge, ever since Ely. The talk was about crops, rainfall, how the fens were drained, etc. The other man did seem less interested in agriculture. He asked me if I was traveling alone, and why my husband wasn't with me. He wanted to know if I didn't find it lonely. Both men had to get off at Spaulding. When the little one left, the large man—he might be only fifty—stayed behind. He said, 'You'd better let me go on with you to Lincoln. I could make things very pleasant for you in Lincoln.'

"I truly don't know what I said to him, but it got him out of my compartment in a hurry. I usually don't say one word on a train to a man, but those two men looked so safe and elderly and they did know all about the fenland, which interests me so much.

"Well, back to my N.Y. rule. Never open my mouth to any male except one so young that I look like grandma—or auntie, at the very least."

I wasn't by nature or training capable of making a European tour with the light-heartedness of an Erica Jong in *Fear of Flying*. There was no need, however, of my being so shamefaced. I acted as if I were a male-chauvinist judge blaming a woman (I was the woman) for inciting a man to rape. What had I done to bring on so immodest a proposal? Talked with too much eagerness about a countryside that impressed me? Confided that in the cathedral at Ely I had liked Bishop West's chapel best of all because I had been born a West? Why couldn't I have smilingly refused a smiling proposal? This was no Trask, but a man who, judging by the way I had burbled on, believed that I would like the talk to continue. Why have to humiliate him? Why not agree? "I am sure you could, but I have made other arrangements." Which would have been both a refusal and the truth.

Was I the product of a male-chauvinist era, or area, and trained to blame myself whenever what seemed unseemly in a man's behavior occurred? I did blame myself. "I must be doing something wrong; I must appear to be a vulgar, bawdy, sex-obsessed creature." It did not occur to me that I was as strange to the English as they were to me. My speech was different. My dress was different. I was dressed like a college girl—sweater that fitted, fine silk stockings (the bobby-socks age hadn't arrived)—married but traveling alone, energetic, hoisting my bags like any porter; a Californian, and everyone knew how *they* lived. But none of this did occur to me. I blamed myself. I tried to remake myself: I stopped using lipstick; I tried to keep my mouth shut; and, finally, a real wound to my vanity, I bought lisle stockings. Someone should have told me that European men hadn't been brought up in an American Quaker community, and that they weren't accustomed to married females traveling alone, willing to talk their heads off about any subject but the one they considered important. No one had told me this. No one I knew knew it.

I had an inkling of my peculiarity later, in Edinburgh, when two American girls, after I told them that when I finished the Summer Session at Oxford I would go to Paris for a month, said, "Don't settle for less than a senator." They had just come from Paris, and I suspected that they spoke with authority.

Why did I write of this to Max but not to my parents? First of all, my parents would have worried about me, alone in a country where men like that fenland lecher existed. Max wouldn't. I hadn't been an all-Southern California basketball guard for nothing. He knew I could take care of myself. And, in addition, I may have been boasting a little: Would you have guessed I had so much sex appeal? For a sophisticated European, at that?

I continued my letter to Max from my Lincoln Hotel. If I still felt shamefaced, it didn't show in the letter.

"I have had a hot bath and am resting cosily in the cleanest of beds in the pleasantest of rooms. This is a hotel much patronized by Americans. Do you know how I can tell? Coat hangers in the closet—I mean, in the wardrobe. These rooms never have closets—always wardrobes.

"The cathedral was closed for the day when I got here, so I washed, put away my things, then tromped about the cathedral. It is supposed to excel Ely in its balance, etc., but nothing, nothing will ever equal Ely for me, rearing itself up as it does out of those ancient streets and above those meadows so near at hand.

"Lincoln is on a hill, the only hill for miles around. Its spires, they say, can be seen for thirty miles on a clear day. This was a walled Roman town; the wall still exists in places, wide enough and strong enough for a taxi to use as a road. I suppose that it would surprise me less to see a Roman on the wall than it would surprise a Roman to see a taxi. I know about Romans; they have never heard of taxis. If I saw a Roman, I would shout, "Ave, Caesar!" If they saw a taxi? Run, I think.

"On the slope of the hill below the cathedral is a large flock of sheep, each one marked with a red numeral on its flank. Why? 'Kill this one'? There is also what is called here an 'arboratorium' below the cathedral, and on it are sprawled one thousand people trying to cool off. England is having what it thinks is a heat wave. No rain recently and the temperature did go up to 80° one day.

"I have a double room with two beds. Did the fenland man phone ahead? Bunny, Bunny, I wish your curly head was on that pillow, not the fenlander's grizzly one. I don't really. I wish your head was on my pillow.

"This letter is not for family consumption. Don't send it home. They think Europe is nothing but history and scenery.

"This is the third week, going on the fourth, of summer school at Berkeley for you—and not one word from you. Maybe the fenlander had second sight and knew that I was not just a wife traveling alone, but an abandoned wife. Tell me he was wrong.

"Honey, I had a dish of ice cream tonight. In London they put sugar on their ice cream. Here they poured thick cream over it.

"Honey, I asked the conductor on the train for the name of a good hotel here. He said, 'Do you want to go to one of those grand places with a lift?' I said, 'No,' and here I am, liftless, at the White Hart Hotel.

"Honey, they never give you a napkin here except at dinner.

"Honey, you have to fight to get water to drink here.

"Honey, there are one million babies in England and each has a baby carriage the size of a Ford roadster. And each baby has a big round John Bull head.

"Honey, did you know that bread, butter, and Bovril make a perfect sandwich?

"Honey, did you know that Bovril puts beef in you?

"Or that Iron Jelloids give women the strength they need?

"Or that there is a Woolworth's store in every town in England?

"Or that England train whistles don't sound like American ones, which say, 'I'm on my way.' Instead, they have a piteous wail that says, 'I'll never make it.'

"Honey, do you know I love you?"

"This is the White Hart in Lincoln. Mama, your not writing will not stop this ceaseless bombardment of letters from me. I know you *do* write. You always have. Where do your letters go? I spent so much money on food yesterday, tonight my dinner was two scones eaten in my room.

"Lincoln Cathedral is thought to be finer than Ely. Nothing can ever equal Ely in my estimation. The English people with whom I have talked all say Ely is very slow, very backward. 'A cathedral town is always very slow,' they say. When I ask them if the cathedral does it, they shake their heads and say, yes, they don't know why, but somehow it is true.

"I'm too sleepy to write, and the cathedral was closed when I arrived. Tomorrow, the cathedral.

"Everyone complains of the drought and heat. 'See,' said the conductor on the train coming here, 'our fields are dying!' They looked like green lawns to me.

"Every human being in England, male, female, child, adult, carries a brown case similar to our now defunct vanity cases. They call them attaché cases, and what they carry in them, I know not.

"A knock on the door. Maid saying my bath is ready. The bathroom is some distance from my room, and baths have to be scheduled, otherwise we'd all be swimming together. I'll write in the morning, clean and awake."

"1:00 P.M., I am sure. Thursday, I believe, July 18, a date you probably remember better than I do. This is a day on which I want to write you. It is also an hour in which I need to rest my weary legs. I am in the courtyard of Lincoln Castle, alone, alone. All the other crazy Yanks are off eating lunch somewhere.

"How can they? They probably had the same breakfast I did: 1) Porridge. 2) Fish. 3) Toast and rolls. 4) Ham and eggs, eggs nicely fried and heaps of ham. 5) Marmalade—no breakfast yet without it. 6) Coffee—sure sign that this hotel has many American visitors. In Ely, nothing but tea in cups the size of washbasins.

"No sounds but the sad whistle of distant trains, the rustle of leaves. Even the birds chirp quietly.

"After breakfast I went at once to the cathedral, though no one in Lincoln called it that. To them it is the 'Minster.' The building is so enormous, I thought that for my first time round I'd better join a tour group conducted by the verger.

"I lagged behind, as usual, but here are some of his remarks. 'I could say we are the greatest church in England—but I leave that for others to say.'

"I'll disappoint him. Perhaps it is only because Ely was my first that I have so much feeling for it. I doubt I'll ever feel the same about any other minster.

"Then, the verger said, 'All Americans want me to show them what they call "the Kodak saint." I didn't know we had one, but here she is.' She was carved in stone, of course, a female figure holding in her hand a square box in just the position a Kodak is held, apparently sighting it at *us*.

"I won't attempt to tell you all the verger had to say about arches, bays, flying buttresses, vaults, early English, Norman, and Gothic styles. You have an *Encyclopaedia Britannica*. If you want to know about them, look them up. These letters are about how I feel about what I see, not descriptions of what I see.

"The verger, in spite of saying that he wouldn't call Lincoln the greatest and best, did tell us why York has more stained glass than Lincoln. One of Cromwell's officers was a Yorkshireman. At the time when Cromwell was razing all buildings having to do with the Catholic Church, this officer told his men that if anything was touched in York Minster, there wouldn't be enough trees in Yorkshire to hang them on. So York's glass was saved; Lincoln's destroyed. The verger hinted that except for this chance of a Yorkshireman among Cromwell's soldiers, York wouldn't be able to hold a candle to Lincoln.

"I didn't tell you that in Ely Minster, there are hundreds of small statues in the recesses, having to do with the life of the Virgin Mary. These were all decapitated by Cromwell's men as being too worldly—so all we see today are these headless, unworldly bodies.

"I can understand how in the anger and fear of a battle, human beings are slaughtered. It's kill or be killed then, a soldier thinks. But who is benefited by tearing down buildings, smashing stained-glass windows, beheading stone virgins? Objects that might be of value to the conquerors are destroyed. What the conqueror thinks he is destroying, I suppose, is an idea. It is not very Quakerly to suggest that the world would be better off if more Incas and Aztecs had been slaughtered by the Spaniards and fewer of their buildings and art objects destroyed—but I suggest it.

"Time to be on my way if I am to see the castle, get a bus to the station, and catch the train to York. I could not fail to write you, Mama, on this day. Twenty-seven years ago, after two and a half days of labor, your hands bloody from pulling on strips of cloth fastened to the footboard of your bed, you, aged nineteen, weighing ninety-eight pounds, were able to give birth to me, weighing twelve. The doctor had said that morning that the baby, if the mother were to live, must be 'taken.' Your mother, not a woman who gave up easily, said, 'Try harder, Grace.' You did, and here I am, seeing what you have always longed to see. Thanks for giving me life and eyes.

"I tell you of the beauty of the cathedrals. On the outside, that is what you see. On the inside is death. I copied for you the names of three or four of the engagements in which soldiers fell. I could have copied dozens.

"Indian Mutiny 1857–59

"Campaign of 1845–46 of the Sutlej

"Campaign of the Punjab

"Nile Expedition 1898

"Campaign of 1899–1902 in South Africa

"I don't know what a visitor from Mars would think: these great buildings erected to the glory of a god who preached 'love thy neighbor as thyself,' and crowded with the records of men who slaughtered their neighbors. You could have one or the other, I suppose; a monument to the 'Man of Peace,' a monument to the 'Men of War.' Trying to combine the two doesn't make much sense. The Quakers at least saw that.

"Beneath an old flag was this verse:

" 'A moth-eaten rag on a worm-eaten pole
It does not look likely to stir a man's soul.
'Tis the deeds that were done 'neath that moth-eaten rag
When the pole was a staff and the rag was a flag.'

"What stirs my soul is not the rag or the pole, but the thought of the dying and suffering. The British Empire is an island floating in a sea of blood. All great empires have been, I suppose. Our hands aren't clean either."

"10:30 P.M., York. Under the eaves up ten flights of stairs in Waites-Laws Hotels Limited. My room is about six x six, just enough space for a bed and my two suitcases—if I get into the bed, which I have done.

"Next morning. I intended writing more last night, but fell asleep. I'll continue with Lincoln where I left off, in the castle garden. On the train to York I passed through one of the richest districts of England. Here the abbots settled. Because of the great strife between the different Catholic sects, a building war was waged; each abbot tried to outdo the other. As a result, this countryside is now littered with ruined abbeys. I told you about the dead who are memorialized inside Lincoln Cathedral. Outside, the workmen let their fancies play; grotesques of every kind: imps, dogs, a cat, a tiny mouse, monkey heads, no two alike.

"I paid 6d for the privilege of climbing to the rood tower. Halfway up, I would have paid anyone ten guineas to get me down. You know the song 'The Monkey Wound His Tail Around the Flagpole'? That's what the stair was like: narrow steps not as big as my feet around a central column with a rope to cling to. The trouble was, with coat and purse, I didn't have enough hands to cling with. There was no light whatsoever, which was just as well; if I could have seen the distance I would fall if I had slipped, I would have.

"That climb (and getting down was just as bad as getting up) has kept me in bed late, worn out as a steeplejack. But there's a lot to see in York—twenty-one ancient churches; and a lot going on in the town itself. The streets are already crowded. Rountree's Chocolate Factory people are having a holiday, and from 9:30 to 12:00 P.M. there is a tattoo. A tattoo is, I think, a military parade.

"With so much to do I may not write again before Durham. But no more climbing towers, I promise you."

"Max, I hate to confess to you that my fidelity is not to be banked on. I swore that I would never love another cathedral as I did Ely, that ship on the fens. Here in Durham, with a cathedral like a fist raised to the sky above the river Wear, I am wavering.

"This is the third time today that I have started a letter to

you. I'll finish this if it takes all night. I am in my room at
the Waterloo Hotel, Old Elvet, whatever that means, in Durham. My room was made for me: casement windows, Windsor
chairs, pictures, a chintz-covered sofa. From my window there
are as many signs to be seen as in the whole of Los Angeles,
though what they advertise is different.

"1. Lochsid's Celebrated Mild Beers and Bitter Ales

"2. T. Hislop, Meat Purveyor

"3. Noted House for Atchinson's Sparkling Edinburgh Ales

"4. Powe Petrol

"5. Boots the Chemist

"6. Three Tuns Hotel

"I now have a new procedure when entering a town. I check
my bags at the railway station, then proceed on foot, keeping
my eye out for hotels. I have now bought a guidebook,
Baedeker's *Great Britain*. $4.00. I hated to spend the money,
but it's a joy, a comfort, and a foot-saver. It has maps, plans
of cathedrals, lists of hotels. So with hotel list in hand, I walk
about and, as I come to one that's listed, I inquire about
'accommodations.' Tonight I asked at two hotels before finding
this place. Then, with a room 'booked,' I find the bus or tram
that takes me nearest the station, go back, pick up my bags,
and return the same way to the hotel.

"Before this, I've taken a taxi to a hotel, which, in the first
place, cost me a lot of taxi fare and, in the second, convinced
the hotel people, when they saw me with bag, baggage, and
waiting taxi, that I would pay any price for a room rather than
go on. If you are merely inquiring, foot-loose and ready to
inquire at another hotel if their price doesn't suit you, they
quote you a reasonable price. So I save money at the expense
of my legs. Since my legs are sturdier than my purse, this
new plan is an improvement.

"Now that I have a Baedeker, I can give you authentic news
about the cathedrals, in case that's what you want. 'Durham,'
said B., 'is dedicated to the Blessed Virgin and is locally known

as "The Abbey." It is one of the most important and the most grandly situated of the English cathedrals.' "

"Dear Ones and All: I am writing you as I sit on the bank of the river Wear, eating my lunch, which is a ham-and-beef pie, 6d, two Sunkist oranges, 4d. The water is only ten feet from me. Above me towers the cathedral and the castle. The cathedral clock chimes the hours and quarter-hours. Children splash in the river. Farmers in town for the Saturday market eat lunch with their wives on the benches behind me.

"I've just been talking with a red-haired ten-year-old and his brother of two. They stood watching me, so ragged and yet so clean as compared with the other smoke-blackened children. When I said 'Hello,' they came over to talk to me. The older boy's name is John Angus. I thought he was Scotch, both by looks and by name. He says not.

"His father is sick and on 'Benefit.' He gets four shillings. 'A day?,' I asked. 'A week,' said John Angus.

"His brother had a leg cut off saving a fellow worker in a factory. This brother is on the dole. His sister works in a mill. His older brother can't read and for this reason can't get work. 'I can read already,' says John Angus. 'I am already in the third reader.' He speaks very deliberately and slowly, as one tends to do to a foreigner. He says, 'I believe this or that is so,' never 'It *is* so.' If he doesn't understand you, his 'I beg your pardon' is automatic.

"I asked him how he happened to be so much cleaner than the other boys. 'I keep myself clean with soap,' he said. 'Some of the boys don't use soap.'

"Ten or twelve boys were swimming without suits just below. I asked John Angus if anyone could do that. 'No,' he said. 'It's against the law. Those boys will get a summons if caught in their bare skins.'

"John wants to be a sailor. 'They kill sharks and sail to distant lands,' he said.

"I gave an orange and a shilling to each boy. 'Oh, will Mom be surprised when she sees this money,' John said. I felt like kidnapping John Angus, he was so sweet and soap-clean. He and his brother ran off, toward home, I suppose. I hope he sails to distant lands and no shark ever gets him. When the bare-skin boys saw me opening my purse and guessed what was going on, they hustled out of the water and into their pants. And I, seeing *them,* hustled away. I didn't have shillings by the dozen to give away; though after he had left, I wished I had given John Angus a pound."

"Friend and Husband, I have an idea that you skip all parts of my letters having to do with cathedrals, so I'll be brief about Durham and rush on to more stirring subjects. Durham is a Norman cathedral, built when a church might have to withstand a siege, so it looks as much like a fort as a cathedral, simple, rugged, majestic.

"Here the people fought both the Scots and the Normans. William the Conqueror made a bloody path between Durham and York. The Scots never took Durham. The roots of Durham go back into an England difficult for us to imagine: wild, bloody, and savage. The minsters in this region once teemed with life: forty masses a day were once said.

"O.K. No more cathedral. How about a drought? The papers list cities and the days they yet have of a water supply. Manchester has only enough for eleven more days, and its people are using water only for necessities. No washing the car, the dog, or watering the lawn. It is hard for a Californian to believe that there is a water shortage when you see these heavy full-running rivers. But in England they haven't any systems of dams and reservoirs to husband their water. When it comes to water, they've always been millionaires. We've been water poor all our lives and have had to save every droplet.

"The Durham paper records as news the fact that there were fifteen hours of uninterrupted sunlight yesterday, plus a 'devastating heat of 80°. People traveling in England can't complain this summer of England's wet gloomy weather.' Wet and gloomy is what I expected, but 80° doesn't devastate me. I've taught with the thermometer at 115°."

"Dear Mama: Please note my new address, 'The Royal British Hotel, Princes Street, Edinburgh, July 20. G. Eglinton Adams, Prop. Telegrams, Venus.'

"If you want to send me a cable, you now know how to address me—Venus. Princes Street has been called by many the 'first street' in Europe. I look across the canyon of Princes Street to the steep cliffs behind, where Edinburgh Castle is silhouetted against the pale grim sky. It is 10:30 P.M. Off near the other end of Princes Street, but not visible from here, is Hollyroodhouse, the home of Mary, Queen of Scots. I'll see that tomorrow and, if you're lucky, I won't tell you a thing about it.

"*I'm* lucky as all get out. In the cathedral at Durham, a man told me that the Royal British was a lovely hotel, but that I should call ahead for a reservation because Edinburgh was full of tourists. I didn't call but here I am anyway. I'm paying the most I have for any hotel yet, 12/6; but two days won't bankrupt me, I hope."

In the sitting room at the Royal British I spoke my first contentious words to anyone since I had left home. I wonder now at the nature of the girl (though she was by then twenty-seven, I still think of her as a girl) who was calm enough with Trask, the pseudo-husband, and the propositioning fenlander but who flew off the handle, loudly and publicly, at the words I heard spoken by two young couples, also occupants of the sitting room at the Royal British.

I was seated at a table near where two English couples sat on lounges. I had with me my purse, my Baedeker, and a copy of I. A. Richards's *Principles of Literary Criticism,* which, in spite of its price and its weight, I had bought. I was reading Richards on T. S. Eliot and copying, as was my wont, pertinent paragraphs into my journal.

One of the young women of the quartet, in a voice pitched for me to hear, said, "A typical Yank, copying notes out of Baedeker to pass off at home as her own, so Pa and Ma will be impressed with her knowledge."

Not more than a half-dozen times in my life have I had flashes of anger of the kind I had then. It is not an enjoyable feeling. All alternatives are blotted out. "Two seeing eyes, see one, see one." For that kind of anger nothing needs to be decided. It is as involuntary as an orgasm. Fortunately, probably, for me, I am a woman, and fisticuffs and firearms do not suggest themselves as a suitable expression of anger. Words do. And because I am a woman, those to whom I have spoken in anger have not, so far at least, replied with anything but words.

Without any debate as to what was right or wrong, suitable or unsuitable, I marched over to the four on the lounge and said, "Here is the book I was reading and here are lines I by chance was copying into my journal. I. A. Richards is the foremost British critic. How many of you have read him?" No answer.

I held out my journal so that they could see and read the last lines written in my journal. Had I had any choice, those lines would not have been my choice as examples to these deriders of American taste and erudition. I copy them from my journal now. "It illuminates his persistent concern with sex, the problem of our generation, as religion was the problem of the last."

"Richards," I told the four, "is here talking of Eliot's *Waste Land,* as of course you all know."

Before any reply could be made to that, I continued. "I have traveled six thousand miles from California to England in order to learn something about the English. Until you have made a like journey to California and have learned something

at first hand about Americans, I wouldn't make pronounce-
ments of the kind I just heard. Travel teaches. Each day I
learn something new about the English. I'll try to forget
what I learned today."

With those words I took myself off very fast. The quartet
was showing signs of recovery. Although I can be angry very
quickly, I can also quickly calm down. If I lingered, I would
find myself involved in a sensible discussion of the differences
between English and Americans: more sensible but less satisfying than attack.

Nothing of this encounter went into either letters or journal.
I did not wonder then, though I do now, why I could not or
did not lift my voice in outrage when I was approached as
an easy pickup or installed in a hotel bedroom as a pseudo-
wife, but did publicly explode when accused of being a plagiaristic phony, sending Baedeker quotes home as compositions
of my own.

The reason, I now think, is that in spite of Richards's declaration that sex was the problem of our generation, I was not
born far enough into the 1900's to be at ease in talking of sex;
let alone to be publicly denouncing advances I considered
sexual. Sex, like constipation, was not a ladylike subject for
conversation.

There may have been more to it than that. There may be,
even in the most unwanted approach of the male, a touch of
flattery that, ladylikeness aside, reconciles the female to it.
She rebuffs it, but does not feel the flash of anger I felt when
called a plagiaristic American show-off. If a man in the
Royal British had said to another, "Let's ask her over for a
drink. These American girls don't come to Europe to see the
scenery," would I have rushed over in anger to read him
something edifying from my journal? Why not? Though I
didn't know it then, and am not sure that this is the answer
now, I would not, because sex was the subject one didn't talk
about. Not exactly shameful or dirty, when practiced by a

legally married couple, though even under those circumstances a subject a bit too carnal for conversation.

"Dearest Mama: 10:00 P.M. The Royal Hotel in Glasgow— 150 miles of the Trossach Tour behind me. I know now why Scottish sheep have such long wool—it's to keep the bone-shivering Scottish wind out. I'd like to have been covered by wool myself today. We went by auto, by steamer, by train, by hoss. We saw everything: Loch Katrine, Ellen's Isle, Ben Venue—in fact, everything mentioned in *Lady of the Lake*. My marrow was congealed but my soul soared. We saw Scott's home; abbeys at Melrose, Jedburgh, Dryburgh. They were impressive. More beautiful were the Scotch hills and villages: stone houses vine-clad and surrounded by flowers. When we see pictures of this kind we think they are too pretty to be true. They're true. I saw them with my own eyes today.

"All this country is rolling. At one point the driver ceremoniously stopped the bus and told us, 'We are now 1,200 feet above sea level.' Many gasps from the English. All but two on this tour were English. I've seen more sheep today than I've seen in my entire life before. And if you're going to be a sheep, this is the place to be a sheep in.

"We met perhaps ten cars all day long. We did pass heavy two-wheeled carts, each occupied by one man smoking a pipe in the rain. Not one sign or billboard or petrol station or snack counter. The British Isles, our geographies tell us, are densely populated. Where they keep that population, I don't know. They're very neatly stowed away, especially in the Midlothian hills. Of course they've been killing each other off here for centuries: the Scotch and the English, the Scotch and the Normans, and, before that, the Scotch and the Romans. We passed the site of a Roman camp kept up for a hundred years, and then abandoned because of constant Scotch attacks.

"The Scotch are handsomer than the English, brawnier, more color in their faces. You have a son and a nephew who, with their red hair and craggy faces, would be taken for natives here any day.

"I made the acquaintance of Bonny Johnnie Gordon, the sweetest six-year-old in all of Scotland, today. His mother, for some reason, had spent her early years in Russia, so when I tired of looking at sheep or abbeys, I could listen to how it was in Russia twenty-five years ago."

"Dearest Maxwell: Here I am in the land of your forebears, seated in the Royal Hotel in Glasgow, and I'll tell you how I got here. The Trossach Tour ended here at 6:30 this afternoon. Glasgow is dirty and ugly, a great shipbuilding town; we passed ship after ship under construction as we came in. Glasgow is the second-largest city in Great Britain.

"So there I was at 6:30, though my train for Carlisle and Stranraer, where I catch the boat for Ireland, leaves at eleven. I checked one bag (sent the other on to Belfast, where all goods must be examined before entering the Irish Free State). Stuck with five hours to wait and nothing but a bench in an ugly station to wait on, I had a brilliant idea: go to a hotel, tell them my train didn't leave until eleven, and ask if I may use their sitting room until then.

"The first nice-looking hotel I came to was the Royal. I went to the office on the second floor (our first is their ground), and put my question, and was told, 'Glad to have you.' So here I am on the third floor in the cosiest of writing rooms. It is now 7:45.

"I don't know why I was so idiotic as to choose to cross at night. I arrive at Belfast at 9:00 A.M. tomorrow, Dublin, 1:00 P.M., Kildare, 3:00 P.M. I have to be at Oxford one week from today. So I suddenly begin to feel that I must hurry. Kildare has a population of only two thousand. I hope I don't get there tomorrow afternoon and find that they have no hotel. I want to stay there a few days before I explore Timahoe, where the Milhouses lived before they moved to Dublin.

"Now excuse me while I go to the 'Ladies Cloakroom'—never 'rest room' or 'lavatory' here.

"9:30 P.M.; still the Royal Hotel. You could never guess what has happened to me in the last two hours, so I'll tell you.

"When I came back from the cloakroom, there was another woman in the sitting room, forty or forty-five years old, auburn-haired, handsome, very smartly dressed, with a big fur cape. There are many fur capes and coats in Scotland—and with these cold winds they are needed—and at their prices here, $85 for what would be $500 in Los Angeles, I'm tempted to buy one. Well, the fur-cape lady came over and sat beside me. When she asked me my name, I told her. When I started this trip, I didn't tell anybody anything. Now I tell them, if they ask, name, age, weight, matrimonial status, etc.

"When I told her that my name was McPherson, she clapped her hands together and said, 'That's a very good name. Highland Scotch. I thought you were Swedish. My name is Isabelle McPherson-McKenzie. I'm Australian. My father had his way paid to Australia.' (That was a way, I think, of saying that he was sent to Australia as a convict.) Naturally I didn't ask. 'My father married an heiress and added her name to his.'

"Next she wanted to know where I was going. I told her: Carlisle, Stranraer, boat to Belfast, etc. 'May I see your ticket?' I had some idea of her grabbing it and running. She did take it. 'Let me see if I can't get you a better connection.' Off she went with my ticket, as I had feared, but she stopped at a phone booth in plain sight. When she came back, she said, 'Sorry, too late.'

"Then she said, 'Will you have some tea with me?' I wasn't hungry, and I needed to be, for the tea she ordered was 'high,' a supper really. It seemed rude to turn down her invitation, so when the waiter brought tea in, I joined her at the table.

"When she saw me eating with my left hand, my right hand in my lap, because I don't eat British, and I guess it's the Australian style, too, she said, 'Oh, you poor girl! Have you lost the use of your right hand?' I told her I was left-handed, and she had traveled enough to know that Americans don't use two implements at once when eating.

"Next she advised me to skip Ireland. 'It's a melancholy country,' she said. 'The climate is bad, the walled manor house sits next to a cottage with no smoke in its chimney. Irish slums are the worst in Europe.'

"I explained to her my reason for going to Ireland and added that in a week I was due in Oxford for the beginning of the Summer Session. This really made her cry out. 'Name of the Deity! Name of the Deity! First the melancholy of Ireland, then the boredom of those summer-school lectures at Oxford. You are spoiling my image of Americans as adventurous people!'

"As you know, just getting to Glasgow has been quite an adventure for me. Almost too much for me at times. Then she saw my wedding ring. 'You are married? Why isn't your husband with you?'

"There were about three honest answers to that. First, that you didn't want to make a trip to Europe; second, that there wasn't enough money; and third, that you needed to attend the university. I told her only the last. When she heard that, she named the Deity a few more times. 'Married to a school-boy! He could be with you if he wanted to. But that's his decision. Ireland is a bog. Oxford is dry as dust. There's no need for you to choose them for your trip. I'm on my way to Paris. After that, India. Come with me.'

"I told her the truth. 'I haven't the money.'

" 'I have. I wouldn't have asked you if I hadn't. Come with me. Paris, India. What have Ireland and Oxford to offer compared with them?'

"I was too flabbergasted to think of the right answers: the home of my ancestors; the cradle of learning. Then she added to her invitation its most compelling sentence. 'I am lonesome.'

"So was I. But I doubted that Paris and India with Isabelle McPherson-McKenzie would remedy that. I couldn't think of any kind way to turn down so generous an offer. When I was silent, she stood, gathered up her things, and said, 'Good-bye, Yank. You'll remember me in the midst of some dusty lecture at Oxford and wish you were in India.'"

I didn't remember her in the midst of a dusty lecture at Oxford, and there *were* some, all right, but I didn't and haven't forgotten her.

The McPherson-McKenzie encounter and her invitation exposes a weakness I've never been able to overcome: an inability to change horses in midstream; a determination, having put my hand to the plow, to finish the furrow. Because she was a woman, her invitation, though it, unlike the fenlander's, promised to increase my pleasure, did not offend or embarrass me. It may have been rooted as deeply in sex as his, but I didn't know that then. I knew I had been given a choice; and that I was unable to decide between the two possibilities rationally. By nature I was tied to the plow I had put my hand to. *Was* Paris a more interesting place than Ireland? *Would* I learn more in India than in Oxford? I never thought of the two possibilities in that way. I never *thought* of them at all. I *could* have accompanied McPherson-McKenzie. In a letter to Max, I could have said, "Plans changed. Will go to Paris and India instead of Ireland and Oxford. Will be home in October as planned." I couldn't do it simply because I had a prior plan; there was a plow I had put my hand to.

Though I didn't think of it then, I do now. Had I accepted Miss McPherson-McKenzie's invitation, I would have substituted adventure for security. She was a seasoned traveler. Paying for two instead of one was no problem for her. I would have embarked upon a special kind of guided tour. Gone would be the effort to find hotels, to save money by walking instead of taking taxis, to eat pork pies and sultanas in my room instead of buying meals in a restaurant. Little money is enough money, if spent ingeniously; to manage so as to buy a wanted pleasure is a challenge. Mallory could have had as much exercise running as he did climbing Everest. The excitement, the satisfaction would not have been comparable. There was risk in Everest, some fear, even the possibility of death. I now believe that my chief reason for my refusal of so unexpected and generous an invitation was my unconscious understanding that for me the adventure would go out of a McPherson-McKenzie guided tour.

There is one line only in my letters home about this occurrence. "An Australian lady asked me to go to Paris and India with her." No more. I evidently took for granted that those who knew me would understand that I would decline this invitation, and why.

Ireland

"Dearest Mama: July 25, 1929. Kildare, Ireland.

"I'm using Church of England stationery and sitting in the very ancient cathedral of Kildare, no great beauty but the warmest place in town.

"I now know what I'd like to be: the Dean of a cathedral in an English cathedral town; or a Scotch Lord with a boundless estate and castle, a Lord Douglas or Seaforth or Duncan. Or maybe a Scottish soldier. They are noble creatures. I suppose they have fallen arches and dandruff like other males, but their uniforms magnificently hide every defect. I must say, in spite of your Irish ancestry, Ireland and the Irish can't hold a candle to Scotland and the Scots. The Irish may have hearts of gold (we know they have, since we have them), but their exteriors, in Kildare at least, are very slipshod. Be sure to send this letter to Max. It will please him.

"This is how I got here. At eleven o'clock I caught my train to Glasgow. There was an empty compartment. The guard told me to go to sleep, that he would give me a call when we were approaching Carlisle. I stretched myself on one of the long seats and was already half asleep when in bounced a young man, laden with more kinds of paraphernalia than I can name. It took him some time to stow away all this stuff.

Then he began to talk and he turned out to be the most amazing, interesting, good-hearted—and I guess the word is Christian—person I ever met. I wished Merle could've been along to hear him talk and to hear the way he talked.

"The conversation started as do most conversations with men on trains with his asking, 'Do you mind if I smoke?' I said, 'No, I don't mind.' The next question always is, 'Will you smoke with me?' I say, 'Thank you, but I don't smoke.' Then they say, 'I can tell you are an American. How do you like England?' By then the conversational ball is rolling—and with Tom Hughes, how! He talked unlike anyone else I had ever heard before. He was Welsh, from Denbigh in North Wales. I could understand him better than the Yorkshire people, or the Cockneys, but to tell the truth he sang instead of talking. He pronounced Chicago Shee-cow-gooo, so long drawn out and in such a nice light tenor, it sounded like high church chanting. He wanted to know if I hadn't been afraid passing through such a dangerous town as Shee-cow-gooo.

"Tom was in the navy during the war; he enlisted when he was sixteen and is now the assistant engineer on a ship. He must be twenty-eight or nine, but he doesn't look it. He had just come from Hamburg for a holiday at home and was leaving in four days for South America. He has been in almost every country and he told me about them all. He was childlike (not childish), simple—I don't mean silly—without any pretense; and so kindhearted, he made me want to cry.

"I told him I didn't know exactly where Carlisle was. He then got a huge atlas out of one of his numberless bags and showed me its location, exactly. I tried to give it back, of course, but no, I must keep it, it was just in his way. He tried to get tea for us and, when he couldn't, took several heavy black bars of German chocolate out of one of his bags and gave me some.

"Then he showed me pictures of all his family, from a nephew who had just won a prize as the prettiest baby in Birmingham to his father, who was lost at sea twenty-two years ago. He showed me programs of concerts he had heard and told me, with a little humming, which compositions he had liked best. His taste in music is good. He showed me pictures he had painted, and they were awful. Never, never have I seen the like of such a person, so much simplicity and trust. I had the feeling that this was the open, generous way people should be, perhaps once were.

"As we neared Carlisle, he said, 'I suppose you have many friends in England.' 'No,' I told him, 'I'm a stranger in England.' Then he said, 'Please write me telling me you arrived safely in Kildare. Just drop me a line. It needn't take much time.'

"Then he gave me his picture, which I am sending you, with his name and address written on it. I have too much luggage already, without adding Tom Hughes's picture to it. But I can't bear to throw it away."

I never wrote Tom Hughes a line. Why not? I did not know how to be a friend to a young man? Did I think, and perhaps rightly, that friendship between young males and females was impossible? Did I think that if I wrote a note saying, 'Safe in Kildare,' that there would be a reply and that a correspondence between a young married woman and a foot-loose sailor would not be seemly? I don't know. It did not occur to me that here was a young man for whom, after a long voyage with fellow sailors, a woman with whom he could talk was a special treat.

In fifty years I have not forgotten Tom Hughes, but I had forgotten that I had sent his picture to my mother. I ate his chocolate, lost his atlas, but here in the big carton with the letter I wrote home is his picture—no snapshot, but a professional picture in an elegant folder by "Ward's Studio, 139 High Street, in Uxbridge."

On this, in the handwriting of a man who likes to make marks with his hand, is Tom Hughes's address, "6 Mydllton

Avenue, Denbigh, N. Wales, Gt. Britain," with his inscription, "Very sincerely yours, July 1929."

I gaze now at the picture of a young fellow who looks a
good deal like the young Bing Crosby: fresh face, wide-open
eyes, big ears. I'm not much given to remorse over acts or
failures to act, but I wish that Tom Hughes in N. Wales had
received a card from Kildare saying, "Safely arrived in Kildare, and very thankful for your kindness en route." I didn't
write. The best I can do now is to hope that the beautiful
nephew in Birmingham has had a life that would please the
uncle who was proud of him in 1929.

"Dear Ones and All: I arrived in Carlisle, and ate another
of the Welshman's chocolate bars, then went to sleep on three
chairs pulled together in the ladies' cloakroom. In the compartment of the train bound for Stranraer everyone was also
asleep: a woman at full length on one bench, and a soldier in
each corner of the other. I sat between the two soldiers, put
my feet, I'm afraid, in the woman's stomach. She didn't wake
up, and I was soon asleep, so I guess she didn't suffer.

"At Stranraer we boarded our boat and had a very rough
passage. There were at least a half-dozen nuns on board. I
learned something from watching them. If you plan to be
seasick, don't wear a nun's habit. With one hand you try to
keep your skirts, shawls, headdresses, etc. from blowing off in
the wind; with the other you try to keep what's down, down,
down. You don't have much success with either, and the result
was a holy mess for the Sisters. I don't get seasick, so when
breakfast was announced, I went down to eat. I was astounded
when I was asked for three shillings. I didn't know that you
ever had to pay for food on a boat. I had already embarked
upon it, so there was no retreat insofar as money was concerned.

"The train awaited us when we landed, and in an hour we
were in Belfast. I had to take a taxi to catch the Dublin train,
which left from a station at the other side of town. Perhaps

it was because I was tired and sleepy, but whatever the reason, Belfast looked bleak and dirty to me and the people on the streets looked the same.

"Something funny happened to me on the train ride to Dublin, though. I didn't think so while it was happening. Across from me sat a young Irishman, who used the cigarette ritual. When I said I didn't smoke, he said, 'If you'll sit over here, you'll be out of the draft.' Over there was beside him and I hadn't felt any draft, so I said, 'Thank you,' but didn't move.

"Then the now funny, then embarrassing, thing happened. I had on my full pleated brown serge skirt, which, when I'm sitting, comes down about to my ankles. He was long-legged and I am long-legged, so our knees about met. Then he, so adroitly I didn't know he had done it until I felt the clamp of his two knees about my knee, slid his feet under my full skirt and put a scissors-lock—I guess that was what it was—on my knee. No one else had noticed. I could have yelled, 'Un-knee me, you cad,' and made an exhibition of myself being kneed by a perfect stranger. Instead I just kept talking to the young woman beside me about Arnold Bennett. She wore spats, with gaiters up to the knee—there wouldn't have been any more satisfaction in kneeing her than in kneeing a boot. By this time the Irishman perhaps thought I had a wooden leg. Anyway, he pressed harder and harder, got really red in the face and popeyed with effort and exasperation. Still I didn't give any sign of being aware of what he was doing. I don't think much pain can be caused by the pressure of two knees against another knee; anyway, at least I didn't feel any, and when we reached Dublin that young man tramped over everyone in the compartment in order to be first out. Before leaving, he gave me a very dirty look.

"In Dublin I had to go clear across town again by streetcar and tram to reach the station where I would catch the train for Kildare. On the way to Kildare we passed men cutting hay in the fields with scythes and binding it into sheaves by hand.

"In Kildare I checked my bags at the station as usual, then went walking about the town to find a hotel. I really don't know what's wrong with me. I'm not cross-eyed or knock-kneed. As I walked about, people calmly stopped talking, turned around so they could stare at me. I think that what I look like must be foreign. Anyway, I found the Station Hotel, from which I now write. Then I went back to the station to get my bags.

"In front of the station in a Ford sat an ancient Irishman.

" 'Do you want your suitcases taken down?' he asked.

" 'How much?' I asked cautiously.

" 'Two shillings.'

" 'I'd rather carry them.'

" 'One and six.'

" 'It's not very far.'

" 'Ninepence.'

" 'All right. Come and get them.'

"And so I arrive at this place of faded glory. It has a drawing room, with clock and flowers under glass, a coffee room, with tables large enough for banquets, a bar filled with Irish Free State soldiers. I have a nice room, with breakfast, of course, for 7/6—too much for this forsaken town—for forsaken indeed it is."

"Too full of dinner, too tired from an after-dinner walk to keep my eyes open, though it's only 10:30. The maid who was just in said, 'The evenings are getting so short.' It won't be dark until eleven o'clock.

"Dinner was boiled ham and boiled chicken together with lashings of gravy poured over same. First gravy I've had since leaving the cooking of my old Hoosier mother. There was a vegetable that looked like spinach and tasted like cabbage. Potatoes with their jackets on. The salad was a big bowl of every green vegetable in the world mixed with unbroken (but shelled) hard-boiled eggs and seasoned with oil and vinegar. Dessert was a rhubarb tart—which consists of cooked rhubarb, plus piecrust, plus custard. Dessert is always served, even though it's only a spoonful of fruit, on a full-sized dinner plate.

"I ate so much dinner, I set out to walk it off. My knee, though the clasping didn't hurt, is still rosy. I bet the clasper, because he put so much effort into it, isn't able to take a walk at all.

"Kildare, for all it's such a ramshackle little town, is one of the most important racing and hunting centers of Ireland. I passed many barns and stables full of horses. It is also the center for the Irish Free State's Middle Country Civic Guards. I passed their barracks about a mile out of town. Mr. Conway, proprietor of the hotel, told me that during the war there were twenty-five thousand soldiers stationed here. Now there are one thousand. 'I wish to God we had never heard of the Irish Free State.' Of course his business has suffered because of it. I asked the waitress if there was any chance of their returning to England. 'England won't have us,' she answered sadly. 'She's washed her hands of us.'

"At the station in Dublin a Belfast man made great fun of the Irish Free Staters. 'The trouble with the people in the south of Ireland,' he said, 'is that they have no Scotch blood in their veins, and hence have little sense and less energy.' He himself is half Scotch and may thus be prejudiced.

"I went to see the ancient tower; there are only three like it still standing in Ireland. It is old, old. No one knows how old exactly, or what its use was. It is said to be pre-Norman. Some think that fires were burned at its top to direct pilgrims to the cathedral. The Danes razed Kildare twice, including the cathedral, but the tower was spared. It is 110 feet high, twelve feet in diameter, and made of stone covered with gray moss. After my fright at Durham, I swore I'd never again try to get to the top of anything except by a lift. Once again I was tempted. For sixpence a very old grizzled Irishman opened the tower and let me climb. Only the thought of those who for a thousand years had made the same ascent caused me to feel faint. How many of us? I wished we could meet and talk. Many probably died here when the Danes attacked. *Were* fires lit here to guide worshipers to a cathedral? Why did they need a guide? Was Ireland then a wilderness of trees and wolves? All I could see was flat green land and the blue of the distant Wicklow hills.

"When I came down, I told the man with the keys that some of my people had come from this part of Ireland to America in the early 1700's. I asked him if he knew any Irish people by the name of Milhous. He said he did, but they lived in Northern Ireland and spelled Milhous with an *e* on the end. They were originally Yorkshire men. I don't know whether Yorkshire blood puts as much sense and energy into Irish veins as Scotch blood does or not. We can hope. Some sense I may have, but the supply of energy has run out. Love and kisses. I'm asleep."

"What a day! What a day! The day is over but not daylight. The town pump is just outside my window, and because of the drought, or at least what they call 'the drought' here, wells have gone dry. There is a daylong procession of two-wheeled donkey carts with barrels carrying a supply of water to dry homes. Reminds me of the days in Yorba Linda when we hauled all of our water from the Anaheim lake in barrels: first boiled potatoes in it, then scrubbed the floors with it, and finally watered the flowers with what was left.

"There really is a drought, Irish-style, here, difficult as it is for me to believe, seeing everything so green. Here is an ad that appeared in a Dublin paper. (If there is a Kildare paper, I haven't seen it.) 'Warning to Motor Car Owners: You are Forbidden to Use Public Supply Water for Cleaning Cars. But car owners who use WONDER MIST SPRAY can clean and polish their cars without using water. Wonder Mist is an

American patent now 21 years on sale the world over. It is also a deodorizer and disinfectant. . . .' I think I'll buy some, stop taking baths, and help save precious Irish water.

"All the townspeople, getting water or not, parade by beneath my window. Also cattle, goats, and pigs, herded, and occasionally unherded. The children here are sloppy and dirty. When you are outside, they stop you with 'Give me a penny, lady.' Everyone continues to stare at me as if I were out on the street in my teddies. But not at the races this afternoon, not at the races! I did the staring this afternoon: tweed suits, furs, and diamonds. On the streets of Kildare, I may be urban; at the races, I was a country cousin."

"I would never have gone to the races, because of the cost of the tickets, except for Mr. Conway. Mr. Conway's niece, visiting him from Boston, had a ticket, but she'd gone off to Killarney for the day, so he gave me her ticket. 'Boston's about halfway to California, isn't it?' Mr. Conway asked. I think he thinks his niece and I might have shopped together at a Woolworth's one day.

"Mr. Conway is thirty-eight years old, a widower with two children. He looks like an ideal hotel proprietor—or politician —big, affable, pretty good-looking, florid, bright-blue eyes, and a big mop of curly brown hair. He's a born glad-hander and full of blarney. Anyway he gave me his niece's ticket and I have seen my first horse race.

"Max, you are more interested in horses than people, but I had to get used to the people before I could look at the horses. I don't know where that crowd came from: certainly not Kildare. Dublin, London, perhaps Paris. Every woman wore a hat, gloves, and a tweed suit. If all the furs at the race had been covering their original owners, the grandstands would soon have been emptied.

"Besides looking horsy, the people around me naturally talked horses. This is a great hunting country, and from the talk I heard there is no hunter like an Irish hunter. 'All the great hunters have been Irish hunters, bred in and about Kildare.' What they hunt is the fox, which seems a great waste of a fine horseflesh to me. Even the waitress at breakfast was a horse fan. 'Ah,' said she—all sentences here begin with *ah*—'ah yes, there's not a real man here but would give his shirt for a good horse.'

"A tweed man explained to a tweed lady why fillies never win races. 'The filly is too erotic in her movements,' he said. 'Like all females, she has her eye on the grandstand, and the time she wastes being appealing loses her the race.' At this the tweed lady guffawed mightily—what you might call a horse laugh.

"The Dublin paper is full of the horse show which will be held here next week. This poem is a kind of trademark for Kildare and the show.

" 'Horses she loves, for she
Is come of the old stock
Lords of the limestone rock,
And acres fit to breed many a likely steed.
Straight in the backbone
With head high like her own
A blood, that tamed, mild,
Can suddenly go wild.'

"Ah me, with these erotic fillies and owners with blood that will suddenly go wild, Kildare ought to be pretty full next week.

"I've seen how the other half lives today—the two other halves: the moneyed half, with their tweeds, furs, diamonds, and chauffered Rolls-Royces; the penniless, who will stop you on the street to ask you for money. I'm somewhere in between, some money in my purse but no diamonds in my ears.

"I did see the horses, in case you're wondering. But I'm no judge of horseflesh, and a racing horse goes by so fast he's nothing but a blur of color in front of your eyes. I was the only person there who didn't bet.

"I plan to stay here a night or two more, then try to get to Timahoe. Timahoe is seventeen miles from here and the only way to get there is by hiring a car and a driver. It will be expensive, but my chief reason for coming to Ireland was to see Timahoe. Mr. Conway thinks I am a fool to go to Timahoe. 'You'll pass through it without knowing it's there.' When a Kildare man says this of another village, it has to be pretty insignificant. 'The graves of my ancestors are in Timahoe,' I told Mr. Conway. 'Oh, if it's the dead you're looking for, Timahoe's the place,' Mr. Conway said."

"What a night! What a night! No sooner had I stopped writing last night and turned out my light than there came a soft knock knock knocking at my door. I got up, put on my robe, and there was my host himself. He said, insofar as I could understand what he said, for he spoke all in a rush with much 'meself'-ing and 'quite all right'-ing,' that he hadn't seen me come in, and he was worried about me and wondered if I was safe. I thanked him for his concern, told him I was safe, and said good night. I had time to notice, though, that his curly hair was very neatly combed and that he smelled sweet as a rose. It came to me that Mr. Conway thinks he's a devil with the ladies of Kildare—and he may well be.

"After half an hour, knock knock again. At first I didn't answer. Then I thought, That's silly. So I stayed in bed but said, 'Who is it, please?' 'It's Mr. Conway,' says me landlord. 'What is it, Mr. Conway?' 'You were a little tired when last I saw you. I thought maybe a little drink would be restful.' 'No, Mr. Conway,' says I, 'I'll ring if I need anything.' Then in about another hour some more knock knocking, which I didn't answer. I wasn't the least frightened. I had no idea he would come in unless invited. He saw that I was alone and, after the long-skirted, shapeless, sad women of Kildare, I probably looked quite dashing to him; so he had decided to see just how dashing I was."

Mr. Conway's knocking made me decide to go back to

Dublin and to hunt Timahoe from there. You can, by train from Dublin, get to within five miles of Timahoe. I've seen the tower, the races, and Mr. Conway here; and I think they're about the best of their kind Kildare has to offer. Having made this decision, I had a quiet night of sleep.

"When I came down to breakfast, no sooner had I seated myself than up comes Mr. Conway, bold as brass, offers me the morning paper, and sits himself down at my table. 'And how are you feeling this morning, Mrs. McPherson?' he asks, as if he had been the doctor who had seen me through a bad night.

"'Fine, Mr. Conway. Well enough to return to Dublin, thank you.'

"And in thirty minutes more, I'll catch the 10:15 train to Dublin."

I was getting calmer about knee-squeezers and matrimonial pretenders. Why should I have been so distraught in the first place? The reason was, I think, on reading these letters fifty years after they were written, that the experience was new for me; as it would not have been for most or at least many American girls. My sister, Carmen, with her almond eyes, blond hair, and olive skin, was younger than I, but early on she warned me that men "made passes" and "had a line." She has been hearing that line and fending off those passes since she was ten. She was not surprised, embarrassed, or shame-faced when what she expected happened. Let down, perhaps, if it didn't.

I had not heard the line or been the target of the passes as she had. I was not, I think, an ugly girl, though plain may have been a just word to use. I was a bookworm, a basketball guard, and a female debater who had never lost a debate. These are drawbacks for the teen-ager who would be seductive. She can probably outjump the male who makes a pass and assuredly outtalk the boy with a line.

Add to these qualities the fact that at the end of my freshman year in college I, aged seventeen, was engaged to be married, and perhaps my reaction to what I was encountering in Europe can be better understood. The twenties was the age in America of "going steady"; and engaged was not only going steady, it was as good—or as bad—as being married: all the restrictions and none of the privileges. When I was a sophomore, Max left college to be a cowboy for a year. I once dared, with Max absent, to have a date with another boy. All the girls in the dorm where I lived gathered at the foot of the stairs to greet me and my date, when he arrived, with this song:

> "What if Max could see you tonight,
> Playing around while he's out of sight?
> Wearing his ring and his promised wife?
> It doesn't add up to an honest life."

Outside, the boy earnestly told me that he was Max's friend, had never intended to stab him in the back, and gave me the tickets to the play we had planned to see. I spent a chilly evening on a bench in the honeysuckle arbor, ashamed to let my dorm sisters know how effective their song had been.

So there I was, as good as married at seventeen, inexperienced in coping with lines or passes, and meeting a few at twenty-six. I did not know how to laugh them off, berate the offenders—or accept them. It was then my opinion that truly nice girls did not elicit responses of this kind. So what was I doing that was wrong? Convincing landlords and radio commentators that I was a loose woman? Was I, at heart, a closet floozy?

My self-regard was sustained in part by the myth, if it was a myth, of the predatory European man. Look at Byron and Shelley; and even Herrick and Donne, who were clergymen, were also womanizers. European men, unlike the good Quakers of Yorba Linda and Whittier, had mistresses and fathered bastards. Simply being a female set them afire—

and femaleness was a fact I couldn't disguise, though I tried
to tone it down by discarding lipstick and silk stockings.

The choice of episodes to report in my letters, and which
report should go to whom, interests me. Some, like that of
the radio commentator at the White Hall, were never mentioned at all. What he had done, and I had accepted, made
me look a fool—and I may have been—but it was no part of
my policy to reveal this to parents or husband.

Some happenings were reported to one or the other by
chance; and, simply because, having told one correspondent,
retelling it to the other would be tiresome for me, it was not
repeated. There is, however, in reading now, a clearly visible
practice. A funny episode (or one I thought could be made
funny), an episode in which I came off well and in which no
feeling except outrage was expressed, I sent to Max. If, as with
the Welsh seaman, great regard, respect, even affection were
felt, I sent the account to my mother. I tried to do as I would
be done by. I would not have cared to have received from
Max the picture of a coed classmate of his at Berkeley, dear
decent Christian though he assured me she was, but hellbent
on providing him anything of hers that she thought he could
use. I would have torn her picture into shreds and returned
it thus to Max. So good-hearted Tom Hughes's pictures, which
I could not bear to destroy, went to Mama, not Max.

Into my journal went no reports of such encounters. I left
Kildare on June 26. On June 28 I sat in my room in Dublin
and wrote in my journal. "A heavy rain is falling. The drought
is broken. I dressed to go to church, but without an umbrella
I would have been soaked. On the table before me I have
*The Cornhill Magazine, The Voyage Out, Rossetti, Michel-
angelo's Life,* Alfred Noyes's *Poems,* and *Selections from
Modern Poets* by J. C. Squire, which I bought. Also Katherine
Mansfield's *Letters,* which is mine.

"The rain drips down the chimney. A maid hums in some

back room. I am far from home and much I would not
be. . . . 7:15 P.M. I've had tea and an hour's walk. I've finished *The Voyage Out* and am reading *Mrs. Dallaway*. Rachel
died just as she discovered companionship. I cry out for someone to talk with.

"A Buick like ours just passed under my window. I could
have kissed its fender. Free State soldiers go by arm in arm.

"Thank God for Katherine Mansfield. I am terribly alone
here. Being alone when you are traveling isn't bad; you're too
busy figuring out train schedules, making connections, finding hotel rooms to notice it. Once you find your room and
look out your window at other people arm in arm and with
friends to talk to, loneliness sets in. I look out my window at
sliding treetops and wish each tree were labeled 'This is an
Irish tree.' That would cheer me up, for that's what I'm here
to see. I'm afraid Rose Bruno's father was right. 'Grass is
grass the world over.' "

None of this ruminating went into my letters. In them I
reported how I got to Dublin and what I did, not what I felt
or read. They are narratives. Even so, they might be labeled
by some present-day reader 'Puritan's Progress.' What would
my life have been like had I gone to India with McPherson-
McKenzie, written Tom Hughes a note, or had a drink with
Conway? Existentialism had not yet been, insofar as I then
knew, invented. In any case, I was not, by breaking the old
pattern of my life, discovering who I might become.

It was considerate, I think, to try to keep the mournfulness,
when it existed, out of my letters and to soft-pedal history and
architecture. On the back of one of my letters that my mother
sent on to Max, she wrote, "Max, read this as many times as
you will, but send it back, *please*. Do you have a letter about
an Australian woman who asked her to go to Paris with her?
She said to ask you for it. I'll return it. Her letters are like
diamonds and pearls to me."

·   ·   ·

"Here I am in Dublin, as I told you in my letter yesterday I planned to be. In my compartment on the way to Dublin was the wife of one of the officers of the Irish Free State Army. She was able to read the signs in Gaelic and says that all children in school must study Gaelic, with the expectation that soon all Irish literature will be written in the earlier language.

"We reached Dublin about noon. Since I'd been in Dublin before, I checked my bags at the Knightsbridge Station and went on foot to the O'Connell Bridge and the Nelson monument at the center of the city. I had decided, remembering the help the Friends Church gave me in London, to go to the Dublin Church and ask for their recommendation of a good hotel. I didn't want to get into another Station Hotel or meet another Mr. Conway.

"When I asked for the location of the Friends Church, people just shook their heads. Not until it occurred to me to ask for the Friends Meeting House did I get an answer: Eustace Street.

"I got lost looking for Eustace Street, and asked a fatherly-looking man if he could tell me how to find the Meeting House. He may have been a father, but he was also drunk, jolly drunk. 'That I can, me darling,' says he, 'but I can do better. I can take ye there meself.' So he put his arm around my waist—and he really needed something or somebody steady to lean on. He knew the way, though, and we marched straight to the Meeting House, where he tipped his hat as if he'd brought me in a cab, and went off singing. I hoped no one had seen how I arrived.

"The only one I found at the Meeting House was, I think, the librarian, a man about sixty-five, no more than half my size and with a red beard almost to his knees, a real leprechaun. When I asked him to recommend a hotel, he said he was just going out to lunch and would walk me to the Standard, a hotel run by a Quaker. So out we started, he holding me by the elbow, so that I felt like an elephant being guided by a flea. He (Mr. Flannery) was very kind, witty, and knowledgeable. He told me the history of Dublin as we went along, pointed out places of importance, and showed me buildings riddled with bullets by the revolutionists in 1922. I don't know how far we walked—miles, it seemed to me, since I had already done a good deal of walking that morning. We passed Dublin's famous Trinity College and finally, when I'd begun to think the Standard Hotel was a leprechaun's dream, I saw those sweet words, 'Standard Hotel.'

"Mr. Flannery introduced me to the lady at the desk as 'an American Friend. Let us try to make her comfortable,' and off he went, and I *have* been made comfortable. This is by far the nicest hotel I've been in yet: drawing rooms, writing rooms, smoking rooms, sunrooms. More, perhaps. I haven't been everywhere yet. My room resembles a room in a home rather than a hotel room. I'll write again after tea."

"Tea over. They won't let me have tea here again, I'm afraid. I ate so much. But tea is only one shilling and dinner is three, so it's a temptation to fill up at teatime and call a couple of oranges dinner."

"As I penned those last lines (I was in the writing room then), a young woman, after looking at all the books in the bookcase, said, 'Why, there's nothing here but murddah stories.' I offered to lend her some of mine, not a murddah in them. After that she asked me to go 'for a run in the country' with her and her uncle in their car. She drove, I sat by her, Uncle had the jump seat. They are English, not Irish. Uncle is a professor at the University of Belfast—a scientist who recently made a trip to Canada, a member of a scientific staff of inquiry, investigating something. Niece keeps house for him. She was a censor of American mail during the war. She said that American soldiers, after every sentence, wrote 'Haw, haw.' She, like me, had eaten a large tea and was feeling 'liverish.' I've read this word many a time in English novels, but I never heard it said before. I've had pangs in most of my organs, but

I have no idea how you feel when you feel 'liverish.' I wanted to ask her but it didn't seem polite.

"Uncle gave up trying to explain his scientific field to me, and when we passed a cricket game, tried cricket instead. I think I understand cricket now and would like to try to play. Uncle says he doesn't think that there are any ladies' cricket teams in Ireland. At least I want to see a game.

"I bought a shawl for you today. Don't thank me. Papa gave me the money for it. It's pure wool, made in Western Ireland, by hand, of course, and is used by nursing mothers to put around themselves and babies when the baby's nursing. It's called 'a modesty shawl'—but it's not immodest to wear it just to keep warm. I think you'll like it, since it came from the land of the Sharps, McManamans, and Milhouses.

"You know how much I'd love to have you and Papa with me—but I'm used now to living without you. It's Max I miss terribly. I'd gladly cut off a toe sometimes just to see him for thirty minutes.

"I have a reading light by my bed here—first time since I left home. It takes an Irish Quaker to know that beds are also made for reading."

"This is your jaunter. That's what I call myself, because across the street is a stand for jaunting carts, the kind where the passenger sits on a shelf on one side of a cart while the driver balances your weight by sitting on a shelf on the other side. The horses are all bays. Why? The horses travel at a clipping pace and, except for the price, I'd like to try jaunting.

"Street bands station themselves outside this hotel, too. Last night one played, 'All by Myself in the Moonlight,' and in memory of your addiction to that on the radio, I threw them two pennies.

"The Standard Hotel juts out onto Harcourt Street, which in a block or two becomes Grabton, the Bond Street of Dublin. The people who pass by my window are 99% Irish, I suppose, though most of them might be walking down Broadway in

Los Angeles. Some are what we think of as typically Irish: the others are the 'Black Irish,' with bony faces, marked cheekbones, lank straight black hair; then there are the blue-green-eyed Irish, big-mouthed and round-faced; and in between every mixture of the two. The black type can be very impressive; the light, very charming.

"I am not able to say what constitutes Irishness; and sitting in a chair by my window, I'll never find out. I think I was getting closer to it in Kildare. There the old women wore red skirts, went barefooted, and had hair that had never been bitten by the tooth of a comb. Dublin is more American than Edinburgh, and Edinburgh more American than London. The girls here use rouge. In Scotland they didn't need to.

"There's great poverty here. Many beggars are on the streets; flower sellers who have no intention of selling flowers.

"They say here, just as that Irish tablecloth seller (if she was Irish) said to me in Yorba Linda, 'Honest to God, Lady, the children at home are hungry,' and I gave her our last $15. Here I get off easier, but bang goes another sixpence.

"Fifty thousand people are said to be out of work. One-fourth of Dublin's population live in single rooms. The papers are already filled with worry about how to care for the poor this winter.

"There is a book in the reading—or writing—room here which must have been planted by an Irish-hating Englishman. It is St. John Ervine's *Life of Parnell*. Surely no Irishman would buy this book and leave it where others could read it. I have it here in my room now, and every now and then I contemplate throwing it out the window. Ervine despises the Irish and hates the Americans.

"I've sworn not to fill my letters with quotes from books and descriptions of cathedrals, but I can't resist some lines from St. John Ervine.

" 'A sense of humor has been denied by heaven to the Southern Irish.'

" 'The woman, who seems to have been one of those strong-minded, outspoken silly women, more common now perhaps in America than anywhere else . . .'

" 'Parnell was of Anglo-Saxon blood, the blood of authority and leadership, while his followers were Celts, in whose veins flowed only the blood of obedience and submission.'

" 'We must not blind ourselves to the fact that the Celts' nature, like the Latin nature, is a cruel nature.'

" 'The Irish, to whom terror and intimidation and corrupt practices and mean bargaining are the instrument of government, are not yet ready for democracy or any rule other than that of a stern dictator.'

"That's a strange book to be reading in a Quaker hotel in Dublin. So now, having digested an Irish breakfast big as a meal for threshers, I'll go out onto the streets and investigate Irishness as it exists outside of books. This is my plan for the day:

1. Visit Trinity College and see its famous library with all the illuminated manuscripts.

2. Visit the Irish National Gallery.

3. St. Patrick's Cathedral.

4. Woolworth's.

5. See a cricket game if possible."

"10:30 P.M. The streetlights are just being lit—gas or acetylene. A lady in Edinburgh told me that in June it is never really dark all night long.

"I've walked ten miles today and still don't comprehend Irishness. Here are some facts, though, about Ireland.

1. Bacon in Dublin is called 'ham' and, call it what you please, I never ate anything so savory.

2. Fish is always served for breakfast.

3. Lentil soup is always served for lunch.

4. There is never any cream for your coffee.

5. Stores are shops.

6. Mongers monger everything, fish and steel being the commonest commodities.

7. There are no department stores, only drapers.

8. The English King and his operation got two lines in an obscure corner of the paper.

9. The English names of towns have been effaced.

10. The porter is a boots.

11. People do not say good-bye, but 'cheerio' or 'righto.'

12. I am having a cream bun in my room for dinner.

13. English money is good here, but Irish money is not good in England.

"I hope that there is word from you when I get to Oxford. I have not had a word since I left, five weeks ago tomorrow. I carry the two letters I got from you at the St. James and the one on the ship with me all the time; but they are ancient history. I need something modern. Write, write, write. I hope that you are well and happy. But not too happy with me gone. Cheerio."

"I'm going out to the library in the Friends Meeting House to copy some material they have about the Milhous clan for you. But I'll write you a note to mail before I go. I've just had tea and am in the writing room. Everyone here is English and, now that the Belfast girl and her uncle have departed, I'm the only one here under forty. Maybe under thirty. I am more of a curiosity to them than they, now, are to me. At the beginning of this journey, I thought it was no one's business who I was, where I was going, or why. How I have mellowed! I don't volunteer information, but if asked, I'll exchange life stories and tell how we do it in America. You remember in my first letter how disgusted I was with the ladies on the train who wanted to know all about me? Now, if asked, I tell my age, weight, and number of filled teeth without flinching. Travel is very broadening.

"For instance, in the hotels where I stay, I don't have a

private bath—or toilet. The public toilets are not designated for 'Ladies' or 'Men.' They're just toilets (water closets here), equally useful to both sexes; and when you come out, a gentleman may be wanting his turn; and neither of you blushes.

"The toilets, since we seem to be on the subject, are works of art, great enormous bowls with the insides decorated with flowers, vines, and blossoming trees. It embarrasses me to sit down on one. They also have fancy names: Geyser, The Rapids, Puritas.

"I am anxious to get to Oxford, where I hope to find mail awaiting me. Not one word from home yet. Anything could have happened, but I hope and pray only the best has."

"Mama, I have decided not to try to go to Timahoe. I hope you won't be disappointed. Mr. Flannery says that there will be nothing left to mark the graves; that the Quakers used nothing but small wooden slabs as grave markers, and they would all have disintegrated long ago. Timahoe, the town, would be nothing but a smaller Kildare, and that I've seen. Also, there is no rail service from Dublin going anywhere near Timahoe, and hiring a car for the day might cost two pounds. If you're terribly disappointed, wire me and I'll come back and walk, if necessary, to those unmarked graves.

"So I'll be leaving Ireland tomorrow. Now that I'm going on to Oxford, I wonder what the highlights of the trip have been so far? Cambridge and the backs of the colleges, King's College Chapel, great Ely in the green twilight, Lincoln's spires, York Minster rising above the streets of that bustling town; and Durham, God bless Durham, a clenched fist raised high on a cliff and little John Angus on the banks of the Wear; Princes Street, the bitter wind on the lakes, the lady from Australia, and the night ride to Carlisle with the benevolent Welshman. Thence to Kildare, that desolate wind-swept poverty-stricken place, then back to Dublin and civilization.

"Of all nonhuman objects I've seen, the one I remember most

vividly is this: in the library of the cathedral in Durham was a square stone upon which was carved the imperial eagle of Rome, and under it this inscription, 'Dedicated by Flavius of the Sixth Legion (called the Victorious) to Fortune.' This is from memory; I have the inscription copied in my journal. Think of me hunting for old Quaker tombstones while this relic of the Roman occupation fifteen hundred years earlier than Quakers were invented is here to see. Flavius, I salute you. Fortune, be good to *me*."

"Oxford, 10:00 P.M., Tuesday Eve. I'll be writing you until tomorrow morning if I tell you one-half of the things that have happened to me since I left Dublin yesterday morning. First, we traveled thirty miles by train to reach our boat. I came to Ireland with a boatload of nuns; I left it with five hundred Free State Boy Scouts on their way to the International Scout Jamboree at Birkenhead. The nuns looked like nuns, but these Boy Scouts looked like no Boy Scouts I had ever seen before. They smoked. They had beards, or at least whiskers. Some of them wore kilts. The crossing wasn't rough at all, but many went immediately to the berths below to lie down. Under every chair in the lounge was a flat white receptacle to be used if the attack should be sudden. The Scouts used them. 'Be prepared' is their slogan.

"In the lounge I met another of these traveling-alone ladies— like myself, I guess, though she certainly doesn't look like me. She was large (well, so am I), heavy, not fat, severely tailored, monocled, and coffee-colored. She has spent twenty-three years in India and is the wife of an official there. She has made forty-three trips to England and Ireland in that time. When her sons—she has two—were four and six, she sent them to the British Isles to school. Her own people live in Ireland. It has been four years since she's been home. She made the trip this summer as the result of having won fifteen hundred pounds in the Bombay sweepstakes. She was very interesting. I never saw or heard anyone like her before in my life, and though I say it blushingly, she took a fancy to me. She took me to lunch, and since she had fifteen hundred pounds in her pocket I saw no reason to be thrifty. I was sorry to leave her and the bearded Boy Scouts when the boat docked."

Ireland: Two Epilogues

But I was not sorry to be leaving Ireland. I would be sorry now if I had never seen it. Without that first trip, two subsequent trips, both important to me, would never have been made.

Travelers without a drop of Irish blood in their veins find Ireland charming: I did not find it so on my first visit. I was a resident of Southern California. I loved its brown hills, its sagebrush and cactus; its coyotes and roadrunners. A season of rain followed by a season of sunshine and dryness, to which I was accustomed, seemed a more agreeable arrangement of precipitation to me than Ireland's smattering of rain every other day.

I was offended by the juxtaposition of manor houses in their walled gardens and tumble-down cots, their doors wide open in the wet raw weather because there was no heat inside to conserve.

Ireland was a republic, but its citizens, unlike those in the republic I knew in the west, were, it seemed to me, as aware of gentry and lower classes as was Virginia Woolf, daughter of the Empire.

After the bookstores of Cambridge, the bookstores of Dublin were disappointing.

New to travel, I had not yet learned that traveling knee-squeezers and prowling widowers were not restricted to Ireland.

I did not expect ever to return. I was happy to be taking to my mother a copy of the Certificate of Removal, which had been issued on May 29, 1729 to Thomas and Sarah Milhous by the Friends Meeting at Dublin. In it she would learn that Thomas and Sarah "were educated from their childhood by their religious parents in the profession of truth . . . sober and orderly in conversation as becomes our holy profession." Thomas and Sarah were recommended to the Friends of Pennsylvania, "as deserving their preservation and growth in the blessed truth and welfare in all respects."

Words of my mother's had sent me to Ireland. It was fitting that I should bring back to her words of the first of our kin to make that transatlantic trip.

I did not then know that one's future life is more affected by what one does than by what one says. I was a dedicated word-woman. I said on leaving, "Farewell, Ireland." But the fact of my having gone there was an act in which more than my vocal chords had participated. Without the first trip, which was in a way simply a dutiful time killer before my real life in Oxford began, subsequent trips would not have been undertaken: one, of great interest; the other of lasting significance in my life.

There was no real reason for the second trip. Twenty-seven years later, aged fifty-four, having finished a stint of scriptwriting in Hollywood, Dorothy Jeakins, the costume designer for *The Friendly Persuasion,* urged me, as a respite from work, to go to a place she had recently visited and found delightful, Achill Island, off the west coast of Ireland.

It was not my intention to spend any time visiting Ireland. I would see Achill Island, which, as Dorothy had described it, was irresistible; I would then be on my way to England, the south of France, and Spain. England was still the home of the penmen for me; but in Provence and Spain, the earth's surface, which I loved (I am an earthling), is less hidden.

Trees are pretty things, made by God, not poets, comfortable in hot weather, useful, ornamental in small numbers. Tree-covered England was different. I accepted it, elms and all.

But at fifty-four, I was making many new and nonarboreal discoveries. "You travel," I wrote in my journal, "to discover yourself. At home there is known to you only the girl you remember. Who you really have become, you do not know. When you travel, that person emerges: she is mirrored in the faces of people you meet.

"On the underground a man got up to give me a seat. He did not see the strong, stalwart girl I still thought of myself as being, striding on the hilltops gathering lupine and yellow violets; swimming the length of the pool twenty times each evening. He saw the woman he faced: the swallower of headache tablets, the older woman of fifty-four. Ridiculous, I thought, for him to give *me* a seat. I laughed at his mistake. But he gave a seat to the woman he saw, not the one I remembered.

"All of us read history into the faces we see. Travel is simply an extended voyeurism. Everywhere, without the lifting of blinds, bedroom life is apparent in the faces of couples. Very few show signs of satisfaction or happiness.

"The middle-aged bring to the idea of travel the romanticism with which they once gilded the idea of meeting a new man. Something will happen, they know not what."

Well, something did happen, something unimagined; and at fifty-four, since it still lasts, probably more fortunate than any meeting with a man might have been. The person I met was eleven years old. Older women are no longer excluded from love stories, even women of fifty-four. Fiction, however, has not broadened to include young girls of eleven. And this young person was an Irish girl of eleven.

•　　　•　　　•

Once again, as in 1929, I went to Ireland by ship, first class this time, a seat at the captain's table on the *Mauretania*. At the port town of Cork, I lingered for two days, sightseeing and buying some warmer clothes. I stopped short of the woolen bellybands recommended to me in 1929 by the two Wellesley ladies, but I did buy an Irish sweater, which makes the climate, for the wearer, whatever it may be outside, summer.

I explained to the clerk who sold me the sweater that I was from California, where weather at this time was still warm and balmy.

He understood perfectly. "Ah yes," he said, "California, the one-lung state."

His terminology was strange to me. But since I had been more or less a one-lunger myself for a number of years, I didn't question it.

From Cork, simmering in my sweater, I proceeded by taxi to Limerick. I planned to stay overnight, then take the bus next morning to Galway, the next step on my way to Achill Island. I stayed at the Royal George Hotel, rated the second best in town, but actually, my taxi driver told me (with a rake-off, no doubt, for passengers deposited there), the best.

It was in Limerick, while staying at the Royal George, that something happened. The Royal George, first class though it might be, did not provide soap or washcloths. Accustomed to both, I went to the nearby Woolworth's, which was well stocked with washcloths, Ivory, and Palmolive. After I had made my purchases and was prepared to return to the Royal George for a good scrub, I saw a weighing machine. On my first trip to Ireland, I never had to think twice about my weight: much walking and thrifty eating kept my ribs visible. Thirty years later, all signs of ribs had disappeared. I thought I had better see what the machine said, though its language, speaking in stones, would take some time to interpret.

I did not want to be weighed holding my heavy purse. I did kick off my shoes. While I was looking for some more dignified and safer spot than the floor for my purse, a red-haired girl, short for her eleven years, said, "Would you like me to hold your purse, ma'am?"

It was exactly what I would like. So, shoes on the floor and purse in safekeeping, I found that I weighed nine stone, four pounds, which in an American translation equaled 134 pounds.

The purse was returned to me, and the little redhead walked with me out onto the sidewalk.

In front of Woolworth's, two violinists, feet wrapped in gunny sacks, for it was a wet raw day, were playing Irish tunes on their fiddles. Into the cap on the pavement in front of them, passers-by were tossing coins. Not caring for the role of rich American tourist (all Americans in Ireland are thought to be rich—and by Irish standards, many are), I gave my new Irish friend some coins to put in the players' hat.

As she crossed from Woolworth's to the players' side, I saw the child was less warmly dressed than the mendicant violinists. This kid, I thought to myself, needs money more than those two stout fiddlers. It's a wonder she didn't take the cash and run.

"How about having tea with me?" I asked her when she returned.

She thought it a grand idea.

She had come from where she lived by bus to Woolworth's, without fare, but needing none because she was able, small as she was, to hide behind a seat when the fare collector passed up the aisle. I gave her the money for the return trip.

That was not my last sight of Ann McCarthy. Before we had parted, I had made arrangements to take her to an Irish circus playing in Limerick the next day. I wanted to see an Irish circus myself, but particularly I wanted to see Ann seeing an Irish circus.

Tennessee Williams's *Glass Menagerie* was being presented by the Limerick Dramatic Society the next night. Neither a drama suitable for eleven-year-olds nor a play the ladies of

Limerick's Dramatic Society would find suitable to their talents, one would think. Nevertheless, with Ann by my side, I was seated in the theater when those ladies began emoting. What Ann made of the play, I don't know. But the ladies of the Limerick theater had very clearly seen the emotional likeness between themselves and those Southern ladies with their genteel pretensions.

So, night after night, it went. Achill Island stayed in the north; I stayed in Limerick getting to know Ann and her family.

Mrs. McCarthy was a widow with six children and an elderly mother dependent upon her. The eight of them lived in two rooms: a kitchen–dining room and a bedroom.

It is no more—even less—likely, I believe, for a childless woman to find on the streets of a foreign city a child to whom her heart goes out in the wish that such a child could be hers than for a man to see in a passing woman the wife his heart has always desired. It is even more unlikely for either, being able to claim the yearned-for as daughter or wife, to find the yearning justified.

I did not, of course, in the beginning think of Ann as a possible daughter. I thought of her as an enchanting, witty little street gamine who needed help. In Ireland, children like Ann were finished with school at the age of twelve.

Still I lingered in Limerick. Ann's family dined with me at the Royal George.

In later years, Ann and I have talked about our coming together.

"It used to hurt me," she said, "when people called me 'poor little Ann' and said you brought me here because you were good Samaritans and wanted to see that I had enough to eat."

"You came to live with us because we loved you—and we hoped you'd love us. It's hard enough to live with people you love, let alone trying to live with someone for no other reason than that he's hungry or poor. Remember that 'Miss, Miss'

Mary who rode with us to Galway? She was just as poor as you were, wasn't she?"

"Poorer," Ann said.

"If poverty was all that it took, we could have invited her."

"You wouldn't," said Ann.

"No, I wouldn't. I'll give my money to the poor, but half-hermit that I am, I'll share my life only with those I love."

"I got over that 'poor little Ann' obsession quite a few years ago," Ann confessed. "I'm Ann without an adjective now, once poor, now rich. And I don't mean money, either."

"I know what you mean," I told her.

When I left Achill Island, I went to Dublin, where I stayed at the Shelburne, a hotel that provided soap and washcloths and whose proprietor, if in residence, never knocked once on my door.

From there, I phoned Max. Thanksgiving was approaching and, with it, school vacation. Could he take a somewhat prolonged vacation from his post as Superintendent of Schools and come to Ireland to talk with an Irish girl I was about to ask to come to live with us? I wouldn't ask her until he had seen her and talked to her.

He naturally thought I was crazy. When we were first married, I twenty-one, he twenty-two, we had wanted children. None, and very lucky for them and for me, had arrived. A year after my first trip to Ireland, I developed tuberculosis. The next ten years—the first five in bed, the next on couches—were a struggle to arrest the disease. That fight was over, but I had been marked by it. I was a cautious woman, no romping playmate for a child.

"How old is this girl?" Max asked.

"Eleven."

"A terrible age. Too old to be treated like a baby and too young to accept responsibilities."

He said he would come, which he did. When he saw Ann, it wasn't necessary for me to utter a persuasive word.

He not only thought that Ann should, if her mother was willing, come to live with us, but that her older sister should, "to keep Ann from getting homesick," come also. The older sister was more than willing.

"I've always prayed that I could go to America," Jean said.

"You prayed that you'd win the Irish sweepstakes," Ann reminded her. "And you never did."

"God knows the difference," Jean, with an older sister's authority, told Ann, "between America and the Irish sweepstakes."

Max took practical steps to arrange for the girls' departure. He had long talks with the girls' mother. She was an unselfish woman and had her daughters' welfare at heart. Thinking of them and not of herself, she said yes to our request to take the girls home with us to rear and educate them as our own. The girls, of course, were eager for the adventure. And we, childless for so many years, were eager to have children in the home. Before we left Ireland, Max had taken all steps necessary for the girls' trip to California.

Mr. O'Donnel, a Limerick lawyer, had been engaged to look after legal matters.

Canon Lee, the local Catholic dignitary, had been consulted. Canon Lee had no fear for the girls. He did express some concern for us. Did we, a middle-aged couple, have any idea of the tumult two teen-aged girls, accustomed to life on the streets of a big city, might bring into our lives? We didn't. Later, when complimented on our courage in this undertaking, we told the truth. It was not courage but ignorance that had permitted us to become foster parents.

So we left Ireland expecting the two girls to be with us by Christmas. At the first of December, Mr. O'Donnel wrote us that the girls' flight to America was being delayed because of objections raised in America.

The American objection, we discovered, was coming from someone very near at home: from the Catholic Archbishop of San Francisco.

He had conveyed to the proper authorities in Ireland his, and, at that time, the State of California's disapproval of permitting children of one faith to live in the home of a family of another faith.

Napa, a wine-making community, has in it many Italian vineyardists, owners, and workers. The majority of these are Catholic. Forty percent of the high-school students were, when my husband became superintendent of the Napa city schools, Catholic. There was then one Catholic teacher, hired from out of state by a board that did not discover what they had done until this good mathematics teacher arrived in town. Max began hiring teachers on the basis of their pedagogical, not their religious, preparation.

Local Catholics naturally had approved of such good administrative sense. When they heard of the Archbishop's effort to keep the Irish girls from joining us, two carloads of Catholics, including a local priest, went to San Francisco to have a word with the Archbishop. They were listened to by his assistant. To him they said, "We guarantee that these girls will be loved, cared for, educated, and encouraged to remain Catholic."

The Archbishop's assistant was glad to hear it.

He was reminded of what the future often held for Irish girls forced to hunt for work in England.

This was not news to him.

Would it not be better to spare them these privations and temptations?

What happens to our bodies here is of less consequence than what happens to our souls in Eternity. Better a Catholic in the factories and on the streets of Birmingham than a lapsed Catholic however well educated and fed in a Protestant home here.

The report that we were apparently free of all missionary zeal and would be more likely to attend Mass with the girls than to take them to a Quaker Meeting was not convincing.

The word from San Francisco to Ireland continued to be: "Keep the girls at home."

It was then I had a thought. Could it be that the voice of the Vice President of the United States would carry more weight in Ireland than that of the Archbishop of San Francisco? There was one way to find out.

Richard Nixon is my second cousin. His mother had been a second mother to me. We lived across the irrigation canal in Yorba Linda from each other. His father was my Sunday-school teacher. My father was his Sunday-school teacher.

(When Edward Weeks, editor of the *Atlantic* and a red-hot Democrat, heard this, he said, "All I can say to this is that his father was a damned sight better Sunday-school teacher than your father.") Weeks may have been right. Frank Nixon was a fiery persuasive teacher; my father, a quiet reflective one.

I believe that it is wrong for officeholders to use their position for personal gain: or for the personal gain of their relatives.

Richard knew that he had nothing to gain by helping me—not even a vote.

I had become at fifteen a socialist. Young people not drawn to socialism, which dreams of providing what the Constitution promises, are lacking, it also seems to me, in recognition of the nature of man.

My people, like Richard's (they were the same on our mothers' sides), were rock-ribbed Republicans. In southern Indiana, our pre-California home, which is apple country, bad apples were called "Democrats."

My mother knew that I was a lapsed Republican, but did not dream of the depth to which I had fallen. She asked me, when Al Smith ran for president, if she would have to tell her father that I was voting for Al Smith.

It was not Al Smith's Catholicism or his being a Democrat that troubled this good Quaker woman. It was his announced intention of repealing the 18th Amendment. Al Smith was for liquor. Quakers, believing "that there is that of God in every man," did not doubt that good men had been Catholics and Democrats. They could not believe that alcohol would improve anyone.

I was able to reassure my mother. "Tell Grandpa that I am not voting for Al Smith."

I did not tell her that I could not because my ballot would be cast for Norman Thomas.

By the time I was nerving myself to approach Richard Nixon with my Irish problem, I had simmered down politically into being a Democrat. This Richard knew. He also knew that years earlier, when he was sixteen, I had gone to Ireland, hunting in County Kildare the graves of our common ancestors.

I thought that our shared Irish background might interest him in girls who were trying to make the same journey westward our great-grandparents had made two hundred years earlier. I thought that he might feel a degree of noblesse oblige in helping a woman who had not even voted for him.

I wrote a letter explaining the situation to Richard. I told him that I would ask such a favor from the Vice President of the United States only if he could divest himself of his official robes and, as a plain citizen and long-time acquaintance of the couple who were seeking to take two Irish girls into their home, vouch for their integrity and good intentions.

Reasoning of that kind must have helped lessen Richard's opinions of Democrats and cousins. Did I really think that he could divest himself of the power and influence of his position? That he could write to officials of state and church or both in Ireland saying, "You know me as vice president of the United States. I write you now as Citizen Nixon, born in Yorba Linda, California, great-grandson of former residents of County Kildare. As such, may I be of help to you in providing information concerning Mr. and Mrs. McPherson, with whom the two McCarthy girls have been invited to live and continue their education"?

Vice President Nixon's letter is before me now. Verbally he did what he could to take off his toga. The letter, from the Office of the Vice President, contained what was undoubtedly the needed information. It was addressed to the Honorable William H. Taft III, American Embassy, Dublin, Ireland. Long, and carefully composed, it had this among other things to say:

"As you may know, I follow a practice of not intervening in the orderly processing of individual immigration and passport cases, and I do not wish to make any exception in this instance. However, I understand that one of the factors taken into consideration in passport application cases is the character and reputation of the sponsors, as well as their financial ability to take care of the applicants.

"In this regard I can personally vouch for the fact that the McPhersons are morally and financially able to care for the children, that they will bring them up in the Catholic faith, although they are not Catholics themselves, and that they will give the girls an excellent education and a good home. . . .

"Again, I want to emphasize that the purpose of this letter is not to ask for special consideration in any way, but only to supply information which may be pertinent and helpful in deciding the case on its merits. If you feel that it would be appropriate for you to do so, I shall appreciate your transmitting this information to the Minister of External Affairs in Dublin in a manner in which you deem most advisable."

Mr. Taft evidently transmitted this information to the Minister of External Affairs. Three days later, we were informed that the girls' passports and visas were in order, that plane reservations had been made, and that Ann and Jean would be arriving soon.

The Irish saga now adds another character: Merv Griffin, also of Irish origin. The first encounter with Mr. Griffin, though it involved the Vice President, may have occurred without his knowledge. It may, my date with Mr. Griffin, have been arranged by my publisher, who, upon the publication of a new book, tries to obtain as much publicity for the author as he thinks will accelerate the sale of the book. A new book of mine was appearing, and Hilda Lindley, then a publicity director of Harcourt Brace Jovanovich, told me that I was scheduled to appear on "The Merv Griffin Show." She asked me to try to remember that though the public's interest in Mr. Nixon was greater than their interest in me, my function as an interviewee was to sell my book, not Mr. Nixon. I promised to try to remember.

Now what happened, or, rather, did not happen, on that occasion—since I walked out of it without ever having opened my mouth—had to do with a conviction I have about speechmaking. There is too much of it. I am the opposite of Mr. Burgess and the purple cow; he would rather see than be one. I would rather make a speech than hear one. To make a speech, I have to learn something. What have I ever learned from listening to speeches? How many people remember two lines of any speech they ever heard—unless they have subsequently seen a printed version of that speech? The point of a speech is to persuade: "Vote for me!" "Enlist!" "Accept Jesus Christ as your Saviour." Or to instruct: "A plural subject demands a plural verb." "Two pints of water equal one quart."

The storyteller, wishing neither to persuade nor to instruct, is in an awkward position as a speechmaker. He is accustomed to using words in such a way as will hold, he hopes, his reader's attention. His books are bought and his conclusion is that he has succeeded. As a speaker, what evidence does he have of success? He is not a snake-oil salesman. No purchases will be made. He is not an evangelist. No listeners will hit the sawdust trail. He is not a teacher. The audience will not be scored on their retention of facts.

What procedure is left to the writer, accustomed to reader response? He can either be funny, like Mark Twain, and have the reassurance of laughter, or sad, like Charles Dickens, and measure success by tears.

I tried to be funny. On the occasion of the twenty-fifth anniversary of Richard Nixon's graduation from Whittier College, the school celebrated the event. Speeches were made, and I made one of them. I said, reaching for laughter and getting it, that as the Vice President's former baby-sitter, I was not awed by his presence.

This is an example of the way in which fiction writers use facts. I had at the age of ten, before baby-sitters had even been categorized, kept my eye on the Nixon children, including baby Richard, while their mother was absent for twenty minutes on an errand. I had used those words with effect and forgotten them until the day of my scheduled interview with Merv Griffin.

Mrs. Lindley and I arrived, as we had been instructed, a short time before the program was to begin.

We were greeted by a middle-aged receptionist. "Where," she asked me, "is your shopping bag?"

"Shopping bag?" I questioned. This was New York, and I was dressed for an interview in a TV studio. Even in California, I did not go to the supermarket with a shopping bag. I drove in my car, and a supermarket boy carried my groceries out to the car for me.

"You were asked to bring a shopping bag."

This was news to both me and Mrs. Lindley. "Why?" we asked.

"Have you never seen Merv's show?"

We never had.

"This is the procedure," she told us. "Now, you have never seen Mr. Griffin, have you?"

"Never."

"And he has never seen you. Now, you are presented to him, a totally strange woman. He proceeds to ask you a number of questions. After which he will be able to guess who you are."

"I don't see how he will be able to do that."

"Oh, he is very clever at this. After a half-dozen questions, he will say, 'I know who you are.' "

"Who am I?" I asked.

"Oh, Mr. Griffin knows. 'Richard Nixon's baby-sitter.' Then he will say, 'And what have you been doing since you stopped baby-sitting?' "

"What do I say?" I asked.

"That's where the shopping bag comes in. You take a book from the shopping bag and say, 'I have been writing a book.' "

I am sorry that the scene that followed was never photographed. If some movie producer had seen the expressions of astonishment, disbelief, and rage that I am sure my face reflected, I might have become the TV tragedienne of the sixties.

When Benjamin Franklin was asked how he wanted to be introduced when making a speech, he replied, "Benjamin Franklin, Printer." After fifty years of longing to be a writer and finally achieving, by the publication of ten books, that status, I wanted to be introduced as "Jessamyn West, Writer."

I do not think I was snobbish in my refusal to accept the title "baby-sitter"; or that I would have been happier had Mr. Griffin identified me as having sat for John Wayne or John Kennedy. I did think that a woman of sixty had outgrown being labeled by a profession practiced for twenty minutes at the age of ten.

Mrs. Lindley and I prepared to leave the studio at once. The receptionist wailed, "You will disrupt the program. You are scheduled for fifteen minutes."

"Someone can talk longer or more slowly," Mrs. Lindley told her.

Outside, we went to a place where we could sit down, have a drink, and talk about the strangeness of the literary, TV, and political worlds.

I was not yet finished with Ireland or with Mr. Griffin. My third trip to Ireland was the direct result of my first. Had I never in 1929 attempted to find the graveyard in Timahoe, County Kildare, where lay the bones of my ancestors, I would never, I think, have been asked in 1971 by Richard Nixon, then President of the United States, to meet him and Pat in Ireland at the conclusion of the European tour they would soon be making. If I could do this, I could then return to the United States on Air Force One with him and Pat and the other members of the official family who were making the European trip with him.

Apart from every other consideration, this invitation made sense to me because I had promised to write an article about Pat Nixon for a national magazine. I had no idea at the time of the degree to which every minute of the Nixons' time while in Ireland would be scheduled. There would be, however, some free time for talk, I supposed, on the homeward trip on Air Force One.

I was in Ireland by the time the Nixon party arrived. They had flown that morning from Spain, had paused in London to have tea with the Queen, and in the long Irish twilight were being welcomed by the people of Limerick. Richard was there, able, as he was whenever I heard him speak in Ireland, to make his listeners smile.

"I am very happy," he said, "that my wife has so many relatives here." Pat's maiden name was Ryan, and numerous relations had made the trip to Limerick to welcome the President and his wife.

"A good many people," he continued, "have been opposed to this trip of mine, particularly to my stopping in Ireland. I am grateful to all the Ryans who have come here to greet us. They will not show up on the TV cameras as in-laws and may convince critics back home that in Ireland at least we are appreciated."

The crowd laughed at this. A thousand times as many non-Ryans as Ryans were present, and some of these yelled for TV's benefit, "Welcome, brother."

This was the Limerick where, fifteen years earlier, I had

met Ann, gone to the circus, seen the Limerick players' production of *The Glass Menagerie*. Now, with streets thronged and buildings obscured by crowds, I was unable to identify places made memorable to me by the happenings of that trip: the Royal George, which had not provided me with soap and washcloths, and F. W. Woolworth, where I had found a daughter.

I was greeted by Richard and Pat. Whatever other virtues may be required, a President, without stamina will be useless. On that long day, they had been present at an official and formal reception in Spain, been subject to the same, plus tea, with the Queen in England, and were now in Ireland making Irishmen smile and welcoming relatives before going off to a formal dinner with Irish leaders.

I, thank God, was destined for Dromoland Castle, eight miles from Shannon Airport. Rosemary Wood, Nixon's secretary, was staying there, as was a male cousin of Pat's. He, no Quaker, brought me a glass of Jameson's, as a nightcap. This, I found, functioned as well for me, long absent from the old sod, as it would have for any native poet or bogtrotter.

What I was to do for the next two days was scheduled for me minute by minute and hour by hour in a booklet printed in Dublin.

On Sunday, October 4, 1970, Mrs. Nixon, without the President, was to visit the homes of *her* living relations and the graves of *her* ancestors. I, from Dromoland Castle, joined her party, from Kilfrush House, an Irish manor owned by the American millionaire J. A. Mulcahy.

We went by helicopter to Ballinrobe, and from there by car we visited Ryan cousins, parish churches, birthplaces, and gravesides.

Pat's cousins, like cousins everywhere, when distinguished visitors arrive, had put their best feet forward. On the buffet at the Naughtons' were decanters and glasses and bottles so numerous they most surely had been brought in by neighbors to grace the occasion. I was tempted, after the good effects of the Jameson's the night before, to have a glass. I also thought that such efforts at hospitality should be visibly rewarded.

I followed Pat's example, though. "If I were to take one sip," she said, "there would be photographs in every newspaper with the caption, 'Pat Nixon and the Irish product she likes best.'"

On the next day, the pilgrimage was to the graves of Richard's ancestors and mine in Timahoe. Forty years earlier, I had come to within seventeen miles of that storied (in our family) spot before widower Conway had convinced me that my first duty was to myself rather than to the bones of my ancestors.

This trip by limousines, American flags on formal display and Irish citizens young and old lining the road and waving their flag and ours, taught me something about the effects of power and recognition and adulation. I began acting like an envoy of some kind myself. I waved the flag I had been given. I stood, bowed, threw kisses. Would Mr. Conway could have seen me. I understood how, as my taste for fanfare developed, a politician might struggle never to be deprived of it.

As we entered Timahoe, we were handed large cards bearing a message for the President. "This is a great day for us," the card read, "a day on which the most important man in the world, the President of the United States, visits us. Many years have passed since the Milhous family left this locality; yet despite the separation of thousands of miles of land and water and hundreds of years in time, we hope that you feel at home and at ease in Timahoe."

I don't know about the Nixons, but I felt at home and at ease. It had taken me forty years, but at last I had reached (though it needed the help of the President of the United States to do so) the goal I had tried to reach earlier.

Had Meeting House and wooden headstones still stood when, forty years before, my journey to Timahoe had been interrupted at Kildare? I do not know. In 1970, there was no sign of either, though the location was still well known. There Richard, where the Meeting House had once stood, dedicated a memorial stone; thus the name of a Milhous was returned to the place where Thomas and Sarah Milhous had worshiped 250 years before.

After the return from Timahoe, the whole of the President's party was invited to have dinner at Kilfrush House. The food was Irish: Irish Smoked Salmon, Clew Bay Oysters, Aran Scallop Soup, Comeragh Salmon, Cealstown Pigeon Crust Pie, Limerick Bacon and Cabbage, Springhill Lamb, Kilfrush Beef, Waterville potatoes, Irish Coffee. Only with apples, spinach, and cheese did we eat unlabeled and possibly non-Irish food.

At the dinner table, I was seated between two members of the President's staff, Dr. Henry Kissinger and Mr. Robert Haldeman. Before dinner, I had been given a piece of information about Kissinger which it was thought that I, as a West Coast resident, might not know. What I was told was not news to the West Coast: Dr. Kissinger was a ladies' man.

With Haldeman, on my right—no ladies' man, by any reports received on the West Coast, long, lank, and bristle-haired, a Californian like myself—I felt more at ease. I was afraid that the President's elderly cousin would not strike a ladies' man as a very rousing table companion. If so, Kissinger hid it. He talked politics with animation.

The United States, he said, was poised to move and would move (without the help of an able leader) in one of two directions. It would become either deeply conservative or sharply radical.

"Upon what, Dr. Kissinger," I asked, "do you base this belief?"

Kissinger's reply was long, eloquent, and emphatic. Either I was too politically uninformed to follow his reasoning or the reasoning itself did not hold water.

In any case, before I could say anything, Haldeman leaned across me to speak to Kissinger.

"Dr. Kissinger, Miss West may understand that, but I don't. And it's a question I've wanted to ask you myself."

There was, I thought, in the conversation that followed between the two men, some acerbity. When it was over, Haldeman apologized to me. "Forgive me for cutting in that way. Kissinger and I have a habit of ribbing each other. Probably it's more fun for us than for someone who has to listen."

After dinner, a program of Irish songs and dances was presented on an improvised stage in the great hall. Daniel Patrick Moynihan, another staff member, sat next to me during this richly costumed display of the great days of Irish history. No potato famines here, bloody clan wars, or clashes with England. Nothing but wit and poetry, grace and song.

When it was over, I, carried away and making after-dinner conversation with a fellow Irishman, said, "Perhaps we made a mistake in ever leaving Ireland."

Moynihan, round pink face calm and baby-blue eyes cold, looked at me with disbelief. "Don't be silly," said he.

I *was* being silly, and I have cherished his reply, defusing my small-talk prattle, as the wisest words I heard in Ireland.

After the dinner at Kilfrush House I walked about the grounds of Dromoland Castle before going to bed. It was to be my last night in Ireland. I remembered my first visit and thought how much hinges upon firsts. The first marks us in ways we don't anticipate: first words, first kisses, first blows. I was at Dromoland Castle because of my first unenthusiastic visit to Ireland. My second trip had resulted in my meeting Ann.

Dromoland was a far cry from Conway's Hotel. It had been the seat of the heirs of Ireland's ancient kings. Here had lived the descendants of High King Brian Boru, victor over the Danes at Clontorf in 1014.

For years, I had thought about Irishness. One did not in the early 1900's, if one lived in southern Indiana, speak of having Irish blood. The Irish were then thought to be shiftless, hard drinkers who lived in shanty towns. An Irish Quaker was a contradiction in terms: overly thrifty, of the wrong religion, living in a neat farmhouse and spurning drink.

On that October night, strolling about Dromoland Castle, I remembered a paragraph V. S. Pritchett had written years before in the *New Statesman*. I can quote it now because I copied it into one of my journals.

There is, says Pritchett, a "foreignness" in Ireland that cannot be found in any other European country. "Ireland has always been the country of goodbyes. That is really what all the ballads are about. Perhaps the real foreignness of Ireland in the modern world has to do, not with race history or climate—but is created by its emptiness, the only emptiness in Europe—a spaciousness tragically made by all those goodbyes."

Thomas and Sarah Milhous, 250 years earlier, had said their good-byes. The McManamans, the Foleys, the Sharps, of my family, the Ryans of Pat's, my Ann, had said that peculiarly Irish word.

There were streaks of light in the eastern sky before I went inside to sleep in the hall of the high kings. Before I did so, I added my good-byes to the millions that already clotted the Irish air.

On Air Force One, I found myself seated behind Moynihan, who was surrounded by books. Moynihan reminded me of other of Pritchett's insights about the Irish. "Unlike the English," says Pritchett, "the Irish do not wear their hearts on their sleeves. They prefer comedy: it hides the self from vulgar definition.

"The Irish," he continues, "have an almost morbid quickness of mind: they listen to half your sentence, guess the rest and cap it, getting their blow in first."

Moynihan did not cap any of my sentences; he would hear me out, then if necessary contradict me. I respected him for it.

The Nixons had agreed that on the return trip I could interview Pat in preparation for an article I was to write about her for one of the large popular magazines.

Pat had just come through ten trying days; being interviewed by anyone, perhaps especially by an in-law, didn't, I'm sure, strike her as the R and R she needed. She was willing to give me statistics: how many state dinners, how many foreign countries visited, how many prayer breakfasts attended.

I wasn't interested in information of that kind and doubted that readers would be. I was less interested in what she had done than in who she was: we had both grown up in the same part of Southern California. She, like me, had gathered yellow violets and Indian paintbrushes on the hills in spring; had listened to coyotes sing and watched roadrunners sprint. She, too, had experienced the excitement of the big-shouldered Santa Anas pushing ahead of them their hundred-headed crop of tumbleweeds.

She, too (early orphaned, as I was not), had needed to make money as a teen-ager. She had earned hers with a roadside stand selling fruits and vegetables; I, mine, in an orange-packing house. About such things, she did not want to talk.

Talk with Richard was easier. But then, I wasn't interviewing him, and we had a background of shared memories. I told him of my hope to get Pat to speak of herself as a person, rather than as First Lady.

"I assured her," I told him, "that I would send the completed article to her and that she could blue-pencil anything she dislikes."

"Don't send the manuscript to her," he said.

"To whom, then? To you?"

"Send it to your editor. I don't want to see it."

Though ten years his senior, and politically of another cast of mind, I felt close to Richard for a number of reasons.

At the time I was lying in a sanatorium with far-advanced tuberculosis, his older brother Harold was dying of the same disease. Harold, with my brother, came one night to visit me.

The next day, fellow inmates said, "You had another lunger visiting you yesterday." I did indeed. In a short time, Harold was dead. Harold was larger, handsomer, seemingly more outgoing than Richard. He liked the girls and the girls liked Harold.

After Harold's death, his father said to my father, "Why is it that the brightest and strongest, handsomest and best, get taken first?" This may or may not have been true. Death hallows the dead. It may have been the statement of one stricken father to another whose first born was not expected to live. In any case, I had often wondered whether or not Richard had encountered that same attitude in his own home. The best had been taken, and he, a substitute, a man on the second team, would have to struggle untiringly to take his place. About this, I don't know, and I did not speak to Richard about it.

We spoke of members of the family no longer alive: Great-uncle Amos, with his skullcap; Great-grandmother Milhous, who in her nineties had developed a bristly mustache which we children were loath to kiss.

We spoke—I don't remember why; I the bookworm probably brought it up—of E. M. Forster's declaration that "if I had to choose between betraying my country and betraying my friend, I hope I should have the guts to betray my country."

"Forster was not in a position to be called upon to betray his country," Richard said.

I was surprised to find that Richard knew Forster. Actually, that may have been all the Forster he knew. It is an often-quoted sentence.

"If Forster had been President, you think he wouldn't have said that?"

"I think he shouldn't have."

I didn't ask the obvious question of the man the Timahoe welcoming card had called "the most important man in the world." We were halfway across the Atlantic, far too high to see the water below us, though Richard peered down toward it.

After a minute or two, in a calm voice, stating a fact, not complaining or asking for pity, he said, "I haven't a friend in the world." It was a cold, sad statement. Did he mean that one way of avoiding the risk of betraying one's country, if one were President, was not to have friends? I named a man or two with whom his name had been associated. "Companions," he answered.

Were there happenings at that time which made Nixon feel particularly friendless?

The *Irish Independent,* on the day after Nixon left Ireland, announced in its headlines, "Nixon's Irish talks may end the Vietnam War."

The *Washington Post* of the same date noted that "Mr. Nixon's sentimental trip to Timahoe had been marred by several eggs hurled against his limousine." He was greeted at Andrews Air Force Base with a welcome "arranged by the White House. Tourists had been invited to the rally by fliers distributed at White House request at monuments and tourist centers."

Meanwhile, there were those who were saying that Nixon, in his trip to Ireland, had been trying to "pull a Kennedy," to "out-Irish Jack." How could a man with the name Milhous be Irish? Being Irish was no longer a liability. It suggested a quality of dash and wit, which it was felt Nixon sorely needed—and was assuming for political reasons to have.

What part this criticism had to do with my second invitation to appear on "The Merv Griffin Show," I don't know. I was asked to bring with me some documents, if I had any, attesting to the early residence of Milhouses in Ireland. I had the documents. I had voted for John Kennedy, but not because he was Irish; nor did I think now that his memory could be enhanced by stripping others of their Irish past. So, forgetting my earlier shopping-bag experience with Griffin, I flew down to Hollywood, where his show then took place.

Griffin had abandoned his earlier routine of guessing who

guests were. He knew who I was, where I had been, and why I was at that minute facing him.

After some preliminary talk about my visit to Ireland in 1929, I was asked to produce my document.

The document I had thought would be most telling in demonstrating that Timahoe was no figment of the President's imagination and that forebears of his had indeed lived there before coming to America in 1729 was the statement sent by the Friends Meeting in Dublin to Friends in Philadelphia.

After speaking of my visit forty years earlier to Ireland, I unrolled my document, on which I expected to read, "The Certificate of Removal of Thomas and Sarah Milhous from Dublin, 5-29-1729."

What I read instead was, "Whereas Joshua V. Milhous and Elizabeth Price Griffith having declared their intention of marriage . . ."!

In my haste, I had grabbed the wrong document. I felt myself a second McCarthy, waving papers and saying, "I hold in my hand. . . ." But I was in worse case than McCarthy. He was not faced by cameras capable of zooming in close enough to reveal the very words on the paper I held.

I did not pretend to read from the document I held. I knew its contents well enough to relate them without reference to the written words. But the camera *was* zooming in. I never knew whether or not Merv Griffin was aware of the mistake I had made. In any case, he leaned closer and closer to the somewhat faded ink of the marriage agreement, crying out, as he read the names, "Here's another Milhous. Here's William! There's Joshua! Here's Thomas!" I do not know what Griffin saw. I do know that all the camera could see was Griffin's leonine head, nose deep in that un-Irish document of a hundred years later.

I have not seen Ireland, Merv Griffin, or Richard Nixon since the Irish trip of 1970.

Richard, demonstrating the Irish wit his detractors maintained he could not honestly have inherited, sent me his autobiography with this inscription: "For Jessamyn, the most noted writer of the Milhous clan, from the most notorious. Richard."

And Ann, the Irish daughter who came to us as the result of Richard's help, had the last word to say about my Irish connection.

When Richard resigned, she sent him a telegram saying, "An Irish girl you helped will always bless you. Ann McCarthy."

Oxford at Last

No Air Force One took me away from my first trip to Ireland. First by boat, with the bearded Boy Scouts, then by train to Chester. From Chester I wrote my mother.

"I am going to try not to write you about Chester. If once I started, I would have to write all night and you would have to read all day. Ely and Durham are my loves, but Chester is my wonder, an English town built high on the stacked ruins of Rome. I'll write you a Chester letter sometime when things are slow in Oxford. But now I'm in Oxford.

"I arrived in Oxford at 9:40 P.M., got a taxi to take me out to St. Frideswide's, where I have reservations for the Summer Meeting. After a lot of bell ringing by me, an aperture the size of a matchbox was opened in the door and a very pretty girlish nose could be seen. 'Who is it, please?' 'Mrs. McPherson. I have a reservation here for the Summer Meeting.' We had more talk. She couldn't understand me. I couldn't understand her. Finally she said, 'I will ask Grandmother if she has a crack or a crevice in which she can put you.'

"Grandmother, I took to be the nun in charge, an abbess of some sort; though such a name surprised me. St. Frideswide's is run by Catholic Sisters for Catholic girls in attendance at Oxford. For the Summer Meeting, when many regular students are absent on their 'Long,' they take in outsiders like me.

"After some minutes, the pretty nose came back and said, 'Grandmother will see you.' There then followed a prolonged unlocking, sliding of bars, rattling of chains. No one was going to see Grandmother, Grandmother didn't want to see. I got inside, but I never saw Grandmother. The nun with the pretty nose let me sit down while she told me the news. My reservation wasn't until Wednesday, and Grandmother didn't have a crack or a crevice I could use before then. She took me out onto the porch, where the taxi driver was sitting, waiting. To him she told the sad news: there was no room for me at St. Frideswide's. 'Take her to either the Randolph or the Mitre; both are good respectable hotels where she will be comfortable until she can come here.'

"The porthole was then closed, the door locked, the bolts and chains rattled. 'She is safe for the night,' the taxi driver said. When we reached the taxi, he said to me what he hadn't said to her, 'Those are big expensive hotels. I won't take you to either of them. I'll take you to the place where all the Americans stay, a more private place. You'll feel right at home there.'

" 'Take me to one of the hotels the nun told you to take me to.'

" 'Oh, no. I know more than those nuns do about hotels. They don't have to pay for anything and they think Americans are made of money.'

"Travel was making me a liar. 'I'm not made of money, but I have plenty of money for a good hotel.'

" 'You want to be happy, don't you?'

"I did. And nothing at the minute gave any promise of happiness that I could see except the Randolph or the Mitre. How to get there short of throwing myself out of the cab or banging the driver on the head with my purse, I didn't know. The driver was a long-nosed, long-jawed, small-eyed man who didn't look to me like a man who had the happiness, let alone welfare, of young female travelers at heart. What he looked like to me was a professional procurer of white slaves for the South American market. I was frightened. I continued to protest. The driver continued to assure me that he was taking me to a place where I would be happy."

Why did I sit, shaking and scared, but quiet, while I was being convoyed to distant dens of iniquity? When money, or anti-Americanism, or doubt as to my intelligence was the subject, I could immediately raise my voice. I wasn't too thin-skinned or delicate-minded to speak up when I thought my cash was endangered. I had made quite a scene when I was regarded in Edinburgh as a typical stupid American tourist. But let sex, or what I thought was sex, be involved and I became too ladylike and prudish to raise my voice.

At this distance, I'm not sure whether this attitude was the result of nature or nurture. Fifty years ago young women, rural and Quaker, had certainly been brought up with as much ignorance of sex as was possible in a world where sex existed. Added to the ignorance was the belief that any public outcry on the subject would be unseemly indeed. On the other hand, was I willing, as the result of strong but hidden sexual desires, to keep quiet and see what would happen? Or was my attitude in part the result of modesty? Knowing as little as I did of the world, of men, and, finally, of myself, did I think that I might be judging as sexual, overtures that were not? And thus flattering myself into believing that knee-squeezing and taxi-abduction were ways of saying, "You look good to me," when actually they were the moves of an arthritic and the commercial enterprise of a businessman whose private opinion was, "Not good, but passable."

At this date, impossible to say. The letter about the taxi ride away from St. Frideswide's continues.

"Residences here look grim, made of stone, built flush with the street, without gardens or front yards and with nothing to show, unless it's a change in the color of the stone, where one house ends and another begins.

"In front of one of these dismal buildings—it could have been a poorhouse, a reformatory, or a factory—the taxi stopped, and the driver shouted, 'Emma.' Down the steps came a plump woman. 'Look what I've got for you, Emma,' said the taxi driver.

"Then, indeed, I felt like a piece of merchandise. I think I would surely, with the taxi stopped and the door opened, have grabbed my bags and run except that Emma said, 'I'm sorry, but every room I have is booked.'

"I would have run anyway except at that minute two young men put their heads out of an upstairs window and one of them shouted, 'Emma, no American is ever turned down at Wellington Square.' I hadn't said a word, so I must look American. Then out of the front door bounded two young men about twenty-two or three.

"The oldest, at least the largest, said, 'Emma, a gallant American will give a fellow countrywoman his bed. I'll move in with Ted.'

"'If you two want to double up, that gives me an extra room.'

"So I had a room, at about half hotel price, just as the taxi man had promised me—and with, just as he had promised, jolly Americans for company. I didn't know whether to tip the driver for kindness or berate him for scaring me to death. I guess you know I tipped him. The boys carried my luggage up to my room and then had enough sense to leave without a word but 'Good night.' They could see that my eyes were closing.

"This morning at breakfast I saw the two young men of the night before plus one more. Of all strange things, they had been on the *Minnekahada* with me. They have a car rented for two weeks, and if I want to pay my share of the gas (petrol here), they'd be glad to have me go with them on their sightseeing trips. Today we went to Kennilworth and Warwick castles. I'll tell you about them tomorrow. My chief conclusion about castles is that I wouldn't want to live in one; though if you lived there, I don't suppose you'd be required to walk through every room every day. I'm getting blisters again.

"The oldest of the three young men is twenty-four. His name is Crandall and he is a master (teacher) at a boys' school in Connecticut. He is handsome and full of advice. He says I pronounce my name wrong. It should be McPherson, not McPhurson. We stopped at a bookstore in Oxford and I bought a secondhand copy, first edition, of D. H. Lawrence's *Pansies*. Mr. Crandall didn't think I should buy *anything* by D. H. Lawrence. He thinks Lawrence is a dirty writer. I haven't found anything very dirty in *Pansies* yet. Mr. Crandall is inclined to treat me like one of his pupils, though I am older than he is, and was just as much a master at Harmony as he is in Connecticut. Also, I think he believes that the West and particularly California is about one hundred years behind the East in learning and culture.

"Crandall drives. In the front seat with him is a young man who says nothing and, insofar as I can find out, doesn't know anything.

"Riding with me in the back seat is a pipe-organ player who is going to be an Episcopal minister. He does a good deal of nudging, patting, and squeezing; but he does this with everyone, male, female, young, old. So I don't take it personally.

"Tomorrow we are going to Salisbury Cathedral, and Crandall says it will make me forget Ely and Durham. He hasn't seen Ely and Durham himself, but he has read all that has ever been written about everything.

"I begin to be sorry that I have to leave Wellington Square for St. Frideswide's and the nuns. The taxi driver was probably right: the boys are more fun than the nuns will be. With the boys and their car, I might never see Oxford itself, though. While I'm at Oxford attending lectures, they're going tomorrow to Stonehenge and Old Sarum."

    •   •   •

"Where to begin: First, letters from home at St. Frideswide's from you and from Max. I was so excited, I shook. The first since I left New York. This is the way I got them. I had given up hope about letters, but was trying to find my trunk. I had had the trunk sent from London to Oxford when I left London for Scotland and Ireland—and now no trunk. I called the London-American Express from the American Express here. They couldn't understand a word I was saying in London. I spelled my name ten thousand times: M as in mincemeat, C as in cowslip, P as in parsnip, etc. Finally, they said they would write me about my trunk.

"All my spelling and bellowing didn't do much good in London but it brought results in Oxford. After hearing my name shouted and spelled so many times, someone had an idea. He looked in a pigeonhole, found a packet of letters, and brought them to me. 'Are these addressed to you, Mrs. Mincemeat, Cowslip, Parsnip?' No, of course he didn't say that: that's me, still light-headed from actually, after so long a wait, having mail from home. I've read each letter ten thousand times and have them here with me to touch in the library at St. Frideswide's. It's a room I love, dark, quiet, book-lined, looking out onto a garden.

"I wrote you about Warwick and Kenilworth. Kenilworth is a ruin, more beautiful in its broken arches than Warwick in its complete ones.

"On Wednesday I couldn't resist, even though I missed opening day at the Summer Session, going with the boys to Salisbury to see the cathedral and to Stonehenge—to see the stones, of course. Salisbury is about sixty miles from Oxford. We left Oxford at 2:00 P.M., and Crandall and I both had to be back at 8:30 for the first lecture. Never, never have I seen, let alone experienced, such dangerous driving. The road was a lane, with a thousand twists and turns, and these were obscured by hedges; and the surface was wet with an intermittent downpour. Along this dangerous road Crandall sent the Morris-

Cowley (which is something like a light Dodge) at fifty miles an hour, missing bridges, stone walls, steamrollers, telephone poles by inches. God loved someone in that car; nothing on earth could have saved us.

"By the time we got to Stonehenge I just wanted to lie down on the ground at the foot of one of those great slabs and let it be my tombstone while I still lived because I doubted we'd ever make it back to Oxford alive.

"We did—and in time for kind Crandall, the dangerous driver, to dump me and my belongings here so that I could get to the first lecture. It was by Dean Inge on the history of Oxford and certainly not worth risking death for. The Dean has an unpleasant voice, a repellent attitude, and a snarly face. I heard him again tonight on the Cambridge Platonists. He is a better essayist than lecturer. In fact, his lectures *are* his essays, and we'd be better off if he'd have someone else read them to us.

"Send this on to Max. I can't keep my eyes open any longer. I'll write him tomorrow. This is a beautiful place. I'll sleep well with all the home letters by my side tonight—old though they are."

For a day or two, entries in the journal and letters home contradict each other. The letters home report, as usual, sights seen and people encountered. Into the journal went some lamentations. I did not yet know anyone, and after the hurly-burly of travel and the companionship of Wellington Square, I was alone as I hadn't been since I boarded the train at Chicago bound for New York. Also, I had traveled across a continent and a sea for one chief purpose: to see Oxford, to be in Oxford; and I wasn't yet able to bring Oxford, the city or the university, into focus.

In my journal I wrote: "9:15 A.M. in my room reading Katherine Mansfield's letters, which I found last night in W. H. Smith and Sons' library. There is a lecture this morning on St. John the Baptist and I sit reading Katherine Mansfield. Thank God for Katherine Mansfield. I am terribly alone here. Being alone when you are traveling isn't bad; actually you aren't alone most of the time. It's only bad when you stop in a place like this and find all other people arm in arm. I would link arms with any talkative guttersnipe and walk proudly down the street.

"I look out of my window into the sliding treetops and through them to the open fields beyond. I wish the entire landscape had a sign, 'This is England.' I wish each tree were labeled 'This is an English tree.'"

Three nights later I was writing, "When I first arrived I was so busy seeing people, I had no time to see where I was. Now I've burst through the barrier of people to this Oxford and its dreaming spires."

A week later I wrote in my journal, "This book is being neglected. Why? There's the question of time, of course, but that isn't the whole answer. It's more a question of feeling. 'Poetry is . . . emotion recollected in tranquillity.' There has been little tranquillity, much to do, much to feel. I cannot write and feel at the same time. Here, swept over by a thousand emotions ranging from excess joy to abject sorrow, I cannot journalize. But if I do not write, all of these scenes, these encounters that mean so much to me, will be forgotten. It cannot be helped. I cannot put them down.

"These days are in some respects wasted. I could get much more from a book in the same length of time than I get from these lectures. Lectures are a sanctimonious hangover from pre-Gutenberg days, when if you learned anything you learned it by word of mouth. Lecturing professors are our modern gods, and we offer them, just as the Aztecs did, the living bodies of our young."

Next day: "I take myself from my window seat and from as typically an English scene as can be imagined. For an hour, ever since teatime, I have been hanging out of the window saying, 'There is England, exactly as I imagined it.' First, I look down onto a walled garden, green turf, graveled walks, regularly laid out flower beds, rose arbors, and garden chairs.

"Over the wall to the right lies the playing field of New College, a large green handkerchief embroidered in white: a foolish way of saying that a game of cricket is being played there. The men in white suits, the decorous clapping, the bowler's slow graceful movement: this is surely England.

"Beyond the cricket field and its pavilion, I see the tower of Magdalen College. And that's not only England, that's *Oxford*! To the left of the garden flows the river Cherwell; and over all, the good English sky, pale blue and cloud flecked.

"As I watch, I hear the crack of cricket ball on the bat, a duller sound than that of baseball on bat—at times it is no more than a thud.

"Today has gone so fast: two lectures, shopping, nursing my broken heels, tea. I feel that I should have gotten more from it. But you can't squeeze a day like an orange. And I have dulled my ability to feel lately by seeing and hearing too much.

"Now I must bathe with the bar of soap loaned me by the good Frieda. I can't let dear John Angus outdo me in cleanliness. I, too, will wash with soap."

The letters home have other things to say.

"If anyone asks you, 'Where is Jessamyn now?,' you may not be able to tell them the town, but because I always describe my room, you can always tell them where I am staying. I've sent you pictures of St. Frideswide's itself, but I haven't told you about my room. The Sisters didn't want me to have it, because they think it's one of the poorer rooms. It hasn't a wardrobe or a big double bed with a fancy brass headboard, and that's the reason I chose it. It looks like a sitting room. The bed is a couch. There are two tables, a really nice desk, at which I'm writing, two well-placed mirrors, a fireplace, a Morris chair, a chintz-covered box, and a ditto footstool. Also, a bookcase which is almost filled with books I own or have borrowed from W. H. Smith's circulating library.

"I could live in this room forever, but it's a good thing I'm not going to, otherwise I'd waddle home unrecognizable. Four meals a day! How do the English do it? Do you want to know what we had for breakfast this morning? Great platters of cold boiled ham, pork pies, sliced tomatoes, hot rolls, marmalade, coffee. Did I tell you how the coffee is served? A tall nun with a pot in each hand, one filled with coffee, one with hot milk, pours two streams into your cup at the same time. I don't know whether she or the order disapproves of coffee, but what you get is three-fourths of a cup of hot milk, one-fourth of a cup of coffee. To get one-half of a cup of coffee, you have to drink two cups of liquid.

"Tonight at dinner I sat with a German lady on one side of me, an Englishwoman on the other. The German lady asked me, pointing to a dish of squash, 'What do you call this?' 'Squash,' said I. 'Vegetable marrow,' said the Englishwoman. The German lady asked, 'What do you say makes the bread so good here?' 'It's fresh,' said I. 'It's new,' said the Englishwoman.

"We are served at the table by nuns. They make our beds, shine our shoes, mop our rooms. They belong to a teaching order and in term time they are either teaching or studying. Now in vacation time they wrap their skirts and veils up high and neat and work hard and fast. The cooks are nuns, and I'd probably learn more that I need to know if I were to stay in the kitchens with the cooks as teachers for the time I'm here instead of going to hear lectures that don't tell me much I don't already know.

"D. Crandall, the dangerous driver and know-it-all (I shouldn't say this; he's an intelligent boy, but can't stop teaching), asked me to go with him yesterday to Stratford-on-Avon to a play. I felt guilty about missing so many lectures here, even though most of them bore me. So I said no. He took me to tea at New College, where he is staying, afterward, and there I heard my third lecture of the day: on Bernard Shaw by Crandall.

"Shaw was at Stratford and shook hands twice with Crandall. I don't know why. Shaw then asked him to dinner next week. Shaw, says Crandall, is the kindest, most pleasant man he ever met. He says he will, on his death, leave the hand Shaw shook to his alma mater, which is, I think, Princeton. He shook my hand so that I could experience at least at secondhand some of the Shaw ambience. Alas, since I am left-handed and Crandall shook my right hand, you are getting the same old stuff."

"After dinner I talked with Dr. Schmidt, a German lady. She was in Cologne during the American occupation of that city and lived in a house in which American soldiers were quartered. 'They spat,' said Dr. Schmidt, 'all over the house, so that I had to lift my skirts when I walked about.'

"Mme Soutelle, the French lady, when she heard this tale of spitting, said, 'Let me tell you what your countrymen did in the house I lived in in France.' Since this has to go through the mail, I'd better not write it out. But, believe me, what the Germans did in her home made spitting seem a charming function. It's a good thing that both these ladies are Catholic, so if they come to blows, they will have to go to confession and suffer for their sins."

"If I am going to continue reporting the sayings and doings of the other residents of St. Frideswide's, I'd better identify them for you. I have now been here a week, and there are three I now consider friends. First, I'll write you about Billie Rendle. Her first name is really Gladys (you wanted to be called Gladys Waneeta when you were little, didn't you?), but no one would think of calling Billie 'Gladys.' She is small, under five feet, square, brown, and muscular. She is English, but her family lives in South Africa. She was sent to England to be educated at four, and hasn't seen her father or mother now for two and a half years. She has been on her own for so long that, compared with her, I am a baby. Her father is some kind of an official. She lived in Switzerland during the war and is now 'reading for honors in French' here at Oxford—that means that she is majoring in French and competing for honors. She is going to France when the Summer Meeting is over and will stay in the International House there. She says I will learn more and twice as fast in Paris as in Oxford.

"She couldn't be kinder to me. The way I got acquainted with her was through her volunteering to take my shoes to a shop that would put a pad in the back which would prevent blisters. She is not the soul of kindness about the townspeople, though. She thinks that they are boobs, one and all. We went to a play last night, which was a miserable bore. Billie said that it was inferior because it was put on during 'Vec,' and since few students were in town to attend, the play management didn't trouble to put on a first-rate production. When students were attending during term, excellent plays were to be seen. Townies couldn't recognize trash when they were given it, so that's what they got.

"You can imagine how different this attitude is from what I knew as a student at Whittier. Class still survives in England. Oxford students are not the children of fathers who are 'in trade,' and they look down their noses at mongers and drapers and meat purveyors and the like. I say that my father is a rancher, which he is, and which they consider a Wild Western occupation suitable for colonists. I haven't yet told them that he also owns a dry-cleaning plant. I don't know what they would make of that.

"From an absolutely selfish viewpoint, I couldn't possibly have made a friend more useful to me. Billie is the coxswain of the Oxford varsity crew—female, of course—and has rowed twice against Cambridge. She has the keys to the boathouse during the 'Vec' and can use any boat stored there she likes. She has been trying to teach me to punt. I think that she is about to give this up and try me on canoeing instead.

"In punting, you push a boat along with a pole, which you ram into the bottom of the river and so shove the boat forward. The river is the Cherwell, which is about the size of two Anaheim ditches. The first time out, a very embarrassing thing happened—to her and to me. I overrammed: that is, I pushed my pole so deeply into the mud—or whatever is at the bottom of the Cher—that I couldn't get it out. I didn't have enough sense to abandon the pole and to shoot on ahead with the boat, but clung to my pole. So there I was, clinging to a pole in midstream that was beginning to bend under my weight. If Billie hadn't quickly and cleverly, with her paddle, got the boat back to me before I or the pole gave way, I would have had a fully dressed swim. The Cherwell is always filled with boaters. The English are a polite people, but when something sidesplitting happens, they do laugh—and I suppose that the sight of me clinging to a slowly bending pole in the middle of the Cher was pretty sidesplitting. Anyway, Billie has given up trying to make a punter out of me. I'm like a left-handed pitcher, all power and no control. Punting looks so easy—even graceful. For me it is awful. I can no more steer than fly.

"Billie would soon be the cheerleader in any American college—or at least they would want her to be. She might refuse. She is a far more profound student of English, history, philosophy, French, than anyone I knew in college. I would like to introduce her to D. Crandall, the wise man from Connecticut; but she is engaged and he would rather shake hands with Shaw than hold hands with a girl. (This is not sour grapes, Max.)

"Billie bought me an elementary French textbook, something used by ten-year-olds, I think, in England. She says that since I will have to pass French and German tests before I can get my doctor's, I should be studying now in time that is wasted during waits for buses, lectures to begin, etc. Since she speaks French as English and Frieda speaks French as German, they both tutor me.

"Frieda Brunner is a German girl, aged twenty-two, who is studying John Dryden. Somebody in Germany knows why; I don't. When the Summer Meeting is over, she is going to London to photograph Dryden manuscripts in the British Museum. She is probably the prettiest girl here, the typical picture, as we have it, of a 'Dutch' girl: flaxen hair, perfect complexion, big soft-blue eyes. Besides being a student, very pretty and kindhearted, she is very religious. I have seen her quickly, when she thought no one was looking, kneel and kiss the hem—I guess—of the robe on the Virgin Mary's statue that stands in the hall here. Even if American soldiers had spat all over her home, I don't think she would have told an American about it as Dr. Schmidt did. In repose, you would think Frieda the most dignified, unapproachable girl you ever saw. Instead, she is full of pranks and quips. She hopes to be a teacher. This means that she must pass a series of stiff exams. Teachers in Germany are employed by the state. It is a very trying and heartbreaking situation—a poor grade means the loss of years of work. She is very conscientious but not heavy or severe. She has made this trip at some sacrifice on the part of her parents and feels she must get all out of it she can.

"During the war, she was in a school where the chief meal of the day was provided by Quakers. She never uses rouge, lipstick, or powder (she doesn't need to), but thinks it very poor taste to do so. She does smoke and drink. To a Quaker, this seems worse than poor taste; it seems wicked—except that it also seems impossible that Frieda could possibly do anything wicked.

"The third member of the trio I know best is a French-woman, Mme Soutelle. She is thirty-five, a teacher, black-haired and elegant. She is the one who wouldn't let Dr.

Schmidt get away with her story of the dirty Americans in
the homes of the clean Germans.

"If I wanted physical help from one of the three, I'd ask
for Billie Rendle. If I wanted to be prayed for, Frieda would
be my choice. If I wanted something complex explained to me,
I'd ask Mme Soutelle to do so. The three of them speak in
French as often as in English. I am the poor little tongue-tied
colonial."

"Dear Harry Maxwell: I asked Mama to send you my letter
about my three closest friends here and I hope she did. Anyway, I'll take for granted that you know who's who now.

"There is a Quaker Meeting here, and Billie Rendle, the
English girl, went with me to Meeting this morning. I was
never in a more dismal room, or walked down a darker side
street to reach it. There were perhaps twenty-five people present, and for half an hour not a word was said. Just when I
was thinking of getting up and repeating what I heard in
London, 'A dumb world is a dead world,' a man stood and
said, 'I pray for the day when all the columns celebrating
Nelson will be hauled down.'

"I think this is a prayer wasted. It won't happen in England.
It takes some really firm belief in Quakerism to be willing to
meet in so drab and ramshackle a room when as Anglicans
they could be worshiping in the church of St. Mary the Virgin.

"Billie Rendle, the Oxford girl, didn't like any of it. She
said that hearing people speak when moved by the spirit was
like seeing people naked. Good taste required clothing. She
believes that everything that really matters can be expressed by
ritual or in ceremony. But Jesus himself, I told her, spoke
when moved by the spirit and without ritual or ceremony.
Billie said, reminded of this, 'When another Jesus makes His
appearance among you Quakers, let me know, and I'll certainly
come to hear what He has to say. But what comes to mind
for you or me to say has probably been better said somewhere
in ritual.'

"If we were all to be silent except when we could say something in a better way than it has been said before, a great silence would fall upon this earth.

"There are plenty of strange women here. The three I described to Mama are the exception, not the rule.

"1) There is a thirty-year-old thin blonde American with thin blond hair, worn shoulder-length. She is writing, she tells everyone, a study of England and America. The theme of this study was suggested to her by a blind beggar. She does not tell us what this theme is. She has been in England over a year. She talks continuously of superficial things. She cannot be stopped. If you don't want to hear her, you have to quickly and quietly leave.

"2) An American schoolteacher, fifty-five to sixty-five, the color of a sweet potato and truly a bit mad. She is a Catholic and an amateur historian. At lectures, she pushes her spectacles to the final tip of her leathery nose, stands and begs to differ.

"She also passes about notes at lectures on the subject of women's dress, as: A. 'Is morality necessary to civilization?,' B. 'Is women's dress conducive to morality?,' C. 'Should dress effectively conceal?'

"As it happened, she handed the first paper to me. I was sitting with a French group, four or five men and the two Frenchwomen who are staying at St. Frideswide's. They shook and turned purple trying not to laugh.

"She, poor woman, talks so much to herself in her room at night that the Sister in an adjoining room couldn't endure it. So Billie Rendle, who has good nerves, has changed rooms with Sister. Jarvis, the American woman, has pasted a cloth over all of her mirrors. She says good night aloud and at length to all of her numerous and absent family. She is called 'the poor old American,' and does unfortunately have some of the worst American traits: our desire to inform and to reform.

"Mrs. Moore is an Irish lady who has been everywhere. She tells us at what shop on what street in what town you get the best roast pigeons. She is doing gardens this year. Cathedrals, she finished years ago. She is an indefatigable talker and really witty, but the witticisms are so profuse, you fail to appreciate them. Her conversation is all spice and no meat.

"Miss Lindsay is another American, who lives in Italy in the winter and in England in the summer. She, too, is much traveled: knows where the best cures are to be had, best cheeses, etc. She translates Italian verse into American. Billie Rendle then puts it into English. What happens to it then, I don't know. Miss Lindsay says, 'America cares only about materialistic things and makes progress only in them.' For all she knows, we might have changed since she's been home.

"I've met people here in whose existence I never believed, women who spend their time traveling from one place to another, taking cures, making retreats. Women who make serious talk of the best place to get coffee, or cheese, or chestnuts. Women who complain of their health, yet who travel constantly, the most trying of all occupations. Women who wear indescribably awful clothes, who snuffle in a ladylike way and carry cans of 'Cow-Gate Milk' with them. What a pity I have for them. To be forever traveling! To have no home. What a hell! To find your most sympathetic audience, perhaps your only audience, about a strange dining table. To have as your only confidant a fellow traveler. To always see strange hills from your bedroom window, and hear the wind blow through trees you can't name. Why do they do it? What are they looking for? Not romance, surely, at their age. It's a habit, perhaps, as staying at home is a habit. Or else it's a means of hiding from themselves the emptiness of their lives. Traveling, if you move frequently enough, does really occupy you, body and mind. That I have found out. Catch the train, book the room, hail the taxi, hang onto the suitcase: at the end of a day like that, you do have a sense of accomplishment. It's about on the same level, but against a less lively background, as that of a savage trying to survive in a jungle.

"I write like this because I have been without any mail now

for almost two weeks. Not one scrap since the few letters, now over a month old, which were here when I arrived. The last letter was mailed June 22. I am dreadfully worried. What is the trouble? Don't ever fail to tell me no matter what terrible thing happens, for I can imagine happenings worse than any reality. I have written the American Express Company in London (they can't understand me on the phone), visited the American Express Company here ten thousand times. Nothing.

"Miss Jarvis is known as 'the poor old American.' I have become 'the poor young American.' Mail that is addressed to persons care of the 'Summer Meeting' is placed alphabetically in a wire holding frame which is hung in the entrance room of the Lecture Hall. I never told anyone to write me care of the Meeting, so I can't expect any mail there. I look anyway, and have moaned and complained so much that someone, Billie Rendle and Frieda Brunner, I imagine, put three letters for me in the rack. The letters had canceled American stamps attached to them by means of tiny safety pins. Everyone knew about the joke except me and all stood around waiting to see, first my surprise, then my disappointment when I, too, saw the joke. Then everyone insisted that I read them the 'news from home.' The letters from the 'folks' told me that gold had been discovered on their ranch and warned me about the indigestibility of British food. Your letter warned me about international playboys like D. Crandall (who is about as much of a playboy as Dean Inge), and assured me that though you were surrounded by luscious, provocative coeds, you never gave any of them a second glance. These fake letters didn't permanently cheer me up, but they did make me laugh—especially gold in Yorba Linda.

"If the reply from the London American Express is that there are no letters there, I am going to cable someone, probably Mama. She'll cable me right back and I'm not sure you would. If no word at all, I don't know what to do—join the Foreign Legion, I guess."

·   ·   ·

"Mama, instead of whining about lack of mail, I'll just tell you calmly and quietly that if nothing comes from London in the next two days, I'm going to cable. I wrote Max that I'd cable you, not him, because a cable would be more likely to scare you into action. So, I write faithfully on even though forgotten by all.

"I am beginning to feel myself a resident of Oxford. I know where the bookshops are and which are most interesting. I know which lanes are dead ends. I know that postcards that cost 2d at a stationer's can be had for 1d at Woolworth's. I never mistake a half crown for a florin. I always ask for the draper's, not a department store, when I want something in the clothing line. I look with pity on the conducted-tour groups I meet in the streets, poor sheep who'd be lost without their shepherd. If I don't open my mouth, I'm taken for an Oxonian. Just one thing I cannot get used to: fleets of bicycles. They hover together, a half-dozen or more, then bear down upon you, silent and deadly. I know how to avoid cars—but these awful bicycles! I think many of the maimed people I see are not survivors of the late war, but persons who haven't been quick enough to avoid the bicycles.

"Tell Papa, the dry cleaner, that he should come to England and make his fortune. It takes ten days to get anything cleaned here. There is not a single cleaner in Oxford; everything goes to London, sixty miles away. Or, if you happen to take your dress to Pullars, who advertise more than anyone else, your dress will go all the way to Perth, which is in Scotland, and in the north of Scotland at that. When I was in Dublin, I saw signs saying, 'Clothes cleaned in three days.' At the time, that made me smile. I now see that the cleaners in Dublin were truly speedy.

"Dr. Schmidt, the German professor here, took a dress of hers to Pullars. When she was told that it would go to Scotland, she said she would send it to Germany, which was almost as close and did better and cheaper work.

"Dr. Schmidt is not noted for her tact. But she is kind-hearted. The other night when Billie Rendle, Frieda Brunner, and I came home from the last lecture, there was a note in my room saying, 'There are chocolates in my room for good girls who go to lectures.' And there were, too. Lots of them.

"Pullars of Perth have their 'drop-in' shops in every town I've been in—except Kildare. There are a thousand more buildings, monuments, libraries, churches, and gardens in Oxford that speak of age than in Kildare. Yet Kildare seems older, a place where time not only stopped but died. An old, melancholy, wind-bitten, green, and decayed town. What ups and downs it has seen. If only that tower could speak. I want to go back there someday, but never alone. I rejoice that my people, only seventeen miles distant, set sail for California. Ireland was, as compared with Scotland and England, down-at-the-heels, sloppy, and gaunt. Though in Dublin and at the Curragh, I saw some of the noblest, best-looking men and women I ever laid eyes on—to say nothing of the horses.

"Here I am already remembering travels past. I pity tour groups here—but in London, to save money and my heels, I took a tour or two myself. At the Tower of London we were all back in the bus, ready to move on, and still we didn't move. Finally, in hustled our conductor, saying, 'Just be patient, ladies and gentlemen. A lady had to go to the toilet. It was a case of necessity and she'll hurry. It won't take her long, I know. Just wait patiently.' It's a good thing she didn't know when she got back how thoroughly the conductor had explained her plight to us. She may have hurried, but she was gone longer than the conductor prophesied.

"Now for travels present. My heels are healing. I went to a chemist's and asked for Mercurochrome for my blisters which were festering. The chemist said he couldn't give me any without a doctor's prescription. When I told him I didn't know any doctor, and he saw through my stocking my bloody heels, he gave me something he said would be better than Mercurochrome, an antiseptic salve. Better or not, it's working like magic. I should have had it about a month ago.

"I have been boating every day—rowing and sculling; no more punting. With heels healing, I can cover more ground on foot now. I saw the Prince of Wales's room in Magdalen College, Shelly's in University, Gladstone's in Magdalen, Arnold's in Keble.

"Saturday I go to Shakespeare's birthplace, have lunch, and in the afternoon see *Twelfth Night* in the theater there.

"Friday, Billie and I hike to see an old church at Iffley."

"I am writing to you from the garden at St. Frideswide's. A party of Americans is being taken through the gardens by an English couple. An American woman is at pains to explain 'the great rush' of American life. She is upholding tradition. We are supposed to be rushers. She knows it and is being orthodox. I see no difference. Well, yes, there is some, but it is less a difference in our natures than between up-to-date and primitive methods of work. In a town of 50,000, not only are clothes sent to London or Perth to be cleaned, but shoes are sent elsewhere to be mended.

"The sightseers have left. It is six o'clock now. Bells of every depth of tone are ringing out, high and low, heavy and light, sweet and solemn. Here in the garden I hear nothing but birds and bells. My pen makes a slight sound, but even it is un-American, writing slowly as I look and listen. Not a rush in a single syllable.

"The Milhouses may have come from Ireland, but England is West country. I've seen West grocers, solicitors, dentists; yesterday in St. John's College Chapel, I saw a plaque commemorating a student named West who had died in the 1914–18 war after receiving the Distinguished Service Cross. He was nineteen. If it could be arranged, I would give him one month of my life (however long it is to be) to make up, in part, for the shortness of his. We were perhaps kinsmen."

•   •   •

"Yesterday I went alone to Shotover Hill. It's about a mile and a half from the center of town. Shelley often went there, and Keats would have if he had had the money to be a University student. It's a good place to get away from Oxford, the city, which is far from beautiful. Omit the colleges, their gardens and libraries and spires, and what you have left in Oxford is a busy manufacturing town, filled with railroads, cars, and the ever-present and menacing bicycle; and surrounded by suburbs of ugly houses.

"Shotover is also the right place to be alone. I can't imagine any Oxford student who didn't at some time climb this hill. William Penn went to Oxford; and the Griffith who married a Milhous came to America on the same ship that brought Penn. Maybe a Griffith listened to William Penn talk of Shotover Hill. 'Thee poor Welshman,' said Penn to his fellow Quaker, 'thee has never seen a sight in thy native Wales to equal Cherwell vale from Shotover Hill.' To which the Welshman replied, 'Friend Penn, until thee has been to the top of Snowdon Peak, do not overpraise Shotover Hill.'

"I doubt this conversation ever took place. And the reason for coming here is not the view, but the solitude. There get to be, sometimes, just too many books and faces and nationalities and bells and bicycles in Oxford town. There is even at this distance a faint hum, like that of a hive of bees considering swarming. The view is not bad; it is a view of the heart of England; the Cherwell meets the Thames here, and I don't suppose there's a greener valley anywhere in England. In America, I'm afraid a parklike spot of this kind so near a sizeable manufacturing city would be worn bare and bald in a short time. The English know better than we how to use without ruining: take the difference between our baseball diamonds and their cricket fields. Our baseball diamonds are spoiled for anything but baseball. No one, unless he's an ex-baseball player reliving old times, would think of taking a stroll on a baseball diamond.

The cricket playing field, once they lift out the wicket-holding apparatus, is no different from any well-kept grassy lawn.

"The view from here, sedgy and green, is too sweet and dimpled for me. The north of England suits me better; even the Trossachs, twelve hundred feet high, is more homelike for anyone accustomed to the Sierra Madres—not to mention the Sierra Nevadas. Billie tells me the Cotswolds, next door to Oxfordshire, will send me out of my mind with their charm. I have yet to see them. Actually, Cambridge is more beautifully situated than Oxford, and the colleges at least as beautiful. But it never once occurred to me to go to Cambridge. Does Oxford, for other persons in other countries, stand as it did for me, for ancient learning above all other universities? I don't know.

"Birds I can't name chirp here; and a plant that looks like white clover grows here. I am going to pick just two blossoms to send you. (I don't want the British, who already believe we are a wanton lot, very destructive, to think I did anything to ruin Shotover Hill.) Two blossoms won't be missed and maybe they'll remind you of red clover you picked a long time ago in Indiana."

"This is the day I cable, even though the conversation I heard at the breakfast table cheered me up a little. I was convinced that someone was dead or hopelessly mutilated and that out of mistaken kindness it had been decided not to 'upset Jessamyn, who is having such a good time in her travels.' Really, you have no idea how despondent I was, what a fool I thought I had been ever to leave home. But at breakfast, two American women from New York said they had had no mail for a week. They said mail from California might miss a mail boat only by hours, then have to wait three or four days. So I feel a little better, but not enough better to postpone my cable.

"Later. I don't know why my sending a cable makes me feel

almost as relieved as if I had received some mail. Perhaps it's because I have *done* something, not just clasped my hands and waited. It's the same with making a date with a doctor. I'm reluctant to do so until I begin to feel better. Then the date is not a call for help, but a celebration of recovery.

"Frieda, not Billie, goes with me on trips to the outskirts of Oxford. This countryside is old stuff to Billie; it's as new to Frieda as to me. Abbingdon is about eight miles outside Oxford; round trip by bus was one shilling. We rode over rolling hills—not hills really, just humps. The road, as always here, was narrow, winding, hedge-lined; and behind the hedges were green flowery meadows. Abbingdon was the site of a rich Benedictine abbey built in the seventh century. Kings and nobles, at times of sickness or plague in London, came down to Abbingdon to breathe the fresh air.

The gardens of the abbey have a magic now they wouldn't have if the abbey's remnants weren't strewn about: a baptismal font, pillars, bones (not many), statues, a wall containing the outline of a large Gothic window, stone coffins. It's this combination of decay and lush growth that is so strange and appealing. Every flower that flourishes in a temperate zone must be growing there. What we call 'holly' in the Yorba Linda hills must be something else if this is holly. I saw my first laurel, many chestnuts, and a beautiful copper beech. In Germany copper beeches are called 'blood beeches,' Frieda says. This sounds terribly German, but they are a baleful-looking tree. There is an enormous and famous copper beech in the garden of Wadham College. It truly looks like a threat to man, not a shelter. We sat in the garden for an hour, where Frieda tutored me in French. Then on to more churches and almshouses and guildhalls, which I won't bother to name for you."

"We got back in plenty of time for me to keep my date for tea with Don Crandall and his mother, who is visiting with him at New College. I bet his mother has read D. H. Lawrence.

She is less conventional than he is. Crandall is leaving Oxford and will go to Italy with his mother. He says these lectures are a waste of time, unless there is some stimuli to help remember them. And there is none. No one cares whether or not you are there, or tests you to see, if present, that you remember of what you've heard. Besides, Crandall says, what you hear isn't worth remembering.

"He is at least halfway right. He says that the Summer Meetings aren't for students, but for tourists, mostly old ladies (I don't know whether he thinks I'm one or not) who feel it's wasteful to spend money just to travel; but if they combine travel with a little suffering at dull lectures, their puritanical natures are eased.

"I'm not sure whether anyone has ever really made an effort to measure the effectiveness of the lecture as compared with reading. The way to do it, I suppose, would be to have the lectures printed; then have fifty students read, fifty listen, and compare their scores. I'm a reader, not a listener. But apart from that, I do believe that what is written to be read tends to be better than what is written to be spoken.

"I was never able to get Billie Rendle and Crandall together. She's engaged, and busy; and sometimes I think Crandall believes that I'm trying to send in Billie as a pinch hitter for me. He's not even sure, since I'm a married woman, that he ought to be talking to me at all. Here I've been thinking of myself as the prey, and to someone else I may seem the predator.

"Anyway, Billie says that the core of the educational system at Oxford isn't the lecture, but the tutor and the examination. They cause the listener to find jewels in the lectures he would otherwise miss. Maybe the Summer Meeting, without tutor and examination, is just a high-class Chatauqua for the American tourist. Americans have always had great faith in the lecturer, and English writers have known it. I don't know why we thought that a word from Dickens's lips was more valuable than a word from his pen. To tell the truth, I have been disappointed with the lectures. A great many of them are diluted textbook stuff, pap concocted to flow painlessly into a listener's ear. Milton was born in 1608, etc. No lecturer has the right to waste an audience's time with the facts of a man's life or the dates of the publication of his works. All that can be found in any history of English literature. What he wants to see is the lecturer's subject as reflected in the lecturer's mind. What we want is interpretation, insight, comparison. We don't get it very often here."

"Max, all this time without mail has taught me all over again how much I value our home. For two months, I've spent hours climbing up stairs, looking at mangy hotel bedrooms. And there are two more months before I'll be home. Could you, would you, scout around and have an apartment rented in Berkeley by the time I arrive? Please have a homelike place that we can go to when you meet me in San Francisco. Don't worry about money. I promise you I'll have five hundred dollars plus a dime between each toe when I arrive. Don't come down to Los Angeles to meet me, much as I long to see you. We would have to share each other then. You understand, don't you?

"But write, write. This terrible silence. What can it mean? I am actually a little sick from getting no mail. I have a dull pain in my middle: an ache because of the continual disappointment. I am staking all on an answer tomorrow to my cable."

The cable brought an answering cable; then misdirected letters were found, and new ones began arriving from my mother.

"Oh, honey," my mother wrote, "I could have spared you the worry. We were getting your letters regularly, and I quit writing, thinking you were so far away and changing locations so often, you'd never get the letters. If I'd realized how little and young and alone you were, starting on such immense travels, I would have worried more. Maybe I wouldn't. I've inherited the strong faith of Grandmothers Milhous and Griffith and I believe that you are taken care of and watched over as tenderly in Europe as in Yorba Linda or Anaheim.

"It is hard for me to write about what's going on here, because, to tell the truth, we have lived more in your letters than we have in our own lives. The flowers arrived from Shotover Hill. Are your heels still bleeding? See a doctor. Don't ride any more with that dangerous driver from Connecticut.

"I don't suppose England has a Labor Day? September 4th is our wedding anniversary. Twenty-seven years ago, if that gives you ample and respectable time to appear. If not, twenty-eight.

"Get all the books you want, sweetheart. Books will last a century and will be prized the longer you and they last. You can spend dollars and pounds and francs on fol-de-rols, and two weeks later you'll wonder why you bought them.

"My heart aches to think I stopped writing you for three weeks, but I was so sure you would never get mail in such strange places. Dumb me.

"If you run short on money, let us know. Don't eat chips and whetstones as you did on the train to New York. I will personally see you through Berkeley next year. I don't want you back in that miserable little one-room school next year.

"Dr. Johnson said in Sunday school, Sunday, that Westminster and those old cathedrals are covered with centuries of dust and look far better in pictures than in reality. The first thing he went to see in London was Spurgeon's Tabernacle and he stood in the very pulpit where Spurgeon preached.

"Well, you know the nursery rhyme about the Pussycat who went to London. 'Pussycat, Pussycat, what did you see there? I saw a mouse under a chair.' That's the way I felt about Dr. Johnson and Spurgeon's Tabernacle. He went to London and saw a mouse. Your letters are a thousand times more interesting than Dr. Johnson's talk; though I did have enough sense not to say so.

"The Milhous relatives are all so pleased that you stayed at a club for traveling Quakers. How did you find out about it?

[I was willing to tell how, but not why.]

"Don't worry about not making the trip to Timahoe to see the family graves. You keep in touch with the living, which is more important.

"O Petty, it is a happy summer for us. We are so glad about your trip. It is better than any trip we ever took. I say it over and over, 'Dad and I are going to see it all some day.' We won't hunt up tabernacles where Spurgeon preached, but we will go to the places we first saw in your letters.

"God bless and keep you safe. Loads and loads of love. Mama."

I still remember the anguish, the terror I felt when I received no mail. I was not homesick. I wanted neither to be at home nor to have the home folks join me. I was where I wanted to be, doing exactly what I wanted to do. But if the life line of letters was broken, I suffered. Less with Max, because five years of marriage had taught me that no letter from him did not mean that he was dead, or hoped that I was.

It was different with Mama. She ordinarily wrote constantly. I was making a trip she had dreamed of all her life. Perhaps I felt some guilt in making it before she did. I did not feel this with Max, who had no desire to see Europe. In any case, a cable from home, explanations of the silence, and the resumption of letters cured me of heavy-heartedness. I was like a patient for whom the life line of letters was a life-support system. Cut it and I began to die.

"Four weeks come Monday and I will have been in Oxford that long. Unbelievable! I'm not attending lectures today. Let me breathe a secret in your ear: these lectures, while occasionally remarkable for an apt phrase or a pat comparison, and while you are a bit mesmerized by the fact that you are hearing an Oxford Doctor speak, are for the most part, and particularly when concerned with English literature, not news for me.

"So today I, 1) poke about in old bookstores (there are books here I may never lay hands on again), 2) read, 3) go canoeing, 4) eat four meals, and 5) tonight with 'my three,' plus two Dutch girls, read poetry aloud in my room.

"English people have a first-rate sense of humor. Last night at the dinner table, when I told them that Americans think that the British are humorless, they were appalled. 'It's the only way we survive,' they said. Actually they're just about as witty as we are.

"2. I haven't found them any more reserved than we are. In the exchange of life stories, I've heard more while here than I've told.

"3. Indiana, Iowa, and New Hampshire are unknown. Not California: its scenery, climate, fruit, movie stars, earthquakes, gold mines.

"One American lady, who had been in California only once, amazed all (especially me) with her tales of great hedges of calla lilies in Los Angeles. Ever see any?"

"Beginning to pack to leave. My room is on the fourth floor, my trunk is in the bicycle hall on the ground floor. I am tempted to send it home without taking it on to Paris with me.

"Tired with running up and down stairs. Billie persuaded me to go on the river with her to 'relax.' We paddled a mile and a half to the Cherwell Hotel. The river was filled with boats, punts, canoes; the boats were filled with people, their lunch baskets, their gramophones, their violins, their dogs. Billie says the river is 'dead' now as compared with 'term.'

"This, I suppose, will be my last day in Oxford. I've come to spend the afternoon in Wadham College gardens, beneath the famous copper beech. Wadham gardens are much less

lovely than a half-dozen others: New College is perhaps first;
then St. John's, with its rock garden; Magdalen, with its river-
bank flower beds; Trinity . . . But Wadham's gardens are
secluded and filled with great cedars that throw long afternoon shadows across the ancient turf. A student 260 years
ago sitting where I am would see just what I see—except, I
suppose, a smaller copper beech. However that may be, Wadham seemed the perfect place to say good-bye to Oxford and
to tell you my plans for the next few days.

"I plan to leave here Monday morning in time to have lunch
with Frieda in London. She went to London Friday. Mme
Soutelle, the Frenchwoman who has been staying here, leaves
for Paris at the end of the week and has asked me to visit her
in her home. Billie Rendle goes September 1st. Frieda, as soon
as she has finished her work at the British Museum, is homeward bound. But we all plan to meet in Paris.

"Billie Rendle has found me a place to stay in Paris, not a
hotel, but a private home which gives room and board to a
half-dozen or so young women of various nationalities. It is
the owner's effort to make the whole world kin; also, I suppose, to make a little money. The house is owned by a French-
woman, Mlle Brunotte, and her companion, a Miss Dixon.
Miss Dixon's father is an Anglican minister in Rome. Her
brother, maybe her uncle, wrote *The Clansman* and *The One
Woman*. I remember Papa's bringing you *The One Woman*
from Los Angeles as a birthday or anniversary present. I
thought it very romantic of him and I enjoyed the book myself.

"I can get room and board there for $10 a week, a little less,
maybe. Miss Dixon said 250 francs, and the franc is a little
less than four cents now.

Mlle Brunotte is a person of distinction: a graduate of Oxford, a botanist of renown, and decorated by the French government for her work during the war. So I'll be going to a
more interesting place than any hotel. It begins to seem that
you could start round the world with no reservations any-

where and trust that friends in one city would see that friends of theirs in other cities take care of you.

"Even so, I hate to leave here. Not the college, but my room, the Cherwell, my friends, England. I have made myself the laughingstock of St. Frideswide's by filling the top layer of my trunk with Crosse & Blackwell's marmalade. Is there any marmalade in California? I don't remember any. I love this thick and tangy stuff and the stone jars which hold it. Billie says my trunk will be oozing marmalade by the time I reach California and that I will be arrested as a traitor to my native state."

"Max, you don't know how I hate leaving here. I've developed the most frightful inertia. 'Where will I find anything better?' A person who asks that question is not a born traveler. The born traveler asks, 'Where can I find something different?'

"The born traveler shouldn't be a besotted reader. Traveling interrupts reading. Oxford is no place to try to kick the reading habit. A drunkard had as well take up residence in a tavern if he wants to learn to live without alcohol.

"First of all is the library here at St. Frideswide's. If not an exciting library, it is at least a solid one—all the books one should read and a few one would like to read. Then, there is the Bodleian, which has a copy of every book published in England; the city library for 'townies' is drab and shabby beside it. Finally, there is the great Smith's, who have 1,200 bookshops and circulating libraries in England. I am now a certified member of W. H. Smith's in Oxford—two shilling six, a month, one book at a time and keep it as long as you like. I could spend my time reading and know I must not. I can read at home this winter and will, too, once I'm enrolled at Berkeley. I came here to see Oxford, not read.

"But there is nothing like attending lectures to make you remember how satisfying a book is: no accent, no repetition of the known and obvious, no set length, no irritating cough.

"They say you can't see the forest for the trees. I can't see Oxford for the people.

"I haven't told you about the two Dutch girls who are here. They are as inseparable as Siamese twins. They know all there is to know about Americans. 'You can always tell an American,' they say, 'because they curl their hair and rouge their faces. American women think all the time about how they look. We do not.' That last part at least is true. The Dutch girls are dark, swarthy, and in football uniforms would look like linemen; far too heavy for backfield runners. If they kicked an ox, the ox would die. But they are healthy and self-confident and that results in a kind of beauty.

"There have been two new arrivals at St. Frideswide's: a girl who looks like an underfed bird. When she told me her history, I understood why. Within a period of six months, her father and two brothers were killed in the war. Eighteen months later her mother was dead of grief and shock. Now she tries to support herself by teaching elocution. Well, she can certainly teach weeping.

"A tall, bony woman, aged perhaps sixty, wearing trailing black clothes and many rings, but with eyes like topazes or calendulas, has arrived. She is here because of a wartime memory. New College was then used as a hospital. She came here in midwinter to visit her son. The gardens of New College were covered with snow; there was a glaze of ice on all the roofs. The gardens were a mass of beds, and her son was in an outside bed. She sat on the bed talking to him and trying to keep from shivering so hard he noticed.

"Crandall, the man whose hand Shaw shook, and who disapproves of D. H. Lawrence, bicycled over to tell me that he did not go to Italy with his mother. Instead, he has met a twenty-eight-year-old Irishman who, until recently a Presbyterian minister, has repented. He has renounced the Presbyterians—or vice versa—and he and Crandall, on a rented boat, are going to explore the Thames. This ex-Presbyterian sounds exactly like the kind of man Lawrence would like to write about.

"This meeting with other people is what you would enjoy most about travel. Of course I need it more than you, it being less easy for me—but it isn't difficult or formal in traveling, and people—it's the truth—seem to like me. I am pleased, because sometimes in Hemet I think I was taken for an Odd Fellow, even by you, eh?

"You remember the man who asked you the nationality of your wife? Here they sometimes think I am not an American until I speak. Then, said one lady, 'I heard your r's and I knew you were American.'

"P.S. I am going to buy you a wedding ring and send it to you, so that the coeds at Berkeley will know you're bespoken. I wear mine—not that it makes a hell of a lot of difference to some of these traveling rascals, but at least they can see that I'm matron, not maid. Why shouldn't you do the same?

"Do you remember what we were doing five years ago at this time? Gathering pepper boughs from Vernon's ranch to decorate the Friends Church for our wedding. Little did we think that in five years we'd celebrate the occasion separated by a continent and an ocean.

"Good-bye, sweet Greek boy who spells like a barbarian."

"Monday, August 26, 1929

"Max, a few minutes with a cup of tea to tell you what my last day in England has been like. I am in Southampton now and will board the channel boat in half an hour.

"I was up early this morning and over to Bell and Company to make some final arrangements concerning my trunk. Also, to deposit some more marmalade in it. Billie went with me to the railway station to see me off and to plan for our meeting in Paris. I was in London at noon. Frieda met me at Haymarket. While she went back to her work at the British Museum, I did something very foolish: I went to see Laura La Plante in *Show Boat*. Terribly thin stuff. Think of going to see such drivel when London is filled with glories Holly-wood can never equal. Don't let anyone know I was so stupid.

"After the show, I met Frieda at the Museum and we had our last English supper together. At Piccadilly Circus, Frieda saw me onto a bus for Paddington Station. We waved as many fond farewells to each other as if we were never to meet again.

"At Paddington Station, I gathered my luggage, and from there went by taxi to Waterloo Station. In the dusk I passed the familiar and loved buildings and monuments: the Marble Arch, Victoria Memorial, Hyde Park, Westminster Abbey, the Houses of Parliament. Good-bye, England, good-bye! How can I leave what I have yearned a lifetime to see? Traveling, as has been observed, is a series of deaths.

"Eleven o'clock. I must be on board at 11:30. I feel like an eighteenth-century Britisher abandoning the old country."

My journal tells me more about leaving Oxford than do my letters. If there had been no Oxford, there would perhaps have been no journey. I wanted Oxford, the university, its gardens and spires and its monuments and memorials, to become as much a part of me as Yorba Linda or Mt. Baldy. So what had I done during the month I was there? Why, boated and talked my head off with persons even less Oxonian than I, and haunted W. H. Smith's, and eaten ices at Stewart's, and attended the Quaker Meeting, which was possibly the most un-Oxonian organization in the city. A Quaker maiden at the time when the Friends were just getting started had been hassled to death by Oxford students.

Except to go home, I am sad when leaving any place where I have made myself a home. I am a born lover of ruts, and Oxford was the rut I had been looking for all of my life, emblazoned with the names of the famous, with shrines erected to the learned of seven centuries. So what had I done? Bought marmalade, got stuck on punting poles, and been bored by Dean Inge.

I didn't confide these melancholy facts to the folks at home.

Paris

I had gone to Ireland because of my mother's dream. I was going to Paris because Billie Rendle, with four years of Oxford behind her, and knowledge of Paris, persuaded me that there was more to life than punting and Dean Inge.

What that more was, I didn't really know. Art, of course; the Eiffel Tower, the tomb of Napoleon, the Arc de Triomphe. Sin was there, of course. France had probably invented wine. There were shows in which women danced clothed only in a few strands of pearls. In Paris, men had mistresses. France had helped us when we had our revolution. Lafayette had been our ally as Cornwallis had been our enemy. Americans were in debt to France.

By chance, the three I knew best at Oxford would be in Paris during the next month. Billie Rendle was staying at the International House. Mme Soutelle was returning to her teaching; and to her religious vocation, the exact nature of which I had never truly learned. Frieda, the German girl and student of Dryden, was pausing in Paris before returning to her home in Germany.

I would be alone, but I wouldn't, as in England, be living with books that had been my friends for years.

When I went to college, there was no course in American Literature, let alone French. I did have a professor who was crazy about O. Henry, but O. Henry is not a writer to pack in your trunk for reading late at night when far from home.

I did not know that young American writers were flocking to Paris that fall. Why had they left America? In part, because Paris was a cult locale for writers of the twenties. And in truth, what was going on in the United States was nothing to nail native sons to its shores.

The best-known writer in the United States was Sinclair Lewis. But the writers who would be most talked of for the next twenty-five years were in Paris: Hemingway, Fitzgerald, Joyce, Pound, Stein.

I didn't know they were in Paris; and had I known, their names would have meant little to me. Fitzgerald was the only one I had read.

I would make a pitiful refugee. I am a one-language woman. I have two "old countries," England and Southern Indiana. I spoke their language and I loved them both.

Visually and linguistically, Southern Californians have ties with Spain. The landscape of Spain, cactus and grapevines, fields of brown stubble, and snow-covered peaks, reminds us of home. Half the names of Spain are familiar to us: we can say Los Angeles and Vallejo more easily than Baton Rouge and Cincinnati. We went to school with Yorbas, Sepulvedas, Navarros, Padillas.

But nothing had prepared me for Paris. I would never be able to say, as Hemingway did, "If you are lucky enough to have lived in Paris as a young man, then wherever you go for the rest of your life, it stays with you, for Paris is a moveable feast."

First of all, I did not "live in Paris"; I visited there for six weeks. And perhaps most important of all, I was not a young man.

Apart from that, Hemingway was a man with an itch for what he had yet to see or experience. Unlike as we are, I take comfort from the fact that Hemingway, like me, was born in July. We are crabs, sideways movers, for whom travel is supposedly difficult. It *was* difficult for Thoreau, another Cancerian. Hemingway proved that it could be done, July cat though he was, Hemingway was not a "fraidy cat," unless his bravado be interpreted as a timid man's determination to overcome his tremors and that final shot be considered surrender, not defiance.

Though Paris has never been a movable feast for me, it did prove once again, filled with writers as it was, that my unconscious was taking better care of me than my conscious.

My unconscious, helped by Waldemar Trask and the London Friends Meeting, took me to Tavistock Square and Bloomsbury.

Failing fast with tuberculosis, though neither I nor my doctor knew it, my unconscious caused me to read every word written by or about a tubercular. I did not panic with the first mouthful of blood. I knew the meaning before the doctor did.

So though I wrote nothing but letters, journals, and commonplace books, my unconscious told me, "Paris is the place for writers."

Once there, my unconscious more or less deserted me; consciousness itself gave me a nudge or two. I did get to the bookshop of Shakespeare and Company, and I did buy there the one book any traveler in Paris in the fall of 1929 should have bought: James Joyce's *Ulysses*.

If I am to believe letters, journal, and memory, Paris meant little to me. What Paris had to offer me, who had no French, was as nothing compared with England's cornucopia of riches. It was a matter, I suppose, of the reading I had done, of the college courses in English literature. What did France mean to me? Wine, perfume, fashion, loose living? I wouldn't cross a continent and an ocean for any of these.

A year later, working for my doctorate in English at Berkeley, I had to pass an examination in French as a preliminary to my orals. I had had, both in high school and in college, nothing but Latin. I enrolled in an undergraduate class in French. At the rate they were going, I saw that it would take me ten years to have enough French to pass an examination. So I studied by myself, passed the examination, and was told by the professor who did the grading of the papers, "I've heard of people like you, who pass the examination without ever having taken a course in French, but you're the first I ever saw."

The French I learned in Berkeley would have been no help to me in Paris. I could read literary French, but I couldn't pronounce a single word except *oui*. In a department store, hunting for its beauty parlor and wanting, as the Dutch girls had declared was typical of American women, to have my hair washed, cut, and curled, my sign language landed me in the cutlery department with a saleslady who thought I wanted (she could see I needed) a pair of scissors.

Elsewhere I fared better. "Choo-choo" got me to the railway station. Anyone can pronounce the French word for bread; and the smattering of Spanish all Southern Californians know was sometimes near enough the French to get me, after a few trials, what I wanted.

A part of the effort of Miss Dixon and Mlle Brunotte to make the whole world kin was their determination to have us all speak the same language. Luckily for me, with Miss Dixon, an American, and Mlle Brunotte, an ex-Oxford student, the language they had chosen was English. There were some accents at the dinner table; Mlle Brunotte herself had one of the heaviest; but no one was impeded by English, as I would have been by French or German.

It is just as well I didn't write home of my sorrows at leaving Oxford. The next letter they received would declare, "I love Paris," and they would shake their heads and say, "The girl is very changeable."

The first letter after my first night at 6 Rue Thibaud went to my husband.

•   •   •

"I swear at night to stay awake until at least twelve. Last night I wanted to write you, to read, but after the busy day of leaving Oxford, taking a last look at London, crossing the Channel, and arriving in Paris, at eleven o'clock I threw all books and papers off the bed, and opened the Venetian blinds; the next thing I knew, someone was saying, *'Bon jour, Madame,'* and my breakfast is deposited on a bedside table.

"The maid who brings it in is seventeen, from Alsace-Lorraine, has the face of a madonna and the figure of a washerwoman.

"I spring at the food. It consists of:

1. A large earthen bowl of much hot milk and a little hot coffee.

2. Two thick slices of porous yellow bread.

3. A pat of butter.

4. A covered pot of plum preserves.

Gone are the nuns' breakfasts of meat pies, sliced ham, rolls, marmalade. Now I will be svelte, chic, and French. And hungry.

"One thing I do like. Breakfast in my room. No hopping out of my bed, a dream still unexplored to be lost in the instant babble of other meat-pie chompers.

"Later. I love this place. I love Paris. Paris is a bit like Los Angeles. People who know Paris will think I am crazy to say that. At least London is less like Los Angeles than Paris. It's probably the dry sunshine, the wider streets, and the trees that look needed that make me feel at home.

"This 'house' is only a part of a larger building of five stories. Behind the building is a garden. The dining room that opens onto the garden is so pleasant, we linger for a long time after dinner just to enjoy it.

"The dining room has, besides dining table and chairs, small chintz sofas, bookcases filled with French and English books, a lot of brass and hammered copper, many lamps and vases, a big blue vase of heather. And, looking out into the garden, with its dark-green trees, you'd think that, except for the rattle of taxicabs on cobblestones, you were in a cottage in the middle of a forest.

"My room here is the best yet—are you tired of hearing that? It's upstairs, overlooks the garden, has double windows that swing outward (the kind we call 'French doors' at home). The floorboards are wide, dark, polished, uncovered. How good it feels to my bare feet after a day of hot tramping! There is a corner cupboard, a beautiful dark chest of drawers, hanging bookshelves, a huge writing table with a desk lamp, three chairs. There are original watercolors of Paris on the gray walls. I look out on trees, I contemplate the broken shafts of light on the polished floor, I caress the rows of books with my eyes. I eat a juicy pear I bought from a barrow for one franc per pound. Four cents. Think of it. I sing silently, tunelessly, too, I repeat, 'Praise God from whom all blessings flow.' Write often or I may never come home."

"This place, which has no name insofar as I know, except '6 Rue Thibaud,' resembles St. Frideswide's in some ways. I never did see 'Grandmother' there, but 'Grandmother' here is Mlle Brunotte; though she certainly doesn't look like a grandmother. She is fifty years old, gray-haired, tall, spare, and sinewy. She looks more like Grandpa than Grandma; and, looks apart, she runs the place, perhaps owns it. Miss Dixon, with whom I corresponded, is in Rome visiting her father.

"You should see *their* room! I certainly prefer mine. Theirs is huge, dark, and peculiarly furnished. Mlle Brunotte sleeps on a cotlike bed. Miss Dixon's double bed is placed on a platform, a kind of dais. You would feel, I would feel, if Miss Dixon were in her bed and I wanted to speak to her, that I should curtsy before addressing her and then say 'ma'am.'

"So this is like St. Frideswide's in having a head, a staff, and a number of resident females to board and bed. Jealousies no doubt exist in religious orders, but if they were present at St.

Frideswide's, they were well hidden. Since Grandmother stayed out of sight, no one would complain that Grandmother was paying one person more attention than another.

"They so complain here. Miss B. asked me to go with her on a walking and botanizing trip into the country. A Miss Lily Vaughn, from Pasadena, who has been here six months, and has never been asked to accompany Miss B. on a walking trip (if you saw her, you'd know why), berated me for my selfishness and lack of courtesy because I didn't say, 'After Miss Vaughn.'

"Miss Lily Vaughn of Pasadena would now be dead if she had gone with Miss B. on yesterday's walking trip. I am only half alive myself. We left 6 Rue Thibaud at 9:30, went by Métro to the railway station; then by rail, third class, on benches, packed between farmers and their wives, so garlic-scented that we smelled like garlic ourselves for the rest of the day.

"After an hour and a half's travel we reached a small village. We raced; Miss B. walks as if the devil himself were behind her. We trotted down the cobblestoned streets of a village on to the dusty road outside. Under a blazing sun, without ever pausing to look, we passed stone farmhouses, cottage gardens, rows of poplars, wild plum and tame pear trees. Finally we came to a forest. Here the going was easier because we walked on spongy layers of moss, leaves, and ferns. We stopped beside a lily-covered, sedge-banked lake to eat our lunch. I had been carrying the food: a long loaf of French bread under my arm and a knapsack on my back. Miss B. (I'm going to call her Miss B. from now on; it takes too much time to write out her full name) carried her botanizing paraphernalia and a jug of coffee. The lunch had been packed by someone who knew that when Miss B. walked, she walked: cheese, ham, boiled eggs, the loaf of bread, apple tarts, and coffee.

"Refueled, we soon reached the edge of the forest. There we saw a long line of mounted soldiers, men in blue, officers in brown. We were near the St. Cyr military training school and a cavalry performance was being put on for visiting Japanese and American officers. The horses were, or looked, incredibly fragile, legs like lily stems, coats shinier than polished furniture.

"A little way beyond the men and horses, we came upon a terrible sight. First, we saw a small group of men and women standing at the foot of a tree. They were groaning, crying, and pointing. What they were pointing at was a dead man, hanging from a limb of a tree. You could tell he was dead by the way his head fell over sidewise onto his chest. I think a man hanging from a tree with a rope around his neck looks deader than a man stretched out on the ground. The man on the ground might be asleep or resting. But a man at the end of a rope is dead. He was hanging from a limb low enough for us to see his face. He was a young man, well dressed, as if he had prepared for his hanging as he would have (if he could) for his funeral.

" 'He looks as if he wishes he hadn't done it,' I told Miss B. I was horrified, but I couldn't stop looking. 'Tomorrow the letter will come saying it was all a mistake.'

" 'Don't be romantic,' said Miss B. Miss B. was a nurse at Salonika for three years during the war. She had seen heads picked up 'like cabbages' from the beaches there. 'A man who wants to die is better off dead.'

" 'I would have saved him if I could.'

" 'He wouldn't have thanked you.'

"Miss B. took my arm in her hard pinching fingers and marched me away from the dead man, as if I were a child determined to see something nasty. I knew she was right, and she, I think, was sorry, right or wrong, to have been so bossy.

" 'Let's look at something pleasant now for a change,' she said. She stopped botanizing; before this she had run up and down gullies gathering I know not what, to put in the case she carried. Now she took us to a long tree-lined avenue. We didn't saunter. Sauntering is beyond Miss B., but we didn't actually trot any more. The avenue, with its trees, which were trimmed into formal shapes, led to the summer home of the President of France. I enclose pictures which give you a better view of the house than I got peering through the grillwork of the fence that surrounds the place.

"When we reached the village where we were to take the train back to Paris, Miss B. said that since we would miss supper at home, we would eat in a café she knew there. It was a wonderful meal, coming after all the hard walking, the soldiers parading, the poor man hanging, the President's house. The proprietor knew Miss B., and I think he perhaps served us a special meal, complete with a big bottle of wine. When he put a wine glass in front of my plate, I said, 'Thank you, I don't drink.' I thought Miss B. might pinch my arm again and say, 'Don't be foolish. You're in France, and in France we drink wine.' She didn't. Instead she said, 'What would you like to drink?'

" 'Lemon squash,' said I. This was the drink Billie Rendle and I drank on the Cherwell.

"Miss B., pronouncing the words as if they soiled her mouth, asked if they had lemon squash. The waiter said yes, as if ashamed of the fact.

"Lemon squash still tasted good to me—even though the waiters and Miss B. watched me as if I were a chimpanzee eating Fig Newtons.

"We caught our train, boarded our Métro, and were home at 9:30, after a twelve-hour day. Miss B. said we had walked twenty-five miles. I believed her. We had seen military might, the beauty of horses, death in a tree, the home of power, and had eaten a typical French meal, though I hadn't sampled all of it. I hobbled up to my room and rested my bare feet on the beautiful cool floorboards. I took a hot bath and discovered two fleas. Fleas, as you know, don't bite me, but I can feel them hopping; and even if I'm not flea-bitten, I don't like the idea of being flea-ridden. I still smelled like garlic, but I killed the two poor fleas in the process of bathing. I went to bed clean, flealess, and only a little more alive than the man on the tree. I didn't know what to think except, This is France, and by the time I had thought that, I was asleep."

Now, fifty years later, I wonder at that nondrinking young woman—what she missed and what she escaped. She certainly missed learning about wine in the country more famous than any other for its wine, and with the help of a woman who knew wines. True, I had been brought up not to drink. Drink· ing was for drunkards. I did not, however, consider Miss B.'s drinking evil. Nor did I refuse wine for that reason; rather, as a child being weaned wants to keep on with what he knows as good, so I was not of a mind to try something as strange as wine.

Years later, in Napa Valley, the wine center of the United States, where we had come to serve wine as a matter of course with dinner, my father, visiting us, took me aside and said, "Jessamyn, have you ever thought of joining Alcoholics Anonymous?"

"They wouldn't have me, Papa. With one glass of wine a day, I don't qualify."

Papa, thinking perhaps, That early trip to France is responsible for her taste for liquor, urged no more.

Only once in Paris did I drink, and that was of a drink without the stigma of Biblical references, as "Look not on the wine when it is red." A number of residents of 6 Rue Thibaud went to what I think was a nightclub. It was underground, and one approached the place of entertainment through a long passageway lined with human bones, neatly arranged: skulls with skulls, thighbones with thighbones, pelvises with pelvises. A great many people who had once been aboveground in Paris now rested here.

To enter this club, if that was what it was, you had to buy a drink. I was a teetotaler, but, even more, I was thrifty. The

idea of buying a drink and not drinking it was unthinkable.
My Rue Thibaud companions knew the solution: crème de
menthe on ice. "It tastes like candy," they told me, "or toothpaste." What I got was, I think, a French version of the
Stinger. It tasted fine and, served in a minuscule glass, contained about one tablespoon of liquor. It was impossible to
think that anything that tasted like toothpaste could cause
drunkenness; and that tablespoonful certainly didn't. No other
occasion occurred where I had to drink to enter, and I continued to explore the French countryside with Miss B., drinking nothing but lemon squash.

"September 10, 1929
"Dearest Mama, The official name of this place plus telephone number in case you want to phone me, is Foyer
d'Etudiantes Grace Madeline, 6, Rue Thibaud, Paris (XIV).
Téléphone: Ségur 96-28.
"Why Grace Madeline, I don't know, but I think that Grace
is Miss Dixon's name and Madeline, Miss B.'s.
"I didn't tell you when I wrote you about leaving London
for Paris how disappointed I was to find no letter there from
you. I walked about overcome by heat and melancholy. I did
tell you that I went to see the first movie I've seen since I've
been here, *Show Boat*. It was terrible but, foolish as it was,
I shed some tears, more for myself than out of any pity be-
cause of Ravenal.
"Behind me sat an English papa and his daughter. 'Papa,
what does fired mean?'
" 'It means to be sacked, daughter.'
" 'Papa, what's a dollar?'
" 'Five shillings, dear.'
"He was slightly off here. These questions and answers,
mostly right, went on during the whole show. Who says
England isn't being Americanized?
"You already know about 6 Rue Thibaud, if Max sent you

my letter about it. I'm still in love with my room, particularly with the lamp on my desk. Candles would have been better than some of the lamps I've read and written by.

"The food served here is entirely different from what we got at Frideswide's—and better. For lunch today, this was the menu:

1. Served first in a big bowl, potatoes and carrots in a cheese sauce. This was removed.

2. Steak, large tender pieces, and an accompanying bowl of macaroni. Removed.

3. Beets in a bowl with a French dressing of oil and vinegar. Noble. Removed.

4. Cream cheese and bread.

5. Grapes and pears with little brass bowls of water to wash them in.

6. Coffee.

"Dinner is not better, but more. Fruit and vegetables are very cheap here. A cauliflower the size of a volleyball costs five cents.

"There are now living at 6 Rue Thibaud: 1) a Czechoslovakian, aged 18, blond and buxom—she speaks no English, 2) a German girl, tall, silvery-blond, very smart dresser, aged 19, lives in Berlin, has been here four months and is studying French; has no English, 3) Swiss girl, 18, small, dark, and sweet, 4) Miss Lily Vaughn, 40?, has been here four summers; from Pasadena, California; has no English; has a crush on Miss B. (I mean her language is 100% American), 5) M. J. McP., beautiful American, seeing the world.

"Do you see us all? And see how charming, lovely, noble, divine it all is? And all for 250 francs a week = $10.00. In Oxford, I paid $17.50 a week. I wish I had come here a week or two earlier. Oxford was beautiful; visiting England and Ireland was like going home. I am a tourist here, but a tourist in a city whose beauties Oxford can't equal.

"I almost wish I had spent my whole summer here. I can't

understand a word anyone says, but, judging by their smiles and gestures, no one could be more amiable or courteous. And prices are one-half what they are in England. Here you can ride a mile for about four francs (eleven cents). In England, it costs three shillings just to sit in a taxi. For $250 I could spend three months here and have plenty of money left over for amusement. *Vive la France!*

"Mme Soutelle, the Frenchwoman from St. Frideswide's, took me to La Rotonde, one of Paris's most famous outdoor cafés. The other is the Dôme. An outdoor café consists of dozens of tables covered with gay cloths, covering the whole of a sidewalk and bulging—at least La Rotonde was—with people. There was every nationality: Negroes, Arabs, Japanese (many of these), Americans, and even some French people.

"I like the café way of entertaining: no time wasted in cooking and nothing impolite about leaving, as you can't do in your own home, when you've had all the talk you can make or listen to.

"Mme Soutelle and I ate ice cream, which she ordered: this is something I can't do. I can only order things I can imitate—and how can you make a sound or a gesture like ice cream?

"We sat for an hour or two watching the passing people, people who had obviously escaped from books, women who had jumped off posters. The ladies of Paris, perhaps the women of Paris, paint, no matter if the Dutch girls do think it purely an American custom. You see a pair of lips advancing toward you, and presently, as they come nearer, you see behind them the woman who propels them.

"I haven't had time to see much yet. Getting about is difficult when you can't ask directions—Paris is no village, as you know. And the traffic! If I was scared by bicycles in Oxford, you can imagine how I feel at the sight of ten million taxis bearing down upon me and driving as to a fire. And traffic is to the right again, just as I came to expect it to be on the left. I manage to cross streets by keeping my eye out for ancient ladies who step right into the swirl. I am ashamed to be less bold than women fifty years my senior and follow timidly, but determinedly, close upon their heels.

"I am no longer the exotic sight in Paris I was in some of the villages of England and Ireland. There passed La Rotonde, as we sat watching and talking, two young women who were joined together by what looked like a slender gold chain which ran from the nose of one to the nose of the other. They stayed close together; even so, a troublemaking passer-by could walk between them, maiming one or maybe both noses.

"Only once have I been really scrutinized as something odd; and I haven't yet been able to figure out what the oddity was. Once on the Métro in a front seat where I could extend my legs, a middle-aged farmer (to judge by his looks) walked up from the back of the car and stood, without saying a word, and looked at my legs. After a lengthy inspection, he went to the back of the car and returned with, I suppose, his wife. She also looked; they had some conversation, then departed. They never once looked at me. They looked at my legs as if they were sacks of grain I was taking to market, no real part of me.

"The only explanation of their behavior I've been able to hit upon is this: I've started wearing my fine silk stockings again. They are a rather dark tan and so transparent they don't look like stockings at all. Did the French farmer and his wife not recognize them as stockings, but think that they were looking at legs which were of a different color from the rest of my body? Like side-show freaks, half man, half woman; half Negro, half white to them? My legs, as you know, are absolutely normal and unspectacular; not hairy, fat, or shaped like Marlene Dietrich's. What else could have motivated them? Since I couldn't ask them, I'll never know."

"I was a good tourist this afternoon and spent four hours at the Louvre. It would take four hundred days, I suppose, to really see it. It took two hours, walking as hard as I could go, just to take stock of what there is to be seen. The pictures and statues we have all heard of were surrounded by reverent crowds. You could see 'Mona Lisa' or Whistler's 'Mother' only through a barrier of staring people. Miss Lily Vaughn, who has seen 'Mona Lisa' many times, says she likes her less each time she sees her. 'She is too cynical,' Lily says. This is like saying you don't like a picture because the painter had bad breath. I admit you don't feel very original admiring something every panting tourist knows he should admire, but you don't go to museums to be original."

In Paris I was like a woman who can't read, in a library. The nonreader in a library can look about her, admire colors and bindings, marvel at the industry of the people who wrote the words that fill the books and the neatness of those who ranged the volumes, according to subject, she supposes, on the shelves. A library is, of course, wasted on such a visitor; and she wastes her time being there.

I don't know whether my inability to respond to the Paris of museums that housed paintings and statuary, of theaters where music and plays were presented, was the result of nature or nurture. Because I had not heard great music, seen plays or paintings, was I like a nonreader, unmoved when a volume of Keats is opened before him?

Had I seen paintings, heard music, attended plays from my childhood, would I have been able to "read" these riches of Paris? Or was I plastically defective? A word-woman from birth who could see what the words painted more vividly than what any painter's brush depicted? Or sculptor's chisel revealed?

I had once made the effort to leave the orange orchards and barley fields long enough to see an exhibition of the paintings by Rockwell Kent in Los Angeles. But Rockwell Kent was a man into whose painting one could walk as into a landscape.

His horizons were very far; his skies were high enough for stars. You were not asked to regard folds of fabric or wrinkles of flesh, as in some paintings.

I thought then—I am convinced now—that the newcomer to painting should not do what I (and ten thousand other tourists like me) did in Paris: treat a museum like a hurdles race, the winner being the viewer who sees the most pictures in a day.

I thought then, and believe now, had I been given a whole afternoon, seated in a chair, to look at not more than two pictures, I might have been able to find in a picture something of what I find in books.

The reason I prefer landscape to portrait painting is the result, I think, of another conviction: words can tell us more vividly and truly what people are like than paint. People on canvas are static. Painted with words, people declare themselves to us, in acts as small as a lip's movement or as large as the genocide of a people.

Who can describe Turner's seas, or Van Gogh's fields with words as their painters did with line and color? But even these deserve time: the firmament is not a museum subject, to be taken at a lope on museum-burning feet. Until painters can devise some means of requiring viewers to give the time to their creations novelists require of their readers, paintings will never have the influence on viewers great novels have on their readers.

In addition to being unversed in the arts, I had another disability when it came to appreciating Paris, a disability James Morris says afflicts all middle-aged English; though I was neither middle-aged nor English. "Gingerly," says he, "the middle-aged Englishman, tilting his trilby, emerges out of the Gare du Nord into the streets of Paris. He has a couple of hours to spend . . . but he views the prospect with no wild abandon, for deep inside him, however hard he tries . . . there stirs, like a rustle of bones in a dark cavern, an old English antipathy to the place. It stems . . . from the puritan strain that still runs through the English character, and long ago stigmatized this incomparable capital as an anteroom of Purgatory. . . . Americans adore Paris, hasten there to write their novels or paint their violent abstracts, love her in the spring-time, hire her same old taxi-cabs, set themselves up with slinky blondes in desperately expensive garrets."

Perhaps, though not yet middle-aged and without a trilby, I came to Paris more English than American. The puritan strain was perhaps stronger in me than in most Americans. Like the Englishman, I walked, as Morris says, "briskly through the maniacal taxis." I didn't hasten to Paris to write a novel or paint a violent abstract. I came because the "family" I had collected at Oxford, English, German, French, was coming to Paris. And soon I had found myself another family, at 6 Rue Thibaud.

And though I did not truly appreciate what was to be found in the great museums and galleries of Paris, Paris itself stirred me. There was nothing dinky about Paris. It was as big, open, and orderly as a prairie. The buildings of Paris, at least in those parts I explored, did not huddle together. The streets were boulevards; they had been laid out by men, not by animals wandering to find water or browse. Trees grew where trees were needed, not where an acorn had happened to fall or the wind had planted a seed. People lived in the parks: ate, made love, walked their big tomcats trained to take the air on a leash. The sky was not so crowded with roofs as to exclude the sun. It was a city of sunshine. It was a mesa, with edifices instead of buttes and rimrocks to break the monotony. The Eiffel Tower itself might have been a rather large metallic yucca stalk. It was, I suppose, in climate and orderliness, less unlike the uncluttered landscape of the treeless, sea-reaching California I had left than London's hugger-mugger. Nevertheless, I loved London more.

I lived in Paris like an Indian: with a landscape to roam in, but a hogan durable and welcoming to come home to.

•   •   •

"Dear Ones:

"I am getting to know Mlle Brunotte better. She is an Alpinist of note, has scaled peaks which have defeated men. No wonder I had such a hard time keeping up with her on our walk.

"Her accomplishments don't keep her from going shopping, straw hat on head and basket on arm. She comes back laden with lettuce, cauliflower, grapes, pears. She rides third class on trains and is indifferent about sitting next to farmers so garlic-scented they can be smelled two coaches away. Can you imagine a woman with such a record in Orange County quietly keeping a boardinghouse for girls of different nationalities, taking twenty-five-mile walking trips into the country to hunt plants, marketing in apron and straw hat? I think not. That woman, in our country, would be the darling of the women's clubs, lecturing on her war experiences and her travels, on her art and her mountain climbing. Many a woman in our neck of the woods is a small-town celebrity on one-half of this woman's accomplishments.

"Miss B. does not like the Germans. She comes from Alsace-Lorraine, which makes her dislike them even more. 'The Germans,' she says, 'do not play fair in war. They are not good sports.' Katy, the German girl here now, is the first German she has been willing to accept as a boarder.

"Since her best friend, Miss Dixon, is an American, Miss B. is at pains to say nice things about Americans. She says the Americans and the French are far more alike temperamentally than the French and the English. The English, she says, where they themselves are concerned, have no sense of humor; because of that, they are able to keep a solid and serious front in the face of criticism.

" 'An English girl said that she understood that the French never bathed,' Miss B. told me.

" 'How foolish,' said I.

"Miss B.'s retort was, not that the French bathed frequently, but, 'You don't have to bathe to keep clean.'

"Miss Vaughn objects to the *pissoirs* on Paris streets into which men can retire, hidden to the knees, to urinate. She saw one man at the opening of one of these things, emptying his bladder and at the same time leaning the upper part of his body far enough outside to permit a view of a street commotion. This, she said, was disgusting.

"Miss B. was not at all disgusted by this. What disgusted and irritated her was that men were provided with such conveniences while women had to walk blocks to find any 'convenience' at all.

"I must stop sending you so many postcards. The last packet cost six cents, and six cents would buy enough cabbage to keep a French family fed for a week.

"Miss Vaughn has just called me to come up to her room to see the Eiffel Tower. It is being illuminated tonight as an advertisement for an automobile company. Miss B. is right, I guess. The French and the Americans are alike. If we had an Eiffel Tower, that is just what an automobile company would like to do with it."

"Dearest Mama:

"I must not let Paris become an assemblage of objects, just one big museum. It's a place where people live, and have lived for a long long time. Of course, part of their history and their life today is to be seen in the museums.

"I have now made three visits to the Louvre. I walk until my heels ache and my eyes burn. I have seen the 'Mona Lisa,' Whistler's 'Mother,' Van Dyck's 'Charles I,' Murillo's 'Immaculate Conception,' 'The Angelus,' 'The Gleaners,' to mention only the pictures everyone knows—I don't mention a thousand or more I had never heard of before. I think more would have happened inside me if I'd taken a campstool and sat down for two or three days in front of one picture. I actually saw hundreds of rooms of paintings, of statues, furniture, ornaments, model ships, miniatures. I saw the 'Venus de Milo' and the 'Nike' or 'Winged Victory.'

"I saw Venus yesterday morning. As I approached her, standing white and womanly—yes, those are the right words; she and Queen Victoria share those characteristics, though Victoria in not so appealing proportions—she was suddenly engulfed by a swarm of Jamboree Boy Scouts from South Africa. Twenty or thirty of them approached her at a smart trot, paused only long enough to give her a few penetrating glances, then were off to see the next big thing in the museum.

"I am estranged by these universally applauded pictures and statues. I shouldn't be. I don't downgrade Milton because he's been praised for three hundred years. I don't doubt Shakespeare was a genius because every man in a streetcar would agree. But when I see Venus, calm and blond, swallowing every word of praise, I feel like saying, 'Madam, you are a craze, a cult. Don't think for a minute tourists come to look at you as a person, as an individual, or even as a statue. I assure you that such is not the case. They come to see you because of the publicity you have received. You are one of the world's most famous statues. Love doesn't bring the Boy Scouts here, or aesthetic knowledge, but duty. If your name and fame were to be attached to that epicene nymph over there in the corner, you, my dear, would never be looked at. You would become for two-thirds of the crowd what in fact you are: a rather plump woman without arms.

"I try to think of the Louvre not as a collection of objects, but as an indication of man's longing to translate his dreams, opinions, desires into something lasting and concrete. As I look at miniatures, cabinets, pictures, I see a great mass of human hands that have touched wood and clay, and paint and brush in an effort to communicate not only with their generation but also with the next and the next. The Louvre seethes and moans with this painful effort to communicate."

"Dearest Mama, A break for you.

"No museum today. Cemetery instead. I don't know

whether this is an improvement or not. I went with Mme Soutelle, the French teacher who was at St. Frideswide's. It turns out that she is a nun, though not so called or dressed. She said that nuns are not permitted by the French government to run a school of the kind she and her fellow nun-teachers have. So, though they have taken vows, they continue to wear civilian clothes and in that way confound the government. This is what I understood her to say, though she didn't say so directly.

First we went to the Trocadéro, then to the Eiffel Tower. Our last stop was at the Passy Cemetery, where I wanted to see the grave of Marie Bashkirtseff. I don't know when I first bought and read her *Journal*. Because of reading it, which seemed more real than a novelist's novel, I feel that I know her. And because her life was so sad, almost as sad as Keats's; though she hadn't his genius, she had much talent and died young of his disease; I have the mixed-up feeling that because life denied her so much, we can somehow make up for that by mourning her death. Anyway, I cried and Mme Soutelle cheered me up by taking me to a café where we had coffee ice cream and wonderful little rum cakes. Mme Soutelle told me that in baking, all the alcohol in the rum evaporated.

"The only other tomb, out of the innumerable tombs and bones I have seen here, that I remember with as much feeling is that of Jean Jaurès, the great Belgian socialist, who was murdered. He is buried in the crypt of the Panthéon.

"Having paid my respects to Jaurès, whom I still think a great and good man, I climbed from the crypt of the Panthéon to the Dôme. This climb made my legs quiver like plucked strings. So I went into the church of St. Etienne-du-Mont to rest and stabilize my legs. Since I was in the city where they were buried, I thanked God for Marie Bashkirtseff and Jean Jaurès.

"Now I am home on my own couch, eating white grapes and waiting for dinner."

•   •   •

My early discovery of and fondness for Marie Bashkirtseff was akin to my beginning to read Virginia Woolf when, at Tavistock Square, I was living near her without knowing it. We are led, or I am at least led, it seems, to what my unconscious alone knows. Near Virginia Woolf, something said to me, "Read her." Near tuberculosis myself, something said to me, "Acquaint yourself with the lives of these afflicted ones." I did. While cavities were forming in my own lungs, I read of Keats and Thoreau and Emily Brontë, and Chekhov and Crane and Marie Bashkirtseff and Katherine Mansfield; and Emily Shore—who remains unknown to all except me. And I know her because of her *Journal* and her early death.

I read; and never once did it occur to my conscious mind that what I read was a forecast of my own future or a warning to me about symptoms to watch for or a cure that should be taken; but my unconscious knew.

Now I wonder if, aware of this tendency of mine to be drawn by what I read toward what is present, or to come in my life, I might, by looking at the books I am presently reading, learn what my future is to be?

Stacked on two stands near my bed are the books I am now reading. What do their titles tell me of what lies ahead?

The Way of Silence, by Basho; *The Pleasure of Ruins,* by Rose Macaulay; *The World Within the Word,* William Gass; *Silences,* Tillie Olsen; *Stories That Could Be True,* William Stafford; *The Snow Leopard,* Peter Matthiessen.

What message has my unconscious for me in that collection?

A practice never reported in letters or journal, but well remembered by me, is this: I ceased in Paris to think that there was something innately loose and sexually inviting about my appearance. No longer, as in the villages of England and Ireland, did passers-by in the street stop in their tracks and turn to look at me. When it came to strangeness, in a city where girls walked down the street latched together by a chain through their noses, or pushed dogs dressed in beruffled baby clothes in perambulators, I did not rate a passing glance.

So I stopped thinking there was something exotic or erotic about me; and decided instead that men, at least Frenchmen, were of a different breed from the Quakers of Southern California. I was satisfied that I looked neither exotic nor sensual. Still, this did not prevent Frenchmen, when one paused at a corner waiting for a pause in the traffic, to slam on their brakes, pull to the curb, open their car doors, and say what I couldn't understand but took to be, "Come for a spin, mademoiselle." To which I replied in English that I believed he couldn't understand, "Thank you, stranger, but I am not an untraveled fool." Such encounters convinced me that for the French, this was a normal response of male to female.

Believing this, no longer feeling shamefaced or guilty, I decided this might be a game that two could play. When I rode with Miss B. on the Métro, I would pick out a man, neither a grandpa with a cane nor a schoolboy with books, and, if married, without a wife, and look at him. I did not smile, certainly did not wink or smirk or beckon. All I did was catch his eye, then tell my eyes to say to his, "You are one of the most handsome, charming, appealing fellows I ever saw." The response was frequently the same. When I stood to leave, the handsome, charming, appealing fellow also stood, and came toward me. I sent these eye messages only when accompanied by Miss B. As I was approached, I linked my arm in hers. She looked old enough, and actually was more than old enough, to be my mother; she also looked stern and strong enough, too, to be my father. I sent a second eye message to the gentleman, who was now confused, saying, "You have made a mistake, sir."

I was never sure whether Miss B. knew what was going on or not. If she did, she never mentioned it to me; though it wasn't a matter, I am sure, she would have found unamusing.

Memory now tells me something of what two months in
Europe had done for me. They had changed me from a cower-
ing, shamefaced country girl, who felt guilty if a man
approached her, into a sophisticate who anticipated and encouraged his approach and was able, without twinges of
guilt or self-consciousness, to have some fun with it.

What if I had stayed six months instead of four? Would I
have been sending out eye messages when there was no Miss
B. by my side to rescue me from the responder?

"Dear Max: I'm glad you're not traveling. I'd hate to get
reports from you of buildings, museums, paintings. If you
were, I hope I'd understand if you did send such reports.
Actually, you're such a sparse writer, I suppose I'd be over-
joyed to have word of how the dear old Buick is working or
a description of Harmon Gym at California.

"So forgive Notre Dame. I'm still stunned by it. I went
there this morning with Billie Rendle. Notre Dame without
Lon Chaney leaping about like a galvanized frog is not the
Notre Dame Americans know. Pictures fail to give any idea
of its grandeur and nobility. Then, too, its greatness lies for
the most part in its interior. The exterior, except from some
angles, is a bit squat. Inside, I left one age for another. It
seemed impossible that I was inside a building; instead, it
seemed another world. Archway gave place to archway, vista
to vista, and, miles away, candles gleamed on the high altar.
This was all in stone, of course, but stone so delicately carved
I felt that I was in a temple made of lace.

"What I saw was enriched by what I knew. In this building (a cathedral is a building, I suppose), the crusade led by
St. Louis of France started. Napoleon and Josephine were
crowned here. During the French Revolution Notre Dame
was called 'The Temple of Reason.'

"Billie, who has been here many times, was more interested
in my awe and astonishment than in the building. 'Every
European,' she said, 'should travel with an American as a

companion. He will then be able to see again old sights with the freshness of a child's eyes.' Maybe I have a child's eyes. If so, I wouldn't trade them for jaded eyes. I don't love Notre Dame as I did Ely and Durham, but I'm still capable of being astounded.

"General Notes:

"I. Climate. Hot, very hot. Less so here at 6 Rue Thibaud, which is on a slope and where a breeze comes daily. Walking about elsewhere, I'm in a lather. My clothes are not cool enough. Thank heaven I didn't buy any woolen bellybands. Also, my clothes are wearing out.

"II. Paris as an International Center

"Far more than in London, you see here people of every race. Indian women with a jeweled stud in one nostril; swarms of Japanese, Chinese, Spanish, German. At the American Express Company, there is such a press of tourists from every country that getting mail requires queuing up and waiting.

"III. Equality of Races

"Negroes and whites. Many times a day you see a Negro man and a white woman together—a little less frequently, a Negro girl and a white man. Many Negro soldiers are on the streets. I almost always find some Negroes at the Shakespeare and Company bookshop. They are extremely well informed and use better English, at least more formal English, than mine.

"Seeing Negroes and whites together startles me, not because I think they shouldn't be together, but because in California I never saw them together. I scarcely saw Negroes there by themselves. Hearing them talk learnedly of literature (my field, if I have any) collides, I suppose, with some kind of bigotry I had without knowing it. It's just in the air, I suppose, this taking for granted that 'we is the smart ones and they is the backward ones.' A few more trips to Shakespeare and Company, and that smear of bigotry will be washed away.

"IV. Cafés

"We ought to have some. California has the right climate. Here the streets are gay with out-of-door cafés. All day long and until late at night, they are filled with men and women who are reading, writing, sewing, talking. You do need a bed to sleep in, in Paris; but except when in bed, you could live in a café.

"V. Prices

"Cheaper than home. Cheaper than London. The cook here gets $12 a month. Cauliflower is 1 franc a head. My haircut was no giveaway, 20 francs. I had to have it, though, or start braiding.

"VI. Gardens and Parks

"Paris has a network of them, and they are really used, filled with women sewing, reading, caring for their children, walking dogs and even cats on leashes. I never saw a city with so much of its life being carried on outdoors.

"All boats are booked until the end of October, unless there are some cancellations. I have put in for any cancellation. My shoes are in shreds. No more heel trouble. My feet are now hooves. I sound like a pony when I walk barefoot across my uncovered floorboards."

I didn't write home about Shakespeare and Company. It was, after all, another bookstore (though the most unusual one I had ever seen); and no one at home was going to think that time in Europe was well spent poking around in bookstores. Letters are a cross between saying what you can't keep quiet about and what you think the recipient would like to hear. Shakespeare and Company meant more to me than Sacre Coeur, which I did write home about. "It is an ugly church, built as a penitential offering after the War of 1870. Now penance should be done for it. It is a hideous blob of stone. For two cents, I would do no more sightseeing, but sit in the garden and read books; and when bored with that, I would walk down the street and order *café glace*. For two cents."

So I wrote home about the ugly cathedral and skipped the great bookstore; this, I thought, was the news they wanted the traveler to send them, that grandpa would relish and enjoy reporting to the mail carrier.

This is also why I enjoy reading writer's journals more than their letters; that is, if it's the writer I'm interested in, not the edited version of himself he sends to his correspondents.

I went to Shakespeare and Company first because of Miss B., whom I was beginning to call Madeline. James Joyce's daughter had at one time been a resident at 6 Rue Thibaud. Now Shakespeare and Company was publishing James Joyce's book *Ulysses,* and for this reason and because she did not think much of my addiction to W. H. Smith and his bookstore, Miss B. urged me to go to Shakespeare and Company. I do not think that I had ever before heard of Shakespeare and Company. I tremble now to think of the barrenness of my life in Paris without Miss B. as a mentor. Of course Billie Rendle was there—she was responsible for my residence at Rue Thibaud—but she had friends of her own at International House and, although we went many places together, she was no longer, as at Oxford, my guide and teacher.

I would have gone to any bookstore recommended by Madeline, even if it had carried an all-French stock. Shakespeare and Company had many English books and was publishing books in English. Miss Sylvia Beach, the proprietor, was an American.

In the summer of 1929, Paris was filled with English and American writers. Now if my theory of being influenced by what was near has any substance, I would surely have read their books. Or at least I would have learned somehow that they *were* all there, and all frequenters of Shakespeare and Company, in order to catch sight of them.

I did not know that Paris was filled with writers that summer, and my subconscious sent me no message of their presence. And even if I had known, I might not have had the enterprise to watch for and certainly not the courage to speak to any of them. Until I was twenty, I had never seen a living writer; nor had I seen anyone who had seen a living writer. At twenty, my big opportunity came. A living writer was to make a speech in a nearby town. A writer would speak, I supposed, on writing. I tramped three miles to hear this speech, which was, it turned out, not on writing at all, but on "the necessity for the passage in California of legislation forbidding the manufacture and sale of spiritous liquors."

It was not, I think, this speech that lessened my enthusiasm for living writers. I simply did not know that any were in Paris. Considering the fact that for over a month I was at Shakespeare and Company at least twice a week, I must surely at some time have been in the room that looked, with its fireplace and pictures and books, more like a living room than a shop when Hemingway or Fitzgerald or Joyce was there.

A notebook of Fitzgerald's recently published reveals a practice of which Hemingway would never have been capable. From stories of his that Fitzgerald believed would never be republished, he "stripped" what he considered usable fragments for use in other of his writings. This obviously was a thrifty practice—if he, in fact, did use them later. I cannot imagine Hemingway doing such a thing. The "strippings" from Fitzgerald's stories resemble a collection of bolts, springs, and screws from a piece of discarded machinery.

I like to think that at some time I stood in the Shakespeare and Company bookshop when Ernest Hemingway was present; perhaps at the time when he got books from Sylvia Beach's circulating library without having the money to pay for his membership in that library.

Madeline told me that I should buy Joyce's *Ulysses*. I knew that the book was forbidden in the United States as obscene; and, apart from not wanting to break the law, I didn't have money to throw away on a book that would be confiscated the minute I got home. Yet I had more confidence in Madeline's taste than I did in that of censors in the United States, so I bought the book. It was large, more than seven hundred pages long (I still have it), a paperback covered in blue. I do not remember, and I recorded nowhere, what I paid for it. Why I did not, when I was keeping the home folks fully posted as to the cost of cauliflower, haircutting, and taxi rides, I don't know. Well, yes, I do. I was reluctant to tell the home folks that I had bought an obscene book that was against the law to bring into the United States. And I didn't put the cost into my journal because that was not an account book—except of the heart.

At New York, when my baggage was checked, the inspector, after one look at my trunk, half filled, it appeared, with marmalade, shut the lid in disgust. Go all the way to Europe and have no more sense than to bring home as souvenirs jars of marmalade!

So I kept my book, which, to tell the truth, I didn't on first reading like as much as I did the marmalade. I had been brought up in the land of oranges. There were no writers like James Joyce in Orange County.

"I am so well filled with potato croquettes and creamed leeks, this letter will probably dwindle off into snores before I write very much. I talk downstairs with my housemates for an hour after dinner, then I come up to my room to read and write letters. I am well supplied with books from Shakespeare and Company, and even though I sit in a chair for three or four hours, midnight is here before I know it.

"Yesterday I went with Billie Rendle and her friend, the most astounding, bandy-legged, freckle-faced, odd-hatted, erudite, self-assured female I ever saw. Any American girl dressed as she was would have jumped into the Seine before being willing to appear in public, particularly that part of the public that frequents the Rue de Rivoli. Not Hilda. She jolly well had a right to wear what she wanted and to be where she was. She speaks French like the French do and can tell you, does tell you, bits of history the French jolly well never knew or have forgotten. She is clean and wholesome, but hard on the eyes. Nevertheless, she was the perfect person for yesterday's tour: Sainte Chapelle and the Conciergerie. Sainte Chapelle was built to house the relics brought home from the Crusades by St. Louis: the crown of thorns, splinters from the true cross, etc. These have been moved to Notre Dame, and the chapel is no longer used, even as a place of worship. It is rented out to tourists at two francs for a tour of inspection.

"It is now called 'the king's jewel box,' which is a good term. The blues of the windows are so deep and intense that the entire chapel might have been scooped out of an enormous sapphire. I had an underwater feeling all the time I was there.

"Next we went to the Conciergerie, the prison parts of which are a thousand years old and are chiefly known as the place where Marie Antoinette was confined before her death.

"I'm not going to describe that terrible place for you: Marie Antoinette's cell had boards nailed across the top of the door so that she had to bow her head in entering or leaving. She must have been a fairly tall woman; only the tallest of us had to do as she had done.

"We came in out of sunshine to this underground green and gloomy prison knowing that we would walk out with our heads on in thirty minutes. What did Marie Antoinette feel, knowing that she would never leave except to go to the guillotine? Robespierre, who had brought about the Queen's death, occupied a cell next to hers a few months later, and he, too, was carted away to the chopping machine.

"From this prison the Girondists, twenty-one rather young men who were republicans and did not believe in anarchy or tyranny, were taken to the guillotine. One of the young men killed himself with his dagger when the death sentence was pronounced. They chopped his head off just the same.

"So much for an afternoon in Gay Paree."

.   .   .

After an afternoon spent in a prison from which two thousand people had been taken to the guillotine, and an evening spent in telling my family about it, I tried, before I went to bed, to cleanse myself of the guilt which I, as a member of the human race, shared with all its other killers.

I copied some Bible verses into my journal.

"Bless the Lord O my soul and all that is within me bless his holy name.

"Bless the Lord O my soul and forget not all his benefits.

"Who forgiveth all thine iniquities; who healeth all thy diseases.

"Who redeemeth thy life from destruction; who crowneth thee with loving kindness."

Having copied those verses, I preached a sermon to myself. "Dear God, give me a penetrating mind and a pious heart." That prayer, it now seems to me, was powered more by a desire for alliteration than anything else. I would pray now for a loving heart, rather than a pious one, an understanding mind, rather than a penetrating one.

"Miss Dixon has come home from Rome, where she has been visiting her father. She is small, dark, comely. Because her uncle wrote *The Clansman*, which was about the South, Miss Dixon looks like a Southern woman to me. All she needs is a hoop skirt and a camellia in her black hair to be a Confederate belle. For all that she is so small, quiet, and even prim-looking, I doubt that anything takes place at Foyer Grace Madeline that doesn't have her approval.

"They have asked me to go with them on another jaunt into the country. This invitation has somewhat mollified Miss Vaughn. With Miss Dixon gone, she wanted to be first with Miss B., and I, so recently here, seemed to her to be a usurper when I was chosen for botanizing. Now I think she believes that I am crestfallen to find that I am, at best, #2. Poor Miss Lily Vaughn. She looks like a sad, sleek, lonesome little

gopher. She thinks I am crestfallen, and she is contrite because she was rude to me. Well, I'm not crestfallen. I never
did get crushes on girls, even in high school; but I know how
she feels. Miss B. is the nearest thing we have to a boy here at
Foyer Grace Madeline; and, in addition, she is learned, distinguished, and kindhearted, which most boys aren't.

"Miss Vaughn has seen every notable building, painting,
statue in Paris. She isn't built for twenty-five-mile hikes into
the country, so she has invited me to go with her on a 'stroll'
into 'nontouristy' Paris. Don't know what this will be, but I
will tell you when I get back this evening."

"One thing it surely was, was the hottest stroll I ever took.
It is 10:10 now and a little breeze has come up. The trees in
the garden are moving about like fans. I'll sleep under a
blanket tonight. Madeline says this is the hottest weather
Paris has had in September in twenty years. When I was in
London, it was the hottest summer in seven years. Be prepared for me when I come home. I bring extremes.

"Mama, you're a garden- and plant-woman, not an animal-
woman, so I don't know whether you would have enjoyed the
bird and animal market very much or not. I did and I didn't.
Every animal I can think of that is capable of living in a
cage was there, in a cage and for sale. Life in a cage is probably hell for any animal at any time; perhaps it just looks
worse on a hot day, when birds have their wings lifted away
from their bodies and even the tortoises look as if they would
like to crawl out of their shells. There were rats there, ferrets,
merles (blackbirds), turtles, cats (or something like a cat);
and they were all hot and miserable, and being bought by
kids who started jouncing them around in their cages and
making them more hot and miserable. I thought about buying a bird (a cheap one) and setting it free.

"I didn't, because I was afraid if it had been cage-born and
-bred, it wouldn't know how to take care of itself if set free.

"I think Miss Vaughn wanted to see the caged because she

knew how to sympathize with them. When we left the birds and animals, we went to the English tearoom, where we had ices instead of tea—and I listened to Lily talk about Madeline.

"After the ices, Lily went to church, 'Evensong,' I think she said. I walked home along the Seine, rested on the steps that lead down to the river for a while and watched the fishing. I didn't see anything caught, but in the hot weather it was pleasant just to be near water.

"I would rather be a human being than any other kind of being I know; even though we are a cruel lot. One afternoon at the prison of the French Revolution, the next at the bird and animal market, showed me this all over again. And poor Miss Lily, caught in a prison of love. She, I guess, doesn't want out. So I won't waste pity on her.

"I stayed by the river until its water reflected the rusty sunset colors, and the breeze that is still blowing came up.

"Tomorrow I go first thing to American Express to see if there's a letter from you or Max. I had mail on Wednesday, so it's optimistic to expect more so soon; I'll go steeled for disappointment, hoping to rejoice.

"Here's what's ahead of me: Seine River Trip, Versailles, Fontainebleau. There's a Battlefield Tour for ten dollars which I feel I should take. I don't know what good it will do me or the boys who died there. But they did die there, and I feel I should at least go out there and suffer a little with them.

"All goes well. I'm not caught in any cage, unless Paris itself is a cage."

"Don't send this letter on to Mama, Max—she'll think I'm wasting my time in Paris. Actually, I think I saw more of Paris as it is today at the movies than I do in the museums. Miss B. asked me and the German girl to go with her to the movies. Miss Dixon ate something in Italy that didn't agree with her. And I don't think this movie would have agreed with her, either.

"We sat in the upper gallery, and our seats cost us four francs each. Miss B. says, 'The less you pay, the more you get,' and she certainly was right about this movie. We got love-making all around us that far eclipsed any embraces Tom Mix gave, even to his horse.

"A couple just in front of us, handsome in a big-nosed, big-eyed, flowing-haired way, periodically swallowed each other—and they did not care whether the lights were off or on.

"That, by the way, is characteristic of Paris. Men and women kiss with audible smacks as they wait for buses, or just walk the streets. Miss B. says, 'Eet ees very nice in Paris. You kees when you feel like eet. Eef you wait 'til you get home, perhaps eet will no longer make you happy to kees.'

"I don't think Mama would think all that public kissing very nice.

"Public or private, I don't know how that couple endured being near each other, let alone kissing. Honestly, I didn't know anything short of putrefaction could have so nasty a smell.

"And, oh, when the lights went up, she combed his hair and killed the fleas she found there—killed them with joy and French élan, clicking her nails as she pinched their heads or tails off.

"After each flea she killed, he would, out of gratitude, kiss, embrace, fondle, caress her with an abandon that didn't seem possible, separated as they were by the arm of the chair between them.

"The show started at 8:30. At 10:10, there was an intermission of ten minutes. I supposed we would go home, but no, we received readmission tickets, and went to a nearby café. Miss B. and the German girl drank beer, I citronade, terrible stuff.

"Then there was a furious clanging of bells and everyone raced back into the theater. Our flea killer and friend were just where we had left them, though somewhat calmer.

Maybe while the theater was empty she had killed the last flea.

"The second picture was French, all bosoms and eyes that rolled. When it was over, Miss B. said, 'Now you girls may kees me. I am sure after so sentimental a picture, you must want to kees someone.' The German girl did plant a loud smack on Miss B.'s cheek. I said, 'When in Paris, do as the Parisians do,' and hunted through Miss B.'s hair and pretended to find a flea which I killed with fingernails snapping. Miss B. gave me a hug and said, 'No one would take you for an uncouth Yank.'

"I'm so glad I'm staying at 6 Rue Thibaud. What I saw last night was probably more Paris than any museum in the city. Museums are all more or less the same, but where else could I find such kissing and flea-killing, and the two together?

"Write, write. Berkeley is where I am going to live and I'd rather hear about it and you than take a guided tour to every tourist attraction in Paris."

"After a visit to the Russian church this morning, I am glad I was born into a Quaker family. First of all, there is a two-hour service, during which everyone stands. I can walk for two hours, can walk all day, in fact, but standing for two hours without moving goes against human nature. During the two hours, there was five-part singing. This does something to the nervous system—it made me want to throw myself over a cliff in an ecstacy of abasement, or perhaps just to rest my legs.

"Tomorrow I am going into the catacombs. Beneath this section of town are ancient quarries which have been partially filled with bones from the overcrowded cemeteries of Paris. Three million persons—their bones, at least—are thought to be stored there. Miss B. says I will not be upset. It is not like going into a morgue. The bones have been so arranged, it is more like viewing a tapestry of some sort, where legs and arms, skulls and backbones have been used to make the picture instead of different-colored yarns. The picture, I suppose, is death. No, death happened long ago, and not to these bones. Anyway, at 2:00 P.M. tomorrow, candle in hand, I descend to the quarry.

"This is for Papa, the dry cleaner. I am having some cleaning done here. This cleaner has a system by which he gives you a ticket good for a franc when you pay. Since a franc is only four cents, I don't know that that system would have much effect in Southern California. I'm not going to patronize the new family industry. I'll have everything cleaned before I come home. My yellow silk dress, pleats all around, cost only twenty-eight francs. I'm coming home in tatters, but clean.

"Write, write. I long to talk to Carmen, starting teaching, Merle, starting school. You and Papa, carrying on what you started twenty-eight years ago—me, for one thing."

"One month from today, Max, I should be with you in Berkeley. Oh, glory! I hope you count the days as I do. And you haven't any nasty materialistic reason for wanting me home. You can't say, 'My socks will always be darned when my wife returns,' or 'I'll have pie every night next month,' can you? It's just that we'll be together again after this long separation.

"Do you look forward to the rainy months of winter as I do? Studying, reading together? Going up into the hills back of Berkeley? Chocolate cake from the Woodshed when we're not too busted? Raisin muffins when I'm not too lazy?

"I have been terribly lucky and it just happened today. I have a berth on the *Minnesota,* sailing September 21. I leave here on a boat train for Boulogne at 4:00 P.M. a week from this Saturday. This is earlier than I had planned to leave, but it was then or mid-October and I just couldn't bear to wait that long.

"I've seen all the conventional sights except Napoleon's tomb. The Oxford girls have taken me to every museum, palace, monument, and tomb, in the city. I have climbed every tower, dome, and pinnacle and can identify every well-known building in Paris. I can order ice cream, fried potatoes, and lemonade in French. I can shout, *'Zutt,'* at bold Frenchmen, which means, Billie tells me, 'Beat it, you swine, and let an honest woman alone.'

"Tonight I am going to the Casino de Paris, where females hop about in their skins. I'll write you all about it afterwards."

"The Casino de Paris wasn't just nakedness, but if you're not used to it, nakedness is what you see. It wasn't a musical comedy in our sense of the word, but a 'revue,' singing, dancing, and presenting one or two skits—and half of the show was in English. The revue began at 8:30 and lasted until 12:00. Everything in Paris lasts until 12:00. Paris is not a town where all lights go out at nine o'clock.

"It was a spectacle, in addition to the nakedness. Vesuvius erupted, Noah's flood flashed onto the stage, and the females, who had no clothes on to worry about, writhed in the water as if drowning.

"The ten or fifteen maidens (maiden-shaped anyway) wore jeweled G-strings only. And I mean strings, not sashes, or bows, or clouts. Above and below the string, nothing but naked maiden. They were so well trained and graceful, it was easy to think of them as animated statues. From the way fat Frenchmen chomped on their cigars and peered through opera glasses, the idea of statues never entered *their* heads. If the naked ones had been men, perhaps I, too, would have been peering through opera glasses.

"In America, I suppose a show like that would be closed in two minutes, and everyone in it in jail in ten minutes. Is that a sign that we are better than the French?"

. . .

"Breakfast is always served in the individual bedrooms, as I have told you. Usually I don't eat in bed, but this morning I did, and am still there. I'm leg weary from the kilometers I tramped yesterday. We—Grace Dixon, Madeline, and I— left here at 9:00 A.M. and didn't get back until 10:30 P.M. First of all, we went by train one and one-half hours into the country. When we left the train, we shouldered our knapsacks and never ceased tramping (except to eat) until we boarded our homeward-bound train last night at 8:30. My bones were groaning by midafternoon. But with two fifty-year-olds pacing smartly along, and actually covering far more ground than I, because they ran up and down ravines, climbed banks, waded in marshes hunting plants, could I, twenty-five years their junior, begin wailing, 'I'm tired. I can't take another step'? Since I couldn't say it, I took another step and another and another.

"First of all, we went through a forest: beech, elm, oak, fir; ferns waist-high. In the ferns were thousands of pheasants. A roadrunner is a scrawny bird beside a pheasant. I had no idea pheasants were so large: big as a fat hen or a medium-sized rooster. Whenever we stopped, we could hear them clumping about in the underbrush. Elephants couldn't have been much noisier. Some took clumsily to wing or scuttled from the ferns on one side of the road to the ferns on the other. Honestly, the forest was alive with them.

"It was also alive with bunnies! I don't mean our jack rabbits, but Easter bunnies. I don't know whether there were actually fewer rabbits than pheasants, or whether the rabbits were just quieter.

"At 1:30, beside a little lake (not the one I told you about before), we sat down and ate our cheese, eggs, ham, bread, bananas, beer (Miss B. and Miss D.), I, citronade. Then they plunged about the lake gathering more plants, while I read the book I had brought with me. Fernandez, *Messages*.

When they came back they talked with me about literature and particularly about *Ulysses*. Did I like it, etc. I told them that I didn't understand it. They didn't know how this could be. It was to them not only clear writing, but great writing. They thought, and this may have been in part true, that I was put off simply by the fact that I had never before encountered a story told in the way Joyce was telling this story. Most novelists are at pains to "translate," so to speak, the thoughts of their characters into words their readers will understand. Joyce didn't do this. Joyce gave you the character as he really was; not a person constructed for easy understanding by the reader.

Since I couldn't understand Mollie Bloom's final ravings, as I then thought them, and because it was easier to believe Joyce a strange writer than to admit that I was an incapable reader, I quoted Fernandez to them.

"Fernandez," I told them, "says that it is a mediocre art which demands from us effort of reflection in order that we may be in a position to apprehend its images."

They hooted at this and insisted that they themselves didn't care to read anything that didn't require or at least permit some reflection.

We spent an hour there by the lake talking, they asking questions, trying to discover what kind of education and upbringing had produced a young woman who couldn't understand Mollie Bloom. I didn't resent the questioning. After all, it gave me the opportunity to talk about myself—which I, like most people, enjoy. What I regret is that upbringing or temperament prevented me from asking *them* questions. I would have learned; they would have been pleased to teach. I did not do so, I think, because I was backwoods and frontier brought up: the backwoods of Indiana, the barley fields of Southern California. There, "getting personal" was not well thought of. I had not yet read Virginia Woolf saying that she refused to let her time be wasted in a conversation in which she could not get personal; I had not yet read Martin Buber, who says, "We must make the effort to impart ourselves to others as we are." I was, no doubt, without making any effort, imparting myself as I was to Madeline and Grace: a country girl, reticent when talking with women old enough to be her mother.

I regret it now. Grace Dixon had been a Red Cross nurse during the war and it was thus that she met Madeline, another nurse. What had that war been like? Why had Grace decided to stay in France? What did they hope to accomplish with their Foyer for young women of different nationalities? Didn't they find that shared bedroom of theirs, with one bed perched like a throne on a dais, strange? And claustrophobic? What differences had they found between the girls of different nationalities? Madeline knew James Joyce. What was he like? Had their families suffered during the war?

I asked no questions. I lived for over a month under their roof. They would not have invited me to spend those days in the country with them if they had been unwilling to talk to me. What was wrong with me, as would-be writer and as a human being? I would know much more now if I had made use of the opportunity I had with them to learn of a world which had existed before I was born and which had a past much richer than my barley fields and pawpaw thickets.

Now, reading of those who were not only in Paris that summer but in and out of the Shakespeare and Company, I seem to myself to have been lacking in all enterprise. Yet what would I have done had I recognized Hemingway or Fitzgerald? Asked for an autograph? I was there, wasn't I? I did not at that time consider this fact exceptional. I do now. Twelve-year-olds today know more about travel than I did then. Ignorant though I was, I had made the trip. Zelda Fitzgerald and Hadley Hemingway, about my age, were in Paris; but they were there with their husbands.

I had had to leave mine to get to Paris. And neither woman had been very lucky even with helpmates by their side: Zelda lost her mind, Hadley, her husband.

Still it bothers me: I was at Tavistock Square when Bloomsbury was flourishing; I was in and out of Shakespeare and Company when Joyce was being published and when Stein, Hemingway, and Fitzgerald were nearby. I feel like a pioneer who could have heard the thunder of the buffaloes or opened her eyes when the passenger pigeons darkened the sky, but never did so. I feel that I should now make excuses for myself. But why? I saw what I came to see—the old country, the land my forefathers had left. No one in Yorba Linda or Hemet or Whittier had told me that new masters were then practicing the art of writing in London and Paris. "Do you know anyone in Europe?" I had been asked before I started my trip. I didn't, and the pity of it was that even when given the opportunity to know women like Madeline and Grace, I didn't know how to use it.

So there I was in Paris in the decade when Americans were flocking to Paris to write their novels. These were my gods, and I was near them and didn't know it.

It was, I now think, like having gone to heaven without being told where you were. Centuries later, time wasted in drinking celestial lemon squash and playing flinch in the heavenly suburbs, you learn that you have been in heaven. "Why didn't someone tell me?"

But what if someone had? What would I, in Paris with the novelists and abstract painters, have done about it? Not much, I fear. If I had been told that Hemingway was seated at the next table, I would certainly have stared my eyes out. And perhaps been disappointed in what I saw. The best of a good writer—and Hemingway was a great one—goes into his writing. What's left over may be less than an eyeful.

I was too timid to have asked for an autograph. Now I am too wise. Or perhaps that is only the word I use to cover up present timidity, since I now think that timidity in the elderly is as unseemly as thumb-sucking. Wise enough now, at least, to know that when I read a good book, I am getting the best of the writer.

In my journal at the time, I wrote, "I begin to feel more myself, or at least more of the self I like to be. Traveling alone, I become self-conscious, too introspective. Alone, I feel myself the focal point of the universe. About *me* revolve cathedrals, castles, historical monuments. Now, in what amounts to a home with friends about me, the castles and cathedrals are standing still. They have stopped looking at me and I am looking at them.

I have also discovered that unless I am more or less carried away by what I am thinking or feeling, I am terribly self-conscious.

"This afternoon I went to the Rodin Museum. It was intolerably hot and I arrived in a sweltering condition. And Rodin sculptures are not the cooling type. They, too, throb and burn. A pulse beats just beneath the marble surface. There is more passion, honor, reverence in them than many a flesh-and-blood man feels in a lifetime.

"There is that strange figure of a female centaur straining even to the point of self-extinction to separate brow and breast from those heavy, horsy loins. This is a marble symbol for a feeling that may be universal in some women."

In a much later journal, after reading the letters my mother had saved, I wrote, "Suddenly stricken with sorrow tonight, thinking of my first trip to Europe and what it should have been. Then I was frightened, embarrassed, homesick. My God, my God, if that trip could have been taken otherwise, those beauties seen and shared without the need of ink. If love could have been there without the need of my pen for communication. If the laughing could have been shared. What that might have been, hand in hand with love. It never struck me until this evening that instead of being comic, as I tend to think of it now, it was a tragic trip."

Young people should be taught to want more, to ask for more, to know that they deserve more.

To go off to Europe seemed to me then all the magic one could want. It wasn't. Insane. Poor simple-minded girl who should have wanted more.

"Max, will you send this letter on to Mama? It's the last half of a letter I intended to write to her, but I was so tired from the day before's tramping, I didn't have the stamina to live it all through again in words. When Miss Dixon, Madeline, and I stopped for lunch, I stopped my letter. We had a whole afternoon's walk still ahead of us, and I'm rested enough now to rewalk it for her.

"About four o'clock we came to the village where Bluebeard, the Frenchman, lived and killed seven or eight wives. This was the least likely place for tragedy I ever saw. Perhaps the peace and quiet drove him to it. There was a white church with a lofty spire, whitewashed houses with thatched roofs, a shed over a dammed-up place in the stream where the women washed their clothes; little boys played in blue checkered aprons; gardens of brilliant flowers bloomed. I don't know very much about Bluebeard, or this town either, but how so bloody a man could have lived here, spilling the blood of wife after wife without anyone's knowing it, is beyond me.

"Madeline and Grace were thirsty, and I went with them to what was called a 'wine merchant's.' I don't know who they sell to—we were the only ones there and I didn't drink wine. The building was wonderful, thick-walled, painted the most vivid blue I ever saw, and cool as an ice cave. We sat at a clean wooden table and were served by an ancient woman whose chin cleared her stomach by a fraction of an inch. She had one tooth in her head; it gleamed like a monument to her dead youth. She was obviously glad to have customers, and talked at length with her countrywomen.

"We walked for an hour and a half more through the forest, then we were out into the cultivated fields. The air was golden now and cool. We tramped through wheat fields, sugar-beet fields; beside two-wheeled carts piled high with hay, alongside farm laborers, returning from work. We did not pass a single house. It is difficult to believe after a day's tramping through the uncluttered countryside that France is one of Europe's most densely populated nations—and we were never all day long more than sixty miles from Paris. This openness is the result of farmers living in the village. The village is a way of life, not just a place to buy things.

"At 7:30 we had supper in one of these villages, in a little café that looked out onto the village square. Here were the people we had not seen during the day. The pump that supplied their water was in the center of the square and to it came a constant stream of people with their buckets and cans. Women lingered there to gossip; little boys fought, little girls cried. Young men used the pump to display their muscles to admiring girls. And I suppose this pump (or something like it) has been used here for centuries. On one of the hills about the village stand the ruins of the castle of Anne of Brittany. I would like to have been here when she was in residence— for a weekend only. I doubt that villagers were very well used by Anne and her retainers. For today's farmers, for their wives, at least, I think life in a French village is less desolate than on farms and ranches where they are as widely separated from their neighbors as ours.

"While we were looking and listening, we were also eating. We had two boiled eggs each, a large platter of boiled ham, fresh bread, a bowl of butter unsalted (all butter is unsalted here), so new it seemed only thick cream, tea and cakes. The price? Seven francs. Twenty-eight cents!

"Why don't we do anything like this in California? I don't mean get meals for twenty-eight cents, but take day-long walks of this kind? Well, unless we get up into the mountains, there are no forests to walk through, no icy-blue wine merchants' establishments anywhere, no ruined castles on the hills to remind us that we are walking through history. The French really do some things better. Or have done them longer.

"We caught our train at 8:30, were in Paris at 10:00 and at home dirty and tired at 10:30. Besides seeing the countryside, I learned more about Miss Dixon and Miss B. than I have known before. They have lived together for ten years. During that time, they have traveled in North Africa, lived in Cairo, visited Cornwall and America. This Foyer now is their joint act of retribution as citizens of the twentieth century, for the war that their fellow citizens waged less than ten years ago. 'Perhaps after living here, all nationalities together, we will be less willing to shoot each other.' I doubt it.

"Even so, I think I would be serving a good cause if I took up residence here and worked as a char girl. I'd have to give up walks like yesterday's or I wouldn't have the legs for charring.

"Are you counting the days?"

With the date of my departure settled, I began to feel the sorrow that always overtakes me at parting. It is perhaps what Eric Hoffer calls, 'the Ordeal of Change,' and is possibly no more than what he felt when he had to make the change as a youth from picking peas to picking beans. I had cried my way from Los Angeles to Chicago, downcast because I was leaving my family. Now I was returning home and, while that prospect made me shed no tears, it did make me feel that I should say sad farewells to scenes and objects which quite likely I would never see again. I went once again to Jaurès's grave, the man with the vision that, if it could have prevailed, would have prevented the terrible deaths of the Somme, Ypres, Verdun, Passchendaele.

I took advantage of the fact that on Mondays all museums except the Rodin, and all department stores (in the morning), are closed. On Mondays tourists "do" the churches and the Rodin. I was loath to leave my room, which was cool, and *The Greek View of Life,* which I was reading, and brave the heat and the buzz of the buses on the boulevards. I tramped on foot everywhere, was frequently muddled, and about half the time truly lost. I endured the heat and the tromping in order to say farewell to what I might never see again.

I went to Versailles and tried to imagine those rooms as they were when David Lloyd George, Briand, and Wilson had been there drafting the Peace Treaty for World War I.

I went with Billie Rendle to the opera. I heard *Faust.* The opera house impressed me more than the opera. I thought I had heard a better *Faust* in Los Angeles, but never had I seen a more elegant opera house. It was shaped like an enormous red tomato, all red plush and velvety red curves.

Madeline and Grace took me to a section of Paris few tourists ever see: until recently a narrow strip of territory surrounding all of Paris had been kept clear of buildings, so that it would be available for fortifications in time of attack. Now people were permitted to live there in shacks, without plumbing, water, or lights. The rent is almost nothing, because in time of need, the occupants would have to evacuate at once.

Many are rag pickers or garbage snatchers: that is, they go through refuse and garbage searching for articles of value. These they sell in what is called a "flea market."

"If you are tired of living," Madeline told me, "you have only to come here at night. You will then probably live no more."

With the date for my departure only a week distant, I really came down with Hoffer's Ordeal of Change. Paris, gone forever! Had I looked closely enough? Absorbed sufficiently? It was unlikely I would come this way again. Had I been kind enough to persons like Miss Lily Vaughn of Pasadena?

I went with Miss Vaughn to the railway station, where she caught a train to Boulogne, from where she would embark upon her homeward journey to Pasadena. Miss Vaughn still had the look, to me, of an apathetic mole. But she told me, since we were parting and were unlikely ever to meet again, why she had hated me so much. After three years of hero worship of Madeline, as I had written home, she had expected this year, with Miss Dixon absent in Rome, to be chosen as the number two woman in Madeline's life. Then along I came, neither learned nor beautiful, and, insofar as Lily could see, with no merits other than an ability to walk twenty-four miles a day. So she had hated me because Madeline had chosen me as a walking companion. Later, however, she had seen that I had walked for the walk's sake and not to be by Madeline's side.

It was difficult for me to understand Lily's feeling for Madeline. A woman, though noted and honored, middle-aged (or more), gray-haired, scrawny, and with an Adam's apple obvious and active.

I had had crushes on high-school boys. When I was sixteen and eighteen, nineteen-year-old boys were going off to the Great War, boys I had screamed my throat raw for in football games. I could not speak to them during the last of our senior year because my lips in their presence trembled and my voice cracked. That trembling concern seemed natural for boys young and beautiful and headed for danger and possible death. Madeline was neither young nor beautiful and her war was behind her. But the sorrow of departure made me more compassionate. By some alchemy, not understood by me then or now, I was able to comprehend that for Lily, Madeline Brunotte was my Earl Stogsdill, dark-haired, strongly built, courageous, headed for danger. Lily and I kissed good-bye. I shed tears for myself, not for Lily. I promised to send her news of Madeline—and never did.

If I had sorrows, and I soon had a real one, I was unable to put any account of it in a letter home. Perhaps that is the way writers are born. Lacking the ability to confide in individuals, they whisper their trouble to the whole world. My journal makes no bones of what ailed me. To Max, who was the source of my pain, I was somewhat explicit. In letters to my parents, I beat round the bush. The journal tells the story straight.

Meanwhile, I was saying farewell to Paris and planning in my mind and in letters to Max the best arrangement for our new life as students in Berkeley, which was to begin when I got home. Max was already there, a junior working for his A.B. When I arrived, I would enroll as a graduate student, working for my Ph.D. In those remote days, it was possible to go straight (provided you had fulfilled certain academic obligations) for your doctor's without stopping for your master's.

"My own dear husband:

"I am getting used to spending money. At first I did not spend a cent except for travel and food. Now I have decided that this is foolish and am buying several things to bring home—so will have many new things for our home—the one we'll start building year after next.

"Max, I think we must have a three-room apartment when I arrive. You know how difficult it is to eat, sleep, and study in the same room. Please look about, Max, and see if for $25 you can't get three rooms. Read the ads, won't you, and see what you can do? We've gotten along for the six weeks of summer school, I know, with one room. But for twelve months, what do you think? I want you to choose it. I want it to be the home you have chosen for me. Please, Bunny, do it. Write 'Welcome Home' on the door and have a bowl of flowers on the table.

"My heart really bleeds for you, to think of your living on boiled potatoes while I live on creamed leeks and French pastry. When I get home, I'll cream a leek for you.

"I've had two letters from you since you reached Berkeley.

First, about the car's breakdown en route, the other about
swarming coeds after your arrival. I enjoyed the breakdown
more. In three weeks, I'll be with you. Until then, I pray you
love me dearly as I love you."

"Now that the last week is here, I'm trying to stop floating
about and to think. Think, for instance, what's the difference
between Paris and London. One difference is that Paris hasn't
a single beggar. Of course that can't be true. There must be
at least one, but I haven't encountered him. England and
Ireland were honeycombed with beggars. I'd be a lot more
solvent if I hadn't tossed so many sixpences and shillings into
outthrust hats and cans there.

"Nowhere in Paris does there seem to be the poverty there
was in London. Even in this, which is the working section,
and a block from the Latin Quarter. The women in their
aprons shop to buy flowers and ice-cream sandwiches. The
people here look healthier and ruddier; of course they get more
sunlight and salads, more light wines and less tea. There are
fewer lame people, fewer monstrosities, fewer children who
look like big white worms being pushed about in big black
perambulators. I'm convinced that England has too many
children. Never have I seen so many papas in bowler hats
pushing about offspring who look as if they have been carved
out of mashed potatoes. England hasn't room for them. She'll
have to have another war in a few years.

"Was the Great War responsible, in part, for this? Did
England, who resisted, suffer more than France, who was
conquered and occupied? Were more of England's men killed?
And did her women, mourning the lost, try to replace them
with a new crop of babies?

"Something else I don't understand—Paris traffic. It must
have some system, but what that system is, I've never been
able to discover. It keeps to the right, which is some consola-
tion; but it moves at an unholy speed.

"First, I waited for ten minutes on the curb. Then I discovered how to cross a street. You look an approaching taxi driver in the eye; with your unwavering glance, you mesmerize him as you would a wild animal. Then, with your glance never wavering, you continue in front of his now slowing car. He stops. He dares not run over anyone who looks him straight in the eye; should your glance waver, he'd run you down in a minute. So you reach the middle of the street.

"Paris provides an island of safety in the middle of the street where you can rest and convalesce after the crossing you have just made. Now it has to be done all over again, and, for some reason, drivers hate pedestrians who have made it halfway more than those who are just starting out. You are to them the fish the fisherman thought he had hooked and who escaped. The eye-to-eye procedure still works, but these drivers, though they slow, yell at you in French, which I'm glad I can't understand. They are not praising or encouraging you, of that I'm sure. Never for a minute unlocking my glare, I squeeze through to the other side and say, 'Sacre Dieu,' which means 'Praise God,' or something like that in French.

"Paris loves water. Their streets are paved, but they are forever being sprinkled. A dry street must truly pain a Parisian. Great tanks of water roll by squirting water, to the danger of all pedestrians. The drivers of these tanks care nothing for the direct stare. A squashed pedestrian would just help dampen the street. Subways are also kept in a damp and slippery condition. Why all this, I haven't the slightest idea. I'm just reporting a fact.

"I am trying in this last week to look more carefully at French people. I can't talk to them; but an inspection of every museum, gallery, café, and bookstore in France won't show me France. Sometimes I think there is more France to be seen, or at least understood, by sitting for a couple of hours on the steps leading down to the Seine and watching the fishermen and family picnickers than there is to be found in the Luxembourg or the Dôme."

·   ·   ·

Then the letter from Max came, and I was no longer a traveler determined to see and understand all of the country I was visiting, but a broken-hearted wife hoping to survive the three weeks that separated her from her husband.

All relationships that depend upon letters are precarious. Not only are the words written without the accompaniment of voice inflection and "body language," but they arrive at a time when what they say runs crosscurrent to the temper of the moment.

Had phoning not seemed to me so extravagant, saving as I was for "our home" and "our education," a call would doubtless have put all to rights. Instead, I spent three weeks weeping, wondering, imagining the worst. The worst, as I came to understand, was something Max had read in one of the journals I had left at home.

"Sunday, Sept. 15, 1929

"Max, my dear and sweet:

"It is 10:30. I have eaten my breakfast, dressed, and made my room spotless. I have been trying to read Dickinson's *The Greek View of Life,* but it is useless. I think only of you. Of the six days before I sail, the ten days on shipboard, a day in New York, five days on the train. Since my thoughts are all with you, I had as well write, though I doubt you'll have patience to read.

"My journey ended spiritually when I got your letter on Thursday. 'I prefer to taste the ashes of an unsuccessful married life—to salute my boyhood dreams of a perfect marriage. Perhaps you'd better stay where you are or with your folks. I do not fear a life of solitude. No one need be solitary among ten thousand coeds!'

"Max, what has happened? Do you only love me when I am near? No, no. I can't dream of a life in which you and I aren't together. Why are you so unhappy, so doubtful of our life together, so melancholy in recalling the past?

"Oh, Max, it's hard to have a letter like this when I am ten thousand miles distant and at least three weeks from asking you why, why?

"I'm going to the services at Notre Dame this morning, though it's useless to go. All happenings and scenes are obstacles now to be surmounted. I have only one desire now: get home. Your letter came at a time when I was filled with tenderness, planning our life this winter in Berkeley and determined to fill the time that separated us with as much seeing and learning as possible.

"Now I only hope that there will be another letter from you before I leave. I hate to start home with only those sad and foreboding phrases as a welcome."

I have always been better able to confront the disaster that is real than the one I imagine. Our house really burned down: the fire chief said, "You are the calmest woman at a fire I ever saw." The doctor said, "Far-advanced tuberculosis," and I expected to be rid of that in three months. If Max had written, "I have fallen in love with a nineteen-year-old coed," that girl would not have struck me as much of a danger. But "ashes in the mouth," and "boyhood dreams" gave scope to the imagination. What had I done? Or failed to do?

When I got home from Notre Dame, I began writing Max again. "Oh, I pray there will be another letter from you before I leave. I can't bear to start home with only those unwelcoming words to remind me of you.

"Max, I think every woman brought up as I was longs to be desired beyond her ability to return that desire in kind. She may snarl, gnash her teeth, declare to heaven that it is obnoxious that one so chaste and pure as she should be so beleaguered, though her heart delights. She has been brought up too long in the belief that she is the quarry and man the hunter.

"A very good woman, a very truthful woman, might have had the backbone to admit the delight in being assailed. I'm not that good and truthful woman. I was afraid that frank delight would show satiety. Taboos prevented me from showing delight. The woman must appear to repulse and to scorn sex.

"And what a damnable analytical letter this is to write! There are times when I curse myself for ever having embarked upon this trip. True, you were the one who bought the ticket and made it possible for me to stop dreaming and start traveling. I didn't have the slightest idea of the physical hardship involved: the stress, and now the heartbreak of travel.

"They are nothing now—or at least nothing that wouldn't be wiped out by one letter from you."

"It is five after 9:00 P.M. and I'm weeping salt tears. Thank heaven it is Monday night. Only Tuesday, Wednesday, Thursday, Friday, Saturday to be endured. On Thursday when your letter arrived, I had a date with Billie Rendle to go to the opera. People died in droves on the stage, gushing blood and song. I couldn't have cared less. Death was sweet solace compared with the days of waiting ahead of me before I even started home.

"Do you know what I'm going to do when I get to Berkeley? I'm going to attend every class with you. Could you stand that, after having been a debonair young bachelor for four months?

"I hate that P.E. female who spends every afternoon on the playground with you. Does she know that you have a terribly jealous wife? Five more days and I'll be starting toward you."

Can we learn only through pain?

"I went to American Express today and made arrangements about my trunk. I had to pay $6.50 to have it sent from Oxford to London and there put on the boat train. But it is full of wonderful marmalade, and under the marmalade it will be full of wonderful books.

"What I really went for was the mail: a letter from you saying, 'Forgive my letter. I hoped that you didn't take it seriously.' But there was no letter. I promised myself I won't go again until the day before boat time; but I know I'll go every day.

"If I didn't already have train and boat-train tickets, I'd see if I couldn't leave this very evening. Everything is done but packing, and I can scarcely keep from doing that. If that were done, I'd be in a frenzy. You know how impatient I am about waiting. If I were all packed, I'd probably start walking toward you. Senseless, I know, since I'd just have to sit on the sand when I got there and wait. I can't even make a berth reservation ahead of time because ships may be delayed at this season of the year. So I'm stuck here, trying to read in between the lines of your heartbreaking letter."

"They say that misery loves company. I don't know whether my actions following the receipt of that letter illustrate that saying or not. I did begin to see and feel for, as I hadn't before, those who were obviously handicapped and possibly suffering.

"There is at the Louvre a one-legged guard and ticket-taker who, whenever a female under thirty walks by, begins to sing in a low sweet baritone. I could not, of course, understand the words of the song he sang. His song, I decided, was a plea to be noticed. I decided to let him know that I had noticed and did care. I gave him the Métro look out of my eyes. I gave him a 4″ x 2″ American flag which was for sale in a booth outside. I shook his hand in a comradely fashion when I gave him the flag.

"I had noticed, when I sat on the steps that led down to the Seine, an elderly fisherman who never had any luck. His bad luck wasn't the result of a lack of fish. Other fishermen were hauling them in. I decided that his bad luck was the result of his poor bait. I remembered the bait my father had

used so successfully: a tasty mash of meat and flour held together with a little cotton batting. Using this bait, Papa
dragged fish in by the score as he sat on one of the piers
built for the use of Pacific Ocean fishermen. With the permission of Madeline, I made a little jar of cotton-batting fish
bait for the unlucky Seine fisherman. He obviously thought
I was a kook of some kind, but in the sport of fishing, he had
nothing to lose. Using Papa's bait, he caught two fish in a
row. I left then, for fear he would think that I expected to
share in the catch.

"At the bird and animal market, I had noticed a brindle-
colored prick-eared cat who, instead of curling up and purring
in one corner of her cage, paced, cried, and grew thinner. I
didn't know a thing about cats, but food was my solution for
all creatures who eat. It had worked, to their destruction,
with fishes. It worked to her convalescence on the cat. I
bought liver, and when the cat owner wasn't looking, I fed
her. She stopped her whining and pacing."

I am amazed now at the sad secret moans I sent to Max.
Screaming and cursing was what might have worked. He
had bought my ticket.

If I had mentioned knee squeezers or Irish widowers, the
purpose had been to convey a report of my attractiveness,
about which I thought he'd be glad to hear. If he'd looked
into my diaries at home, he might have found a complaint
or two; nothing to elicit talk of ashes and broken dreams.

But if small matters had ballooned for him, for me they
had truly detonated.

"Max, the last four months of my life have been thrown
away: strange cities, foreign lands—that's not living."

Not a word of truth in it, but what I believed at the minute.
I kept up my cheerful letters to my mother until the next

to the last day. Then I wrote her, "To be strictly truthful, I've been so homesick, so anxious to have the propellers start whirling that will move me westward, that I haven't enjoyed Paris for the past week. I had a particularly sad letter from Max at the end of last week. It made me wish I had never left home; feel like a prisoner here marking time, waiting until 5:30 Saturday, when I can get underway. I count the days. Only two more: Thursday, Friday, then Saturday I leave the Gare du Nord for Boulogne. The boat sails at ten or twelve for California, Anaheim, and Berkeley. Hurrah for the red, white, and blue. I had planned to see New Orleans en route home, but none of that nonsense now. Write Max. Tell him I was an egg to leave him and home."

She wrote, all right, but not to tell him what I had asked her to tell him.

"Max," she wrote, "I am ashamed of you. You have spoiled the last days of her trip; made her miserable. She has seen more, appreciated more than any of her family, including her hubby, could have done. I'm mad at you because you didn't have the backbone to stand the separation a little longer without complaining."

"Dear Mama, I'm sorry I wrote you that homesick letter yesterday or the day before. Tomorrow at this time I will already be one and one-half hours on my way home—westward bound, westward bound. Think of that!

"I haven't time to really write now. I'm having a farewell dinner with the Oxford girls tonight and I must wash and dress. I'll write you more after I get home.

"Your letter addressed London, California, arrived at 6 Rue Thibaud, Paris, France, yesterday. Holy Moses in a haymow, was I glad to get it. The Post Office loves me anyway, even if no one else does.

"The last thing I'll do tomorrow will be to go to American

Express to see if there is one final letter from Max. Do you know what haunts me now? The fear that some accident will happen, trains collide, boat sink, so that I'll never hear Max say that he can't understand why he wrote such a letter."

"I couldn't put off packing any longer. Not everything is dry yet: a dozen handkerchiefs are drying, a half-dozen stockings are yet to be mended. Two dozen postcards need to be written. I could skip these, but I *must* pick up my dry cleaning, return my borrowed books to Shakespeare and Company, and go once more, though I swore I wouldn't, to American Express to see if Max didn't say, 'Please forgive me.' It's better just to stay here and to imagine that such a letter might be there than to go and to be disappointed.

"Tomorrow night I'm having dinner at the International Student Hostel with Billie Rendle. After dinner, we'll go to the Dôme, where we'll eat cakes and coffee until midnight. My last night in Paris. Billie and her friend are going to the train with me. We leave here at four, because several ships leave on Saturday and there may be traffic jams near the station.

"I'll write you one note tomorrow. Madeline, who has no idea why I've been so downcast, took me aside, clasped one of my hands in both of hers and said, 'Time heals all wounds.' Then she kissed me French-style, first on one cheek, then on the other. I had just enough backbone to keep from crying on her shoulder."

Into my journal went my tears. "Thursday and Friday," I wrote, "were the most unhappy days of my life. Thursday and Friday I feared that some catastrophe would prevent my ever seeing Max again."

"The days creep by like flies across a page of tanglefoot. I suppose I have prayed a thousand times before, 'Life, give me just this one thing and I'll never ask for another.' Now I make the same prayer once again. 'Let me reach home safely, and I'll never ask for another thing.'"

"I think that it is terrible to want to have your cake and eat it, too. So I put my cake on a very high shelf; always being careful, however, that a tall stool is nearby."

"I am always jumping into the sausage grinder and deciding, even before I'm half ground, that I don't want to be a sausage after all."

"Too dreary and miserable to sleep last night, because of Max's letter. I finished Katherine Mansfield's *In a German Pension*. Awake again before daylight. I finished Van Wyck Brooks's *Wine of the Puritans*.

"I use books to oil the wheels of time and for no other reason these days."

"Sept. 9, 1929

"I believe that I am going to be able to stand it."

"Sept. 19, 1929

"I awakened this morning saying, 'I'm going home day after tomorrow.' Before, it has seemed so far away; now, it has come down to day after tomorrow. Home, home, home, oh, heaven be praised. I'd like to hire a robed choir to chant that. Two more nights and I'll be homeward bound! Hip, hip hooray! Three cheers and twenty-seven tigers, all in the prime of their lives."

"Sept. 21, 1929

"The adventure is over. I'm going home. Have I learned anything? We travel not to discover new lands or new people, but new selves. I suppose that there are still facts concerning myself of which I am unaware. It seems possible, but not likely. A good many qualities which I either supposed I did not have, or, if I had, I would never give way to, have come out in the open. In this way travel is educational—the text-book to be studied is you, yourself, not the country through which you travel!"

Thus ended my sermon to myself on my last night in Paris. Reading it now, I feel sad. Had no one told me that travel could be adventurous or fun? Without being told, had it never occurred to me? Had I never heard the word "pleasure"? Was the whole purpose of travel to learn? To help unsuccessful fishermen, feed underfed cats, cheer up maimed security guards?

With my last two lines in my journal, I gave over sermon-izing. "I spent my last night in England boating on the Cherwell. I spent my last night here at the Café du Dôme."

In my journal, trying to decide what had happened to me, I wrote: "The last two days, and today, have been, with the exception of the period when I got no mail at all, the most miserable of my journey."

Much has been written about journal keeping: Emerson advised it, Thoreau practiced it; Pepys *was* his journal. "A journal is a savings account," said Somerset Maugham, "it's insurance that you won't lose your memories." It is also as-surance that your memories will quite likely be shared by others—readers you never expected or wanted.

John Burroughs's definition of the journal keeper is not true for all. Sir Walter Scott, for instance, who, when he broke off his journal keeping began again because "I'm hanged if I'll be beaten," is not a Burroughs type of lonely introverted journal keeper.

Many writers have kept journals. The greatest have not done so. The greatest were able because of their talent or energy to put all of themselves into their narratives. Who doubts that in Heathcliff Emily Brontë put all of the self she herself comprehended or was willing that others should know? Emily Dickinson needed no journal. What more could she say about herself and life than she said in her poems?

What of the fiction writers who, in addition to a copious output of novels and short stories, fill page after page of a journal? Katherine Mansfield, Virginia Woolf, Jules Renard, André Gide. Why did Virginia Woolf in the hour between tea and dinner when guests weren't present (which wasn't often) fill journal after journal? Her journalizing was not the work of a lonely woman, as some writers or journal keepers have said, using her pen to express thoughts others express in conversation. Virginia Woolf was certainly not lonely in the sense of being alone, without friends with whom she could talk. If her various homes could have been as well taped as the Nixon White House, we would be able to judge the accuracy of Virginia Woolf's reports in her journals—to say nothing of the gain in wit and literacy over our own national product.

Almost certainly, Virginia Woolf did not call Logan Pearsall Smith "buggeristical" to his face, or tell Katherine Mansfield that she "advertise herself" or Hugh Walpole that he was "an uneasy, prosperous vain man."

Is the journal then a means for drawing out venom that would otherwise fester and poison?

Is it a therapist's couch, where, without charge, one can make known by listening to oneself what the trouble is?

Does the journal permit the journalizer to be an Iago, "the smiler with the dagger hidden in his cloak"?

I have had a theory that the great letter writers did not keep journals. Virginia Woolf disproves this theory, as she disproves many. She was as copious in letter writing as in journalizing. This is not true of most letter writers. No man was ever more faithful, open, and revealing in a lifetime of letter writing than Robert Louis Stevenson. Ill, tied to the routine of getting saleable material off to his publishers, separated by years and continents from the friends of his youth, R.L.S. never flagged in getting to them his monthly reports. Able to speak to them and Fanny forthrightly, journal keeping, where one talks (one hopes) to oneself was no need of his. No wonder Thoreau, two miles from home and dinner, living his life talking to himself, was no hero of Stevenson's. Each marched to a different drummer, though the time rapped out was the same for each: death march to an early grave.

Who needs, or apart from needs, wants to be a journal keeper? The Mormon church advises it. These Latter-day Saints known as Prophets urge their fellow Saints to keep journals for two reasons: first, as a means of keeping track of their spiritual development and, second, as a history that will be useful to Saints of the next generation.

There are others who need no urging. Journal keeping is as necessary to them as breathing. The life they live is vaporous and unreal until recorded in words in their journals. They may, like Virginia Woolf, have friends and lovers to whom they may confide. Or, like Thoreau, have none of the one and few of the other. Both would have missed a journal more than an arm. Talk, a disturbance of the air by vanishing syllables, cannot be compared with the solidity of written words. Some journal keepers may feel reticent about voicing the wonder, the joy, the anguish they feel in their day-by-day encounters with the world and its inhabitants; so, cowardly or kindhearted, they put down in ink what they would never permit their tongues to say. But the eyes sometimes see what the tongue would never have said.

Jane Welsh Carlyle writes of the hazards of journal keeping: "I remember Charles Butler saying of the Duchess Praslin's murder, 'What could a poor fellow do with a wife who kept a journal, but murder her?' There was a certain truth in that light remark," she continues. "Your journal, all about feelings, aggravates whatever is facticious and morbid in you; that I have made experience of. And now the only sort of journal I would keep should have to do with what

Mr. Carlyle calls 'the facts of things,' as I now see it—very; and what good is to result from writing of it in a paper book is more than I can tell. But I have taken a notion to, and perhaps I shall blacken more paper this time, when I begin quite promiscuously without any moral end in view; but just as the Scotch professor drank whiskey, because I like it and because it is cheap."

Mr. McPherson had not told me, as Mr. Carlyle told Jane, to stick to "the facts of things" and avoid feelings. If he had, I would have told him that feelings were facts; in any case, I kept on as Jane did because I liked it and it was cheap.

There is a good deal to be said for and against the reader of someone else's journal. Perhaps he should not have done so at all, but, ignoring the rights and wrongs of his illegal entry, what he finds is this: someone who gave no hint of anger or distaste on the occasion of some happening, permitting the reader to believe that the writer was, if not pleased, at least content; now, behind his back, so to speak, he berates and derides him.

What can he think of this? Except that he has to do perhaps with a two-faced double-dealer. Or Iago, smiler with the hidden dagger?

Is the journal keeper more an Iago than most men? In how many do what is spoken and what is felt coincide? Does the listener whose inner summation of the discourse to which he has been listening is "Hogwash" gain points by never putting the words into a journal? Points for greater discretion, surely. Is the admirable participant in conversation or action the one who voices immediately his feeling of disapproval or dismay? What of the man of whom you can say, "You always know where he stands"?

This can be said of some journal keepers. Did anything go into Dorothy Wordsworth's journal she would not have wanted William to read? Did anything go into Pepys that he was willing to have his wife read? Pepys took care of his wife with his code; but counted, I think, on posterity's breaking that code, since the whole of his journal, whatever it might have conveyed to his wife, was a shout of joy he wanted the world to hear. "This is Sam Pepys, man alive and the life he loved."

George Steiner, writing of a needed history of "inner speech," considers journal keeping a part of such a history. "It is in her most secret diary . . . that the young wife and mother voices the epiphanies, disappointments or raw sorrow of her condition. . . . The intelligent woman makes her journal the forum, the training ground of the mind. . . . Quantitatively, there is every reason to believe that we speak inside and to ourselves more than we speak outward and to anyone else."

Steiner connects the decline in journal keeping with the decline in writing by hand. The pen is far more an extension of the hand than the typewriter is. I speak from inside and to myself with it—with this addition: I am able by its use to see what I have said to myself. The left hand, and I am a left-hander, seems nearer the heart. Take my pen away and I would move back to wordless prehistory. With it, I am able to tell what I think, and also in some strange way by the look of the script to judge the state of the thinker: tired or joyous, confused or energetic.

At the time when doctors told me that I was dying of tuberculosis, I had for some reason begun to practice a hand-writing so minute and precise that a magnifying glass was needed for its reading. This was not caused by weakness. By what? A desire for a miniaturization so complete that I hoped that an untoward fate would overlook me entirely? What I now think is more likely: deprived of almost every means of gaining anyone's attention (except a doctor's), by minuscule handwriting I elicited comments from everyone to whom my father took a check or a list of mine. "What beautiful, tiny, almost invisible handwriting."

When he came home, my father would report these comments to me. Thus I would have my success for the day: the writer of an almost invisible script. We were fading away together: body and penmanship.

Of all the ologies, graphology seems to me, left-hander that I am, nearer the heart of an understanding of the nature of the penman.

The sorrow and misery I experienced on reading Max's letter was not occasioned by any feeling that he ought not to have opened that book, or that I shouldn't keep a journal. It was occasioned by my conviction that though what I said was true, I had, as Carlyle told Jane, "aggravated the factitious and morbid." I took sunshine for granted, good health as my due, and wrote only of darkness and pain. So, Max, reading, had the picture of a suffering wife—and what is worse, one who lied.

I thought I would be punished. I would never reach home and have the opportunity to correct for Max the mistaken impression that one paragraph gave.

One thing my misery did for me—and perhaps my misery showed more than I intended it to—it drew me closer to my "family," Billie, Mme Soutelle, Madeline, and Miss Dixon. I told them nothing, but one exhales sorrow like bad breath.

Madeline, older than the others, with one war and perhaps a broken heart behind her, obviously didn't look on me as one whose life had been forever blasted. She knew that wounds heal, are even forgotten. She gave me errands to run which required that I make change, avoid taxis, carry bundles, judge quality of supplies: all tasks that kept me too busy just staying alive and getting my money's worth to brood about marital woes.

Mme Soutelle took me to church. Church is no place for the broken-hearted, particularly when all you hear is in Latin or French. It's a good place to cry, though. No excuses are needed when one faces a man dying on the cross and praying, "Father, Father, why has thou forsaken me?" Tears are the truest response there.

Billie, the youngest of the four, woman of the world, child of foreign capitals, head of a crew on the water, bester of men in the classrooms, engaged to a man whose absence I never saw her mourn, had a solution for my, and her, problems, if she had any: be with people who were merry—the drinkers, the dancers, the singers, the talkers. Paris was filled with places where such people could be found. Billie knew them all, and had the money for herself and anyone she wanted as a companion.

Frieda, about my own age, was wondering whether or not she should take holy orders and become a nun. First, she would complete her paper on Dryden; she was not a girl to abandon a project; and this same purposefulness characterized her as a Catholic. It did not lie with her to give less than a whole self to God.

I knew more about Dryden than I did about God, but after I had run Madeline's errands, shed tears with Mme Soutelle, sampled Paris merriment with Billie, it was with Frieda I sat and talked.

Frieda became a nun. She sent me her picture at the time of her investiture. How she graced that habit! I heard from her until toward the end of World War II. Then there were no more letters. That war, which engulfed millions, took Frieda from my sight.

Billie, I met two or three times on later trips to England. She had married the fiancé, and he, like her father, had become a civil servant in one of the outposts of the British Empire.

Once, in London I spoke of her husband, far off, I supposed, in distant Africa.

"Oh, no," she said. "He lives at his club here in the city."

I felt abashed at having spoken of those two worldlings as if they were adolescent American live-togethers.

I have kept the letters of the two: the bride of Christ, the British matron. What I wrote to them, I do not know. I never keep letters of my own. This double discovery is possible only because my mother kept my letters, as I kept hers.

Letters strike me as an attempt to tell others how you are. Journals are an attempt to discover who you are. Recently a book entitled *The Culture of Narcissism* was published. In it the author, Christopher Lasch, writes of "the extent of a particular person's self-preoccupation." Journal keeping would appear to be one form of this preoccupation. Yet Steiner, as learned in these realms as Lasch, believes, and I think truly, that journal keeping is largely a practice of the past. The letter writer works harder to form and preserve lasting attachments to others. But letter writing, while less narcissistic than journal keeping, is also dying out, according to Steiner. The phone has replaced the pen, he writes, and "one is tempted to conclude that where much more is, in fact, being heard, less is being said."

Since I have both letters and journal at hand, I am able to see the difference, if any, between the two. The letter writer was a good-hearted girl. She was inclined to instruct, but tried for the sake of her readers to curb this tendency. She could fill one page of her journal, and did, with a single sentence many times repeated, "I am distraught," without ever mentioning in her letters the cause of her turmoil. And just as well not, since whatever was the cause, she no longer is able to remember it.

Into neither letters nor journal went much I now remember, largely because I did not have the verbal skill to convey moments of wonder, sights of grandeur. I wrote less to Frieda and Billie than they to me, less willing, apparently, than they to "preserve lasting attachments."

Of my heartsick last weeks, only my journal got the full story. There was also not much point in sending letters that would arrive after I did.

If it were not for my letters to my mother, I would not remember how I got from Paris to Boulogne to the *Minnesota*.

The only information in my letters to Max is that my heart was breaking.

To my mother, I wrote on my last day in Paris, "I am completely packed. To do it, I had to buy another suitcase for thirty-five francs, and it is bulging. After I had finished packing, I went to American Express, where I hoped for more mail and where I needed to cash a check. At the last minute, I found myself running short of francs and was afraid I might have spent my last penny before I was established on shipboard. To my disgust, because I knew it, American Express is closed on Saturday; so if there were any final letters there for me, I didn't get them—and I had pinned my hopes on that final loving letter. If I hadn't been able to borrow fifty francs of Billie, I would have had to carry my bags one by one from the tender to the boat. (All banks were closed, too.)

"The two Oxford girls, Billie and her friend, went with me to the station, the Gare du Nord; from there after a taxi ride across the entire city, we had tea in a room overlooking the tracks. We watched a troop of Zouaves, home from African duty, arrive, and as they embraced plump French ladies, both Zouaves and ladies crying, there were tears in my heart of envy. I parted with Billie at the tearoom. She said, 'I don't know what you'll do without me'—and I don't, either. She's five years younger than I am and a century more experienced in travel. God bless her."

Homeward Bound

"Fri., 1:30 P.M.

"Max, I write, not for your pleasure, but to ease my heart. I started to write you before lunch, but in spite of my best efforts, I would cry, so I went to my room, pulled a curtain over my porthole, climbed into my bunk, and cried—and really howled. My roommate is elsewhere. Oh, how I long to get an oar, sit near a porthole, and row, row, row. I hate to sit here, holding my hands while this scow plows along through the water at the rate of only 345 miles every twenty-four hours.

"I had my seat reserved on the boat train and by nine I was in Boulogne, and went aboard the tender. The *Minnesota* was late, a biting wind was blowing, the sky was clear, a bright moon was shining. We churned about the bay until almost eleven. We had no shelter, no seats save as we bought campstools. A kind woman bought a campstool and a pear for me. (I had no money left, not a sou. My broken heart must show.) So we froze and rocked and I thanked God for my pear and campstool. Finally, just as we were all saying that we could not stand the icy wind another minute longer, the *Minnesota* was sighted. Why did I ever choose a ship with a name like that? Why not Florida? Or especially Southern California?"

"Dearest Mama,

"Homeward bound at last! It was after eleven last night before we disembarked from the tender and, chilled to the bone, boarded the *Minnesota*. I went at once to my stateroom. It was the tiniest, most luggage- and human-filled room I ever saw. I had a top bunk with a pipe actually touching my stomach.

"I thought that my *Minnekahada* room was tiny, but this is truly tiny, a 2 x 4 room filled with 3 x 6 people. I crawled over luggage, undressed without ever bending a knee or an elbow and got into the one empty upper bunk, too tired to look at my dozing companion.

"My companion dozed, I didn't. A pipe, sewage, hot water, engine cooler, I know not what, curved down from the ceiling at just the point where my stomach rose toward it. I could neither breathe properly nor turn.

"Next morning I discovered that the room next to mine was not only much larger but that it had only one occupant. I wasted no time finding the purser and asking to be transferred to that room. The purser was willing, but the occupant wasn't. She was French born, imposing, with white hair and tawny eyes. She didn't fall on my neck with joy when she saw me, laden with my luggage, appear in her doorway. She had been promised, she told the purser, and me, a room by herself. The purser told her about the pipe in my stomach. The *Minnesota*, he told her, could be sued for physical injury of that kind. She cared not a whit for the *Minnesota* or me and my stomach.

"It was my amiability that won her. She now loves me like a daughter. She speaks English, not with an accent, but with so peculiar a construction, it takes some time to figure out what she has said.

"She is married to an American and has two daughters,

twins, Louisa and Marguerite. She spends every summer in France to prevent the hay fever she has in Harrisburg, Pennsylvania.

"The twins are twenty years old, already have their M.A.'s and are now in residence, with scholarships of $650 each at the University of Pennsylvania working for their Ph.D.'s.

"They are undoubtedly clever girls, and beautiful, too, to judge by their photographs, several of which I have seen. I now know all of their witty sayings, early sicknesses, and adolescent triumphs. Madame considers herself the most perfect of mothers; she tells me incident after incident to prove it. Since she is deaf, I must bellow my understanding and appreciation. She is doubtless a very interesting woman, but I hate to be awakened at 6:30 every morning to hear it—once again—from her lips. She loves me dearly, and I wait on her hand and foot, turn down her bed, fetch her books, listen once again to a report of the twins. She kisses me first on one cheek, then the other, and calls me her dear other daughter. It is only the memory of that pipe in my stomach that keeps me docile and listening!"

"Mama, having now traveled on two ships, I have become a ship expert. The *Minnesota,* insofar as food, lounge, and rooms are concerned, is much superior to the *Minnekahada.* However, she is older, smaller, and she creaks and moans with every wave. She is to be put on the New York–Havana run at the first of the year—if, and this feeling is prevalent, she holds together that long.

"Each day the Captain's log reads, 'Strong winds, rough seas.'"

Travel, I now see, had done something for me. There had been a change, whether for better or worse, I'm not sure.

On the Continental Limited, I drank toothbrush water all the way from Los Angeles to Chicago. I was afraid to let the name of my hotel in New York be known. On the *Minne-*

kahada, I believed every word that radio commentator said. I was given an upper berth and I slept there. A pipe in my stomach would have been endured without complaint.

"This is going to be quite a different journey from the one on the *Minnekahada,*" I wrote in my journal. "It is not only the difference in the weather; there's a difference in the people. Everyone on the *Minnesota* is so much more friendly. It isn't 10:30 A.M. yet; I didn't come aboard until late last night and I already know twelve people."

I doubt that there was any difference in the people; the difference was in me. On the Continental Limited, I had cried, eaten my fruit, and said not a word. Since then, I had learned to live with people. I was the one who had become more friendly—not the passengers.

On the *Minnekahada,* I would never have done what I did here, hunted up the purser and said, "I am dented and creased and perhaps permanently injured by having to sleep in a berth that is more than half occupied by part of the ship's anatomy. There is a room next to mine with only one occupant. Transfer me at once."

Mrs. Richtenberg, its occupant, who said she would sue if she had to endure a roommate, calmed down when I said, "Look at these bruises and guess who will sue for the most."

The girl on the *Minnekahada* would never have been capable of such a threat.

"Mama, I told you that I got onto the *Minnesota,* and out of my cell, but I haven't yet told you about my train trip to Boulogne, the kind of a boat this is, or the people who are on it.

"I naturally, as you know, got on the train earlier than was necessary. Being in such a swelter to get home, I took no chances. We were a motley crew in our compartment: two New England females who ate French cakes; a sour gentleman who bewildered us all by reading alternately, the *London Times,* the *New York Herald Tribune,* and the *Paris Matin;*

an American boy who recounted in lusty terms the story of his six months' journey in the Orient; an American woman homeward bound from Budapest who frequently interrupted him to say, 'I have a quart of Scotch in my bag. When shall we open it?'

"I had no newspapers, Scotch, or accounts of Oriental travels; but I did flaunt *Ulysses* to show I'd been to a place or two and knew a thing or even more.

"You already know about Mrs. Richtenberg and the twins. In addition to them, this ship is filled with artists and midgets. I think that there really are more artists than midgets, though with the artists being two or three times the size of midgets, there seem to be more of them. The hold of the ship is swollen with packing cases of painting. I know because I had to go down there to look through my trunk. The midgets belong to a troupe called 'Lester's Midgets,' good Britishers all, and booked by themselves as 'artistes.' The tallest is four feet and the heaviest weighs fifty pounds. You see someone who looks like a six-year-old, then he turns his fine crinkly black French beard toward you. It is very confusing. Especially when you are on the verge of being seasick.

"Our room (Mrs. Richtenberg's and mine) is nearer the prow of the boat than any other. In this picture I am drawing, the black space represents our room, the white the prow of the boat. When the *Minnesota* tosses, we toss twice as much as anyone else. We are at the far end of a sea-saw, and this sea is some rocker.

"They are taking bets as to whether the *Minnesota* will hold together until we get to New York. Portholes have been boarded up, passengers have been forbidden to walk the decks, except at times when the captain says that it is safe.

"I think we'll make it, but I also think that the passengers who disembark will be a wan and sickly crew. Everyone is seasick. When you go down the hall, you hear behind every door an unpleasant retching sound.

"I was seasick myself for ten minutes this morning, the first time in my life.

"This morning, Mrs. Richtenberg talked to me from 7:00 to 7:30 while she dressed for the first breakfast sitting. I propped myself on one elbow in bed while I listened. It was one of the roughest mornings we had ever had and I began to feel queerer and queerer. Mrs. Richtenberg's talk alone makes me feel a little queasy, but this was something different and worse. In spite of the mighty tossing, I climbed out of my bed and started to dress. Dressed, I started down the hall to breakfast—then suddenly I was seasick. I ran madly, handkerchief to mouth, toward a ladies' room. Either the sudden exercise, or the fact that I had reached the middle of the ship, cured me. I was still weak, wet and panting, but in ten minutes my seasickness had disappeared. I surely didn't have a very bad attack, because I was able to go down to breakfast, where I ate with a half-dozen other hardy souls.

"I spent the rest of the morning midship, afraid to go down to my roller-coaster room."

"Dearest Max:

"They were to have had horse racing on deck this afternoon, which means betting; since I'm not affluent enough to bet, I sit in the library and write to my dear husband. Besides, because of the weather, the horse racing has been, as I said, called off.

"Max, you have no idea how time drags. We have twenty-four and a half hours a day and never have I wanted an extra long day less.

"The sea is enormously rough this afternoon. The *Minnesota* is a weak little mouse and the sea plays with us like a hungry cat. A good many of the portholes have been boarded up. Not only horse racing, but walking on the deck has been called off. We are due in New York next Tuesday morning, but no one thinks we'll make it, unless possibly one by one, floating on planks.

"Max, if we do make it to New York Tuesday morning and I am able to catch the Baltimore & Ohio at twelve-something, I'll be in L.A. Saturday night.

"Max, if I make the twelve o'clock train Tuesday, wouldn't it be beautiful beyond words to find you in Los Angeles Saturday night? Honey, I don't suppose you can, and I don't want you to at the cost of your studies, or your job—but if you could, oh, if you could! I'll wire you from New Orleans the exact time of my arrival. I expect you won't be able to do this. I won't count on it, but I can't help imagining your being there.

"This will probably be my last letter to you, not only of this summer, but, if the storm keeps up, of all time. It is now 7:30 A.M. The foghorns sounded all night. At 6:30 they were particularly alarming—so I got up and dressed. If we are going to crash into something, I'll be well dressed for the occasion. The people who have breakfast at the first sitting have all gone down. The others are still in bed, so I have the library to myself.

"Last night we had a real hurricane. Waves swept across the upper decks; all portholes were clamped shut. The boat didn't so much leap about (which she did), as she staggered and shuddered. When a wave hit her, she shuddered exactly the way an auto does when the springs hit bottom. We have tried to worm information out of the stewards about the trip at this time last year: was it as bad as this? Or worse? The stewards say that last year at this time the *Minnesota* encountered a storm so bad that it filled her staterooms with water.

" 'We went about without our shoes last year. As you can see, we still have our shoes on, so last year's storm was much worse. Don't start worrying until you see us barefooted.'

"I'm worried, just the same.

"I remember that on our trip over I tried not to forget that we were traveling on water. It seemed to me that an ocean voyage would be wasted if I didn't remember all the time that beneath me was the Atlantic Ocean. Now the shoe is on the other foot. The Atlantic Ocean is determined not to let us forget that we are not traveling down the Yorba Linda Boulevard."

With half the passengers seasick, the other half staying very quiet so as to avoid being seasick, there was little to do but read and write—and play bridge. Seasickness, I could and did write home about; but I understood that it wasn't a subject a correspondent would want to read page after page about. Seasickness resulted, to use the lingo of Southern Indiana, where I was born, in puking; and this was a word on a par with four or five other unmentionable backwoods words. So, a letter or two exhausted the subject of seasickness.

There was also bridge. But in my home, playing cards were called "the devil's calling cards"; and my parents would not care for the idea of my sinking in the briny deep with a handful of jacks and aces (if I drowned lucky) in my hands.

I had come to the pass of playing bridge six hours a day: ten to twelve in the morning, two to four in the afternoon, eight to ten in the evening. Bridge playing, even to other players, is not an exhilarating subject to write about.

The bookworm can put up with a little talk from another bookworm about what he has read. If the truth be known, he would rather read his own book than listen to a fellow worm's report of his reading.

So there was less letter writing than there had been. In the first place, I would reach home by the time my letters did. In the second, my subjects, seasickness, bridge, and a breaking heart, were, for various reasons, nothing anyone wanted to read about. For these reasons, I talked to myself in my journal.

I made a list of characters and scenes left behind me in France that I would never forget—and I have forgotten all except one.

1. The Brittany mother and her sailor son.

2. The Spaniard bidding the American girl good-bye, saying, "Eet ees very fonny."

3. The girl on the bus with the Negroid lips.

4. The one-legged guard at the Louvre who always sang very low to himself when a pretty woman went by.

5. The young policeman who was sick on duty.

6. The young girl in yellow who watched the crowds pass the Café de la Paix and who waited for someone to notice her.

Of these six, I remember only the one-legged singer at the Louvre; remember him probably because I did more than look: I spoke to him.

"Tues. The most important thing that happened today was this," I wrote in my journal. "While I was taking my bath tonight, it suddenly came to me that if all went well (and I'm not sure it will, the water while I was bathing sloshed out of the tub), I'll be at home one week from this Saturday. Wednesday, Thursday, Friday to be gotten through, then I can say, 'Home in a week.' Surely the sweetest words in the language. Eleven days. Anyone can survive anything for eleven days.

"There was a man at our table tonight I detest. He said, 'When I get home, I have to go to work. Each day here is a precious jewel.' Perhaps I would hate his work, too. But I love mine, and the home I am returning to."

There was one passenger I could write home about: E. D. Burdon, the poet who had been one of the passengers on the *Minnekahada* when we were outward bound. She was still writing poetry and she still copied it in my journal. One, because it had to do with a mother and a daughter, I copied for my mother. E. D. Burdon called it "Encircled."

This little waist contains a host
Of loving thoughts for thee,
Your mother wove them one by one
In this embroidery.

And as this little waist
Your waist encircleth round,
So to your mother's loving arms
Have oftentime been wound,

And just as closely to your breast,
As this to thine
You have been pressed
With mother love divine.

Since Mama was not a woman given either to sewing or to pressing her children to her breast, this was not a very appropriate poem to send her. But I couldn't write her about E. D. Burdon's other accomplishment: bridge playing. It was she who asked me to make the fourth of the group that played six hours a day. Kindness, I'm sure, prompted the invitation. She knew nothing of my breaking heart, or even of my unfamiliarity with bridge. I was competitive, I wanted to win. How she knew this, I don't know; but she understood that once I had learned the rules of the game, I would try very hard not to be bested.

The third member of the quartet was the man I detested, the one who did not want to go home to work. He was the last man in the world any woman (I thought) would want to spend six hours a day with. E. D. Burdon, poet though she was, was a more practical woman than I. Mr. Smalley, the work hater, was probably the best bridge player on the boat. E. D. Burdon took him as a partner. She procured as my partner Eloy Ramos, a Spanish gentleman fleeing political trouble and personal tragedy in Spain. Señor Ramos was my opposite: he was a fine bridge player who didn't care whether he won or lost.

I had noticed him before I began to spend six hours a day

with him as a bridge player. The heavy weather continued. Since I had already concluded that some catastrophe would prevent my reaching home, a storm at sea scared me no more than the dozens of other mishaps that could end my or Max's life. So while the ship wallowed and the waves crashed, I sat in the library with the others, who were neither seasick nor so fearful of seasickness they feared to move around. The stewards still had their shoes on, so I took it that the *Minnesota* had weathered worse storms.

By chance, I had taken *Precious Bane* from the library's shelves, and as usual was copying sentences from it into my journal.

"It was always my custom, if things grieved me or gladdened me, to write them down in full. Because I had no lover, I would lief have been the world's lover, such a world, that is, as I could reach," wrote Mary Webb.

I had just copied "For here was my lover and my lord and behold, I was hare-shotten" when, though I had seen him often before, I had never paid more than casual attention to Eloy Ramos, and he had never, insofar as I had noticed, given me a single glance, now it was as if he had been able to read what I had written. I had looked at him because he did not read, play cribbage or even solitaire. Instead, he sat gazing into space, and holding on his lap a cat. The cat was not his. Passengers' pets were in suitable containers in the hold. This was the ship's cat, gray, densely furred, with a Siamese's crossed eyes but the plump big head of some domestic tabby.

Mrs. Burdon believed that there was some connection between bridge and poetry. She may have been the only person in the world to do so, but I understood her meaning. Poetry makes statements by means of symbols and metaphors. So does bridge. Bridge is not a multiplication table; poetry isn't *Poor Richard's Almanac*. Because I read her poetry, and the poetry of others, Mrs. Burdon thought that I would have an aptitude for bridge. She had already discovered that Five

Hundred was permitted in my home, and, in her opinion,
anyone who could play one of these games could play the
other. So, on the basis of my poetry reading, and perhaps
because she, like Señor Ramos, was kindhearted, I was asked
to play bridge. Mr. Smalley and Señor Ramos were asked
because they were bridge players.

How did she know this? It wasn't hard. In addition to that
characteristic which caused all of us to confide in her, Mrs.
Burdon had eyes; and anyone with eyes could see that most
of the ship's passengers were either sick abed because of the
storm or reading. Smalley was up and about, but not reading; Ramos held a cat, not a book, in his lap. I held a book
that I didn't often read. How Mrs. Burdon knew that Smalley
and Ramos were fine bridge players, I don't know. Asked
them, probably. She was intuitive about partnering me with
Ramos instead of Smalley. Smalley was a dentist, and any
man who chooses to spend his life with bicuspids and root
canals is not the man for me. Ramos, until Mrs. B. told me
his story, was in appearance a Lincoln who had lost Tad and
27,000 men in the Wilderness. Lost *his* mother early on, too;
and it was of her Ramos was speaking, I supposed, when he
once said, "The hand is full of memory." He was unable to
stroke Gatto when he played bridge; but for Gatto, the lap
was a cradle of memory, stroking or no stroking. There he
curled quietly as the game went on.

More and more often as the *Minnesota* lurched toward
the new world, Señor Ramos and Gatto sat beside me after
the game was over.

By this time, Mrs. Burdon had told me more about Señor
Ramos; told him all about me, too, I suppose, though my
story, as Mama would have said, was a short horse and soon
curried. There wasn't much to tell except that I had had a
letter from my husband calling our marriage up to this point
"ashes in the mouth," and suggesting that I might better not
join him in Berkeley.

This wasn't much of a story; enough to make a young

married woman blubber, but nothing as compared with what had happened to Señor Ramos. He was, or had been, a politician in Spain; more than that, he was as near leadership as anyone in that still monarchically inclined country could be. Then, by mistake, assassins, intending only the death of Ramos, killed his wife, the babe in her arms, and their two-year-old daughter.

Mrs. Burdon, I believe, because of her unusual insight, knew that Señor Ramos and I would never tell each other what she told us. And we never did. Mr. Smalley's story, if he had one, other than the extracting, filling, and cleaning teeth, she never told us. And I think she never told him ours.

I talked with Mrs. Burdon about Señor Ramos, though, and even about myself, and she listened patiently.

"If I were Eloy Ramos," I said, "I would never have left Spain until I had seen that the man who murdered my wife and children was brought to justice."

"What do you mean by justice?"

"Caught, and the law enforced."

"Hanged, you mean?"

"If that's the law."

"I thought you were a Quaker?"

"They believe in keeping the law."

"When the law says join the army and kill, they don't do it."

"*I* would if somebody had killed my wife and child."

"So you have written a letter denouncing your husband and saying, 'You will never see me again.'"

She knew I hadn't.

Mrs. E. D. Burdon could see right into you. I didn't practice what I preached. Eloy Ramos was saving his neck, Mrs. Burdon said, by going to Mexico. I was saving my marriage (if it was endangered) by writing conciliatory letters and getting back to California as fast as wishes could speed the *Minnesota* and quiet the storm.

.   .   .

"Dear Max," I wrote. "Last night while playing bridge, an elderly lady at the next table remarked in a carrying voice that all men were untrustworthy and all husbands unfaithful. I wanted to say, 'Not my husband,' but I wondered. Max, was I a fool to leave you? Have I exposed you to temptation, so alone and good looking? Alone at U.C.L.A. with Eula prowling around nearby? Three weeks' silence from you at that time. Now at Berkeley, with numberless lovely girls swarming about you and that oh-so-helpful coed as your assistant playground director. Then finally, and worst of all, that terrible letter. Oh, Max, somehow I will live through the next week, if the boat holds together, and all my doubts will be ended in your arms."

Señor Ramos and I had made Gatto our surrogate in life. What Ramos told me about Gatto, I now believe, was talk about himself. He didn't find it possible to tell a stranger (even one who looked as depressed as I evidently did, and in need of someone else's troubles to think about) his own life story undisguised. He speculated to me about the sorrows a ship's cat must have encountered.

When he took Gatto, on the first occasion of his seating himself by me, onto his own lap, he said, after long silence and much stroking of Gatto, "Old and shabby now."

Gatto looked neither to me.

"And in the beginning, what a difference."

"He looks fine to me," I said.

"Adrift on a ship, homeless, without a friend."

"He has you."

"I have him."

"Will you take him with you?"

"He is better off where he is."

"Do all ships have cats?"

"Yes."

"Why? Cats don't like water, do they?"

"The lost and needy take what they can get. This is better than a gutter or a rooftop."

"If he had stayed in the town where he was born, he might have been chewed up by a dog by now, or run over by a cab."

"He might, he might," said Señor Ramos. "And he might be happier."

"Are the dead ever happier than the living?"

"What do they have to mourn?"

"I'm glad I'm alive."

"You don't look it."

That was as near as Señor Ramos ever got to talking personally to me, about either himself or me. A more experienced or traveled person than I might have told him the truth, and have learned something about myself and about Eloy Ramos. If I had told him the truth, said, "My husband doesn't love me any more," he might, by telling me something of his life, have opened my eyes to the unimportance of a trivial letter.

I didn't. He didn't. He stroked Gatto.

"The hand is full of memory," he said.

Once Señor Ramos, called to the purser's office, gave me Gatto to hold. When he returned, I looked at him carefully. Until then, I had been able to see only my husband at a big state university, surrounded by peppy coeds; and the stewards appearing ready at any minute to throw off their shoes and man the lifeboats.

Now, with Gatto on my lap, I looked at him. It is a wonder that I hadn't seen him sooner. Señor Ramos was Spanish and I had gone to school with Mexicans and descendants of Spaniards. We lived on what had been a Spanish grant.

My father, when he arrived in Southern California from southern Indiana, was called a "greaser": which was Southern Californian slang for Mexican. He had neither Spanish nor Mexican blood in his veins, but he did have an Indian grandmother, and from her he had inherited his black hair, coppery skin, big shoulders, and striding toed-in walk.

When Señor Ramos reseated himself, I looked at him some more—and no longer as a reminder of schooldays and a land that had once belonged to Spain. He had the saddest face I had ever seen: not sad because of a drooping mouth or red-rimmed eyes, but because of eyes that looked beyond our shipboard life and the storm we appeared to be weathering, toward that final storm none of us would survive.

He had no accent, only a quicker, more precise way of speaking than that of most Westerners. He did not talk about himself or where he lived; he asked no questions of me. He talked about storms at sea, cats, and the drought that had caused the Spanish in California to lose their grants. I was ignorant on all these subjects. I had never been in a storm before; we, the newcomers to California, were too busy trying to establish a foothold ourselves to give any thought to those who had preceded us; I had never owned a cat.

"A cat," said Señor Ramos, "is the animal most akin to humans."

"Not a dog?" I asked.

"A dog is unlike a human in every way. A dog belongs to a man. A cat belongs to itself. Whistle and the dog comes. Bark and he barks. Say 'miaow' to a cat and what happens?"

"I don't know."

"Nothing. If you have lost someone, who do you want to replace him: a slave or a companion?"

"A companion, of course."

"Get a cat."

"You will have to leave this cat when you leave the ship, won't you?"

"Perhaps not. Meanwhile, she's the best I can do."

Señor Ramos stroked his cross-eyed cat. He didn't say purr, but it purred. "Hour by hour," said Señor Ramos, "one does the best one can. Very little is forever."

I was still young enough to believe in forever, for myself and those I loved. I was suffering from what I feared was the breakup of my forever.

Meanwhile, when not being beaten at bridge by Burdon and Smalley, Eloy Ramos and I sat in the library, Eloy with his faithful cat, I with first one book, then another. I had finished *Precious Bane* and was reading E. E. Cummings.

I never spoke to Señor Ramos about the horrors he had experienced. He never mentioned my disturbing mail. We were held together by the storm that threatened us all, and by the cat to whom we attributed our own experiences. I noticed that Gatto, obviously as masculine as a cat can be, was always "she" to Señor Ramos.

"She no doubt looked forward to quite a different life," said Señor Ramos.

"Where do you think she was born?" I asked.

"What country, do you mean?"

"No, no. How could we tell that? I mean farm, city, small town."

"Small town," said Señor Ramos. "She's no kitten. City cats get killed in traffic before they reach her age."

I agreed with him, having experienced traffic in London and Paris myself.

"She was born in a small town. A farmyard cat could never have settled down with people the way Gatto has done."

"How did she get on a ship?"

"Some sailor."

"Can sailors bring their pets on board?"

"Depends on the pet. I wouldn't try it with a kangaroo."

"No one would, would they?"

"There is nothing in this world someone hasn't tried."

"What if the sailor that brought Gatto on board found out that he wasn't a very lovable cat after all? What would he do? Throw her overboard? Get rid of her?"

"Not the sailor we're talking about and not the cat we're talking about. Those two were linked for life."

"You just said anything could happen to anyone."

"It can, it can. God knows it can. But I'm talking now about this particular sailor and this particular cat. They stayed together."

"If the sailor went ashore someplace, mightn't the cat think he'd been deserted?"

"Not Gatto."

Señor Ramos was going to Mexico to join an uncle there. "I should have gone years ago. What a life we would have had, eh, Gatto?"

Gatto, a reserved cat, closed his eyes.

The afternoon bridge game was over. We had uninterrupted time to observe the storm.

"They still have their shoes on."

Señor Ramos, who hadn't heard what the stewards had done in last year's storm, didn't know what I was talking about. At the very minute I was explaining, a wave, though it felt like something more solid than water, hit the ship. No one in the library said a word until it appeared that the ship was going to hold together.

"This year we may not be so lucky."

"Can you swim?" asked Señor Ramos.

"I can."

"I also."

"A cat can't swim."

"She won't have to."

After the bridge game that night, I wrote to my mother. I didn't think the letter would arrive before I did, if either was going to make it. But my hand, too, was a remembering hand, and what it remembered was writing.

"We are advancing at a snail's pace," I told her. "Horns blowing, boat shuddering. Unless we are terribly delayed by fog and high seas (and we will be if the weather doesn't change), we are scheduled to reach New York sometime in the night. If we should, I might be able to get the 12:40 after noon train out of N.Y. If I do that, I'll be in Louisville on Wednesday morning, change trains, reach New Orleans Thursday at 10:40, be in California Saturday evening at 5:00 P.M. Think of that, think of that! Boy oh boy!"

This schedule, including New Orleans, was one that I had drawn up before I had learned anything about traveling, homesickness, letters that didn't arrive; and letters that *did*. I no longer had any desire to postpone California for the sake of New Orleans.

I was right in telling my mother that I doubted that we'd make New York that night. Before daylight, a steward, shoes off, was in our room.

"Ladies," he said, "will you please place yourselves on the upper berths? We want to take all of your hand luggage off the floor and place it on the lower berths."

We saw the wisdom of that. The steward was splashing about in water ankle deep.

"Are we sinking?" I quavered.

The steward was disgusted. "The day we sink," he said, "I won't be troubling myself about your hand luggage."

"How the twins would love this," Mrs. Richtenberg said.

"Too bad they aren't here," the steward told her. "We're short-handed."

Mrs. Richtenberg, because of her gray hair, I suppose, was helped into the upper berth by the steward. I was left to clamber aloft as best I could.

The steward, who recognized a real traveler when he saw one, said to Mrs. Richtenberg, "I think the storm is slacking off. There's water in here because some of the boarding on the portholes at the prow of the ship was smashed. Get some more sleep now. Coffee will be brought to the rooms when things quiet down."

That was exactly what Mrs. Richtenberg did, after re-
minding me how lucky I was to be with her, not back in my
original berth, with my luggage now added to the ship's
plumbing on top of my stomach.

She was asleep when I heard a quiet knock at our door. I
slid down from my berth into the water, which was cold,
but shallow, and opened the door. There stood Señor Ramos,
pajama-clad, as I was, with Gatto in his arms.

"There are four of us in our cabin," he told me, "and we're
pretty cramped. Two of the men object to the cat. They think
she brings bad luck."

"He's not black," I said.

"They're superstitious about cats, no matter what color. I
can't have Gatto outside in weather like this. Since there's
only two of you here, I thought you might take her into your
berth until the storm blows over. You know how quiet she is."

I did know. In the half light I saw for the first time that
Señor Ramos's eyes were not a Spanish or Mexican brown
or black, but the kind of speckled green of some cured olives.

"I've made her dependent on me. I believed you would
understand."

I did understand. At that minute, there was no one in the
world I could give any comfort to except the cross-eyed
half-breed of some distant and probably dead Siamese—be-
friended by a Spaniard who had no other family. I held out
my arms. Gatto settled down as into another basket.

"What if we go down?"

"That is not going to happen. Only so much is permitted.
Gatto is going to Mexico with me."

"How will you manage that?"

"You'll see."

Señor Ramos put out his hand for one farewell stroke; and
Gatto, as if wanting to participate, lifted himself from my
arms so that his forehead fitted the outheld cupped hand.

I had supposed that Mrs. Richtenberg, who had been silent
during the conversation, was sleeping. She hadn't been. As

soon as I, with Gatto cuddled under the covers, was settled in the upper berth, she said, "What was to keep him from sitting with that precious cat of his in the library, if his roommates don't want a cat in their cabin?"

"I don't know," I said. I hadn't even thought about it before. Now that I did think about it, the answer was one I didn't believe Mrs. Richtenberg would understand. Señor Ramos's kindness was also his to me. The cat didn't know that the stewards had their shoes off, and that porthole covers were being smashed. I did. Taking care of the cat of a man who had lost so much would keep me from watching the depth of the water on our cabin floor and from counting the seconds between the shuddering smash of waves.

And he was right. I didn't see, I didn't count. The hand learned, comforting Gatto.

"Do you mind having a cat in here?" I asked Mrs. Richtenberg.

"Not at all. The twins have had kittens since they were four years old."

Anything I did that was twinlike endeared me to their mother.

"They won't let him take the cat ashore, will they?"

"Of course they will. They'll never see it."

"How can you hide a cat?"

"I do not know. But never fear, Eloy Ramos will know. His trouble all along has been that he knows too much."

When I awakened, Gatto was gone, the water was gone, Mrs. Richtenberg was back in her lower berth.

"You have had quite a sleep."

"What time is it?"

"Noon."

"Where is the cat?"

"Señor Ramos took it."

"The storm?"

"Finished."

"New York?"
"By nightfall."

We made it before nightfall, while there was still enough
October light to bronze the windows of the New York sky-
scrapers. Looking at them, it seemed impossible that anyone
would leave such a glittering homeland to stand in Scotland
on an elevation of twelve hundred feet, or even to say a prayer
at the grave of Jaurès. The storm so recently survived added
to our pleasure in seeing buildings that waves, we believed,
would never batter.

Those who wished could spend the night on board the
Minnesota. Those who had friends waiting or connections
that, in spite of our tardiness, they could still make were
eager to leave. I had neither friends nor connections; but
the *Atlantic Monthly*'s St. James, haven for women traveling
alone, had been my temporary home and it beckoned me
now. Not only was it on solid ground, but I might find mail
there; though I, never expecting to stop there, had asked no
one to write.

Customs officers had come on board at once, so that those
who were leaving the ship could do so with as little delay
as possible. Those of us who were leaving were lined up alphabetically with our luggage by our side. My luggage was
limited: only my handbag, my thirty-five franc French suitcase, and my steamer trunk. I did not delay the officers long.
One look at my marmalade and they were finished with me.

I had said good-bye to Mrs. Richtenberg earlier; she was
staying overnight on the *Minnesota*, awaiting the twins, who
would pick her up in the morning.

"The twins are intelligent," she told me for the twentieth
and last time. "They will have read of the storm and know
at what hour we are docking. They will know that a night's
rest here will be best for me."

I would have been happy to have had one twin, still an
A.B. only, not yet an M.A., to look after me.

E. D. Burdon was in the line. When they had finished with her, she started saying farewell to friends. "Keep playing," she told me. "You have the makings of a fine bridge player, a good memory and a determination not to be beaten. Practice will supply the rest. Now I must say good-bye to Señor Ramos. He has help from the Spanish Embassy, I see."

He did indeed. The ambassador himself, from the formality of his clothing, was by his side, and some chauffeur-dressed gentleman was busy stacking his bags.

"Is Mr. Smalley here?"

"Believe me, he is. For the night. With a woman."

"Smalley?"

E. D. Burdon shook her head. "You've had a restricted life, my girl; no bridge, no poetry, no experience with dentists."

I had had a tooth pulled. I had read a lot of poetry. But it was true: of experience of the kind Mrs. Burdon had in mind, I was ignorant.

"A dentist," said Mrs. Burdon, "is drawn to orifices."

When she concluded her farewells to Señor Ramos, and before I could go to him myself, Señor Ramos came to me, carrying some of his own hand luggage.

"You were asleep when last I saw you. I didn't want to waken you to thank you for looking after Gatto."

"Oh, I would still be taking care of him if you hadn't taken him."

"No," said Señor Ramos. "Never. She goes to Mexico with me. Never be separated from those you love."

Heartily, I agreed. "How do you take her to Mexico?"

"I am here to show you."

Señor Ramos opened what appeared to be a hatbox, deep enough for a top hat. At the bottom in the center of a circle of fur, of the kind men in cold climates wear as much to look rakish as to keep warm, two golden eyes opened, then closed.

"Gatto," I said.

"Shh," said Señor Ramos. "She will sleep for a while now." He clapped the lid tight on the hatbox. "We will never be parted again."

I had already lost faith in such optimism, but I knew better than to contradict a man with so much need to believe that something, even a tomcat misnamed "she," would never leave him.

In our bridge playing, Señor Ramos had learned that I, like most Southern Californians, knew a few phrases of Spanish: *Vamoose, undulay, pronto, no dinero, adios, vaya con dios.*

"*Vaya con dios,*" he said to me. "Go with God."

Then, seeing that I was going to cry, he quickly opened the hatbox once again, took my hand and put it inside, where it touched the living fur.

"Say '*adios,*' Gatto."

"*Adios,* Gatto."

Señor Ramos' companions beckoned, and I, who had no twin, had written no poetry, had collected nothing but Joyce and marmalade, was left alone with my remembering hand.

Though I had collected little, I had dispensed with much of the cargo I had started with: thrift, for instance. I took a taxi to the St. James on what might have been a fruitless journey. They had a room. I was remembered. There was a letter from Mama. Accustomed to a walk that had to adjust itself to the roll and lurch of a deck sometimes as near vertical as horizontal, the solid floors of the St. James rose up and hit my feet like stones. No give to this boat.

"You don't have your land legs yet," said the porter.

I didn't. And the bed itself was as unyielding as a plank, after a ship's rock and roll.

The letter, since I had not expected to stop over in New York, was a pure miracle. Mama, still remorseful about the weeks she had not written, now shot her arrows into the air, though they would fall she knew not where.

"Petty," she wrote, "I have just had an idea. If you are still filled with wanderlust, don't go off to some strange place like New Orleans. Save traveling like that until Max can go with you. Here's something Max wouldn't want to do with you which will take one day out of your time only. Stop over, the B. & O. goes through there, in North Vernon. I've written Arlo and Ada. They'll drive you out to Sadie Perkins's home; she lives about five miles out of town on the farm her father owned. He's dead now. She has no car, no phone. Except for her, I doubt you'd still be alive. She was what we called a 'hired girl' in those days, and she took care of me, and of you—when you were born. I've told you that story often enough. The doctor had given us both up. Not Sadie, not my mother. She'd be so happy if you'd stop in and she could see that the baby she had fought for had grown up to be a European traveler. She's lonesome, born lonesome, never married and took care of her father and the farm until he died.

"The trip out to her place would be nothing for Arlo and Ada, and it would mean a lot to two old ladies."

Mama, at forty-six, was not an old lady, though I thought so at the time. Sadie, at sixty-six, certainly seemed so to me. Ada was my double second cousin, her father a first cousin of my father's; her mother, a first cousin of my mother's. The trip was inconvenient, for Ada and Arlo, but we were too enmeshed in family ties for them to disregard my request. Arlo had been a doctor during the war, and any event short of legs blown off or of brains turned to soup on a shirt front was minor to him. Both doubted that I was in for an entertaining evening, but they understood Mama's wish and Sadie's lonesomeness. They would drive me out, then pick me up next morning in time to catch the ten o'clock B. & O. for Indianapolis.

"We'll just let you out," Ada said. "If Sadie got hold of us, we'd be here all night. She's hungry for talk, and you and Europe are all she'll be able to digest in one evening."

Sadie *was* hungry for talk, all right; but for more than that. I was as near to her having a child as she had ever come; and Mama had never let her forget the days of labor they had shared.

Mama, with her policy of nothing risked, nothing gained, had written Sadie that I might be stopping by. Sadie had been prepared for this possibility for a week: a good supper was on the table, and she was wearing her Sunday apron, white, with ruffles and crocheted edging, tied tight as a truss around her firmly corseted waist. I felt the corset when Sadie took me into her arms. I was unaccustomed to any such hugging. Mama had no such apron and no inclination for such embraces. I was deep into ruffles and bosoms and crocheting when Sadie, holding me at arm's length, looked at me with disappointment. "Considering the start you had, I had expected someone more sizable."

"Mama," I told Sadie, "had been eating for two before I was born. I try to eat just for one."

I was subjected once again to the pressure of flesh and crochet. "You're your mother's child. You don't look like her, but you talk like her."

We ate supper at once. "Elizabeth ain't been milked, but there's no point being a human if you're the one who has to wait instead of the cow."

I carried the lantern, Sadie the milk bucket and stool. Elizabeth, who had been in the pasture, came into the barn lot when Sadie called, a place, as far as I could see by lantern light, of dead weeds, potholes, and cowpats.

Sadie sat on her stool, and sent Elizabeth's milk hissing into an enamel bucket. I, reminded, held the lantern at a better angle and, unlighted myself, shed unseen tears as fast as Elizabeth let down milk. Both were perhaps a relief. The boat had not sunk. I had seen the land of the poets. I was once again on my native heath, in the very township where I had been born. But never, when embarking on my trip, had I imagined such an end: lantern light, cowpats, and tears in a Jennings County barnyard. Max had sent me no phone number. I was too proud to complain to my mother. A cat, called "Hector" by Sadie, joined us and Sadie shot a stream of milk into his opened mouth. He made me feel better. If Gatto could get to Mexico, rammed into the bottom of a hatbox, I could surely make it, though shedding a few tears, to California.

After the crocks of milk had been put in the cooler, Sadie told me once again the story I had so often heard of my birth. It was a story she, my mother and grandmother loved to recall. To me it was the story of a stranger I had never known, of a villain even, I so large and my mother so small, but I was forced to hear it once again.

Not until we had gone to bed did I wish for some more of it: more talk or more milking or more anything that would get me out of the bed I occupied with Sadie.

Sadie's home, when it had belonged to her father, had consisted of eight rooms, a sizable Southern Indiana farmhouse: kitchen, dining room, sitting room, parlor, parlor bedroom, three bedrooms upstairs.

Sadie had changed all this. She now had a kitchen and a sitting room, which, with a double bed, served as the one bedroom. In the bed, I slept with Sadie. It was a feather bed, as plump with goose feathers as Sadie was with flesh. There was no possible way of clinging to the bedrail and avoiding not only rolling down against but into Sadie, who then clasped me like the babe she had lost a quarter of a century ago. On top of us was a down comforter that increased the temperature, which wasn't low to begin with. There was no way I could think of telling this loving would-be mother that I couldn't endure the heat, or the clasping or the snoring.

"I have to get up," I whispered.

This was a human and not unloving thing to say. Sadie understood. "Under the bed," she whispered, with scarcely any cessation of snoring.

I crept to the kitchen, closed the door to the bedroom–sitting room, and, after searching, found by a combination of memory and good luck matches and the lamp. It was nine o'clock. Six o'clock in California!

Oh, remembering hand. It wanted to hold a pen. But any letter I could write now would reach home after I did. There was my journal, the letter I wrote myself.

Hector scratched at the door. He slept in the hayloft, but the light in the kitchen had brought him to the house. I gave him a saucer of cream skimmed from a crock of milk. He settled himself in my lap, a skimmed-milk cat, happy at his improved status.

I put into my journal messages Sadie had asked me to give to my "Ma."

"Be sure to tell your Ma that you found me right side up and forked-side down. Remember that, forked-side down. That'll tickle her."

"Tell your Ma you didn't find any scarcity of vittles. I've got enough here for a logrolling. It's been that way ever since Pap died. I just can't seem to pare down on the vittles."

"Pap was always so fond of gravy. He was always saying, 'Sis, ain't you got any gravy timber on hand?' "

"I suppose you went sightseeing a lot when you were across the water. Were you in any Catholic churches while you were away? I've been told they're full of didoes and holy water. Didn't do any toe kissing, did you?"

Finished with Sadie for Mama, I wrote of Max for myself.

"I try not to think of Max, in his apartment in Berkeley, getting (I hope) his own meals but subject to the wiles of one thousand beautiful and unscrupulous coeds.

"Is there any virtue in doing a thing just because you decided to do it? Keeping on after it is apparent that what you are receiving is not what you set out to get?"

It was at this moment that the back door to the kitchen opened. Quietly, Arlo, whispering, said, "Am I disturbing anyone?"

"Not a soul. Sadie's asleep. I can't sleep. Come in. Sit down. Talk."

Arlo sat at the table, then handed me a folded slip of paper. "This is a telegram from Max, phoned me from Vernon. I drove over with it. I was overseas for two and a half years. Oh, God, do I know the meaning of mail. And its lack."

I sat down with the paper still folded in my hand.

"Why did this come to you?"

"Same reason your mother's letter did, I expect. She wrote us she'd told you to stop here. Wrote the same thing to Max, I imagine."

"And you drove all the way over with it."

"Five miles. Chicken feed for a doctor. But if you don't intend to read it, I'll take it back with me. Send a return telegram saying I couldn't deliver it."

He was kidding, but it wasn't a subject I could kid about.

"I'll read, I'll read," I said.

"It won't take you long," said Arlo.

Nine words. It didn't. "Flowers on the table, welcome mat out. Hurry."

"Would you ask Ada," I asked Arlo, "to phone Mama, collect? Tell her I'll leave Chicago tomorrow directly for San Francisco. I'll see her at Thanksgiving."

"Ada and your Mom will talk all night."

They were cousins and old friends. "You do the phoning, then."

"No, no. It'll be a treat to both."

I walked out to his car with Arlo. I was crying and I didn't care if he knew. A doctor's business isn't with the healthy. The October night was not California mild. My nightgown had as well have been made of mosquito netting. The wind off the Muscatatuck went right through it, damp and chilling.

Hector, more warmly clothed than I, but also cold, wound himself around my ankles. I picked him up, for my sake, not his. He warmed me and he sopped up my tears.

Arlo said, "I'll be here at 7:30 in the morning to pick you up." He patted first Hector, then me. "Never regret travel. Better see the world and cry, than stay home dry-eyed."

He was a doctor who had seen death on the battlefields. I supposed he knew what he was talking about.

I took Hector to bed with me. He could have been an alligator for all of Sadie. I didn't mind Sadie's snoring any more, and her warmth was a comfort. Hector lay behind me, delicately treading my rump as he had done long ago the belly of his mother. He was asleep before I was.

My journey was over. What had I learned?

Try to learn to live where you are. Don't pine for the land of the poets while in the midst of sagebrush and barley fields. Don't dream of three-room apartments while the Seine and Cherwell flow by.

Wisdom in every word and the lesson in those sentences still unlearned after fifty years.

The three of us slept: the old maid, the hayloft tom, the homesick wife.

"Journeys end in lovers meeting,
Every wise man's son doth know."

—William Shakespeare
Twelfth Night